Significance:
The Struggle We Share

Significance: The Struggle We Share

A Book of Readings

Third Edition

John H. Brennecke
Robert G. Amick

Mt. San Antonio College

GLENCOE PUBLISHING CO., INC.
Encino, California

Glencoe Publishing Co., Inc.
17337 Ventura Boulevard
Encino, California 91316
Collier Macmillan Canada, Ltd.

Library of Congress Catalog Card Number: 78-71732

ISBN 0-02-470740-6

1 2 3 4 5 6 7 8 9 10   83 82 81 80 79

Contents

12 The Transcending Self *281*

Introduction to the Third Edition

It is said there are two things we can never escape from—death and taxes. There is a third—crisis. As one grows older, life appears to become a series of major and minor crises. A crisis in one part of the world that we have no control over can alter our life drastically. As an example, look at how we are all affected by the energy and monetary crises in the world today. Some thinkers have called this the Age of Anxiety; others, the Atomic Age, the Age of Aquarius, the Technological Age. Perhaps we should label it the Age of Crisis.

Among the most crucial crises confronting human beings in these troubled times is what Rollo May calls the crisis of significance.[1] In another work, *The Struggle for Significance*, we have chronicled the conflict of modern individuals as they grope their way out of the welter of confusions and conflicts into the light of Self-actualizing fulfillment.

More than feeling lost, alienated, alone, many of us have experienced the desperate feelings of doubt as to our own significance. We may amass money, invent gadgets, accumulate material goods, gain prestige and reputation, seek and find love, and all of these can be good in and of themselves. But many people continue to feel that their own Selfhood is unimportant. They find themselves in a battle to declare who they are, hoping for that declaration to make a difference.

To feel significant is not necessarily to become important or famous. Far from it. Most of the people to whom this book is addressed will never become famous or wealthy or powerful. But they can attain a feeling of significant Selfhood. They can live their lives in such a full and rewarding way that they will come to know that their being here has mattered, that they have made a ripple on the pond.

In the midst of all the change and chaos of our age, we believe that humans are still struggling to gain a sense of their own personal significance, despite the obstacles. To aid in that struggle, we have added to this edition some readings that further reflect the fight against dehumanizing experiences. As in the first edition, we have drawn not only from scientific thinkers, but from novels, philosophers' works, and poets' dreams. The scientist gives us an objective, consensual view of conclusions he or she has reached about human thought processes, motivations, and so on. Poets, philosophers, and fiction writers may give us a glimpse into the personal

1. Rollo May, *Psychology and the Human Dilemma* (Princeton: Van Nostrand, 1967).

feelings of someone like ourselves. So both kinds of readings are valuable, we think, in the study of psychology.

We wish to thank the countless people who have helped us grow, and all of the authors who have risked writing about life, whose thoughts we have borrowed to make up this book. We wish to thank Beverly Grosenbach for her assistance. We especially want to acknowledge the beautiful help and support we have received from our wives, Bernadette and Taffy. We will always love you.

John H. Brennecke
Robert G. Amick

1 The Crisis of Insignificance

People are born. People die. In between, what? Is there a meaning to this round-robin experience called life? The existentialists have made it their entire theme. Beginning with the realization of the fact of death, we are told that we must shape our lives so that we live them—not simply let them be lived. Decision, commitment, and responsibility are the major requirements of meaningful living.

Without acknowledging the fact of death, we live in a fantasy world. We don't expect that significant human beings will spend every waking moment dwelling on their own mortality, but fully living persons live with the fact of the shortness of life and let that reality so pervade their being that they live their lives more fully, more meaningfully, more richly, and certainly more realistically, because they know that life is limited.

Doesn't this lead to gloomy despair? For some, yes. But for people who know that death is part of the facts of life, it should be something that takes its place alongside the other facts. Having made realistic room for this reality, they can then take on the other less morbid and less frightening aspects of human existence. Human life can be lived joyfully. If life were only a burden, only a struggle, only an assortment of pains, we'd say, "Hang it up" too! But life can be joyful; human beings can know happiness and a feeling of worth.

We begin with a reference to a very happy man, Alexis Zorba. Nikos Kazantzakis has given the world a story of a full and rich man in Zorba the Greek. Zorba, for all his peculiarities and peccadilloes, is a fully human and large-living man, who is flesh and blood to millions of people, including us.

1

The second reading is another fiction piece. Albert Camus, in The Stranger, introduces us to the existential posture in literature, inviting each reader to find his or her own kinship with the hero, Meursault.

The third reading is an intimate view of a young woman's impending death. "Soon There Will Be No More Me," Lyn Helton's personal diary, tells us how it feels to know she is dying.

The fourth article discusses industrialized countries' changed attitudes about death. Robert S. Morison, in "Dying," explores the problems of technology's impact in keeping people alive, and how that interferes with the natural process of death.

We end the chapter with an excerpt from Erica Jong's novel, "How to Save Your Own Life," in which the author describes her feelings about her friend's death.

from *Zorba the Greek*

Nikos Kazantzakis

A young man, half Greek and half English, returns to take possession of his inheritance: a lignite mine on the Greek isle of Crete. He meets a rascally jack-of-all-trades, Alexis Zorba, who promises not only to show him how to reopen the mine and make his fortune, but also how to get a bit more out of life. The scholarly, shy fellow falls into many philosophical discussions with the rough but deep-feeling old worker. In the following excerpts, Zorba and his "boss" are discussing the matter of human existence on earth.

"You don't believe in man, do you?" I retorted.

"Now, don't get angry, boss. No, I don't believe in anything. If I believed in man, I'd believe in God, and I'd believe in the devil, too. And that's a whole business. Things get all muddled then, boss, and cause me a lot of complications."

He became silent, took off his beret, scratched his head frantically and tugged again at his moustache, as if he meant to tear it off. He wanted to say something, but he restrained himself. He looked at me out of the corner of his eye; looked at me again and decided to speak.

"Man is a brute," he said, striking the pebbles with his stick. "A great brute. Your lordship doesn't realize this. It seems everything's been too easy for you, but you ask me! A brute, I tell you! If you're cruel to him, he respects and fears you. If you're kind to him, he plucks your eyes out.

"Keep your distance, boss! Don't make men too bold, don't go telling them we're all equal, we've got the same rights, or they'll go straight and trample on *your* rights; they'll steal your bread and leave you to die of hunger. Keep your distance, boss, by all the good things I wish you!"

"But don't you believe in anything?" I exclaimed in exasperation.

"No, I don't believe in anything. How many times must I tell you that? I don't believe in anything or anyone; only in Zorba. Not because Zorba is better than the others; not at all, not a little bit! He's a brute like the rest! But I believe in Zorba because he's the only being I have in my power, the only one I know. All the rest are ghosts. I see with these eyes, I hear with these ears, I digest with these guts. All the rest are ghosts, I tell you. When I die, everything'll die. The whole Zorbatic world will go to the bottom!"

"What egoism!" I said sarcastically.

"I can't help it, boss! That's how it is. I eat beans, I talk beans; I am Zorba, I talk like Zorba."

I said nothing. Zorba's words stung me like whiplashes. I admired him for being so strong, for despising men to that extent, and at the same time wanting to live and work with them. I should either have become an ascetic or else have adorned men with false feathers so that I could put up with them.

Zorba looked round at me. By the light of the stars I could see he was grinning from ear to ear.

"Have I offended you, boss?" he said, stopping abruptly. We had arrived at the hut. Zorba looked at me tenderly and uneasily.

I did not reply. I felt my mind was in agreement with Zorba, but my heart resisted, wanted to leap out and escape from the brute, to go its own road.

. . . .

When he returned one evening, he asked me anxiously: "Is there a God—yes or no? What d'you think, boss? And if there is one—anything's possible—what d'you think he looks like?"

I shrugged my shoulders.

"I'm not joking, boss. I think of God as being exactly like me. Only bigger, stronger, crazier. And immortal, into the bargain. He's sitting on a pile of soft sheepskins and his hut's the sky. It isn't made out of old petrol-cans, like ours is, but clouds. In his right hand he's holding not a knife or a pair of scales—those damned instruments are meant for butchers and grocers—no, he's holding a large sponge full of water, like a rain-cloud. On his right is Paradise, on his left Hell. Here comes a soul; the poor little thing's quite naked, because it's lost its cloak—its body, I mean—and it's shivering. God looks at it, laughing up his sleeve, but he plays the bogy man: 'Come here,' he roars, 'come here, you miserable wretch!'

"And he begins his questioning. The naked soul throws itself at God's feet. 'Mercy!' it cries. 'I have sinned.' And away it goes reciting its sins. It recites a whole rigmarole and there's no end to it. God thinks this is too much of a good thing. He yawns. 'For heaven's sake stop!' he shouts. 'I've heard enough of all that!' Flap! Slap! a wipe of the sponge, and he washes out all the sins. 'Away with you, clear out, run off to Paradise!' he says to the soul. 'Peterkin, let this poor little creature in, too!'

"Because God, you know, is a great lord, and that's what being a lord means: to forgive!"

I remember I had to laugh that evening, while Zorba was pouring out his profound balderdash. But this "lordliness" of God was taking shape and maturing within me, compassionate, generous and all-powerful.

. . . .

A moment later he decided to speak.

"Can you tell me, boss," he said, and his voice sounded deep and earnest in the warm night, "what all these things mean? Who made them all? And why? And, above all"—here Zorba's voice trembled with anger and fear—"why do people die?"

"I don't know, Zorba," I replied, ashamed, as I had been asked the simplest thing, the most essential thing, and was unable to explain it.

"You don't know!" said Zorba in round-eyed astonishment, just like his expression the night I had confessed I could not dance.

He was silent a moment and then suddenly broke out.

"Well, all those damned books you read—what good are they? Why do you read them? If they don't tell you that, what *do* they tell you?"

"They tell me about the perplexity of mankind, who can give no answer to the question you've just put me, Zorba."

"Oh, damn their perplexity!" he cried, tapping his foot on the ground in exasperation.

The parrot started up at these noises.

"Canavaro! Canavaro!" he called, as if for help.

"Shut up! You, too!" shouted Zorba, banging on the cage with his fist. He turned back to me.

"I want you to tell me where we come from and where we are going to. During all those years you've been burning yourself up consuming their black books of magic, you must have chewed over about fifty tons of paper! What did you get out of them?"

There was so much anguish in his voice that my heart was wrung with distress. Ah! how I would have liked to be able to answer him!

I felt deep within me that the highest point a man can attain is not Knowledge, or Virtue, or Goodness, or Victory, but something even greater, more heroic and more despairing: Sacred Awe!

"Can't you answer?" asked Zorba anxiously.

I tried to make my companion understand what I meant by Sacred Awe.

"We are little grubs, Zorba, minute grubs on the small leaf of a tremendous tree. This small leaf is the earth. The other leaves are the stars that you see moving at night. We make our way on this little leaf examining it anxiously and carefully. We smell it; it smells good or bad to us. We taste it and find it eatable. We beat on it and it cries out like a living thing.

"Some men—the more intrepid ones—reach the edge of the leaf. From there we stretch out, gazing into chaos. We tremble. We guess what a frightening abyss lies beneath us. In the distance we can hear the noise of the other leaves of the tremendous tree, we feel the sap rising from the roots to our leaf and our hearts swell. Bent thus over the awe-inspiring abyss, with all our bodies and all our souls, we tremble with terror. From that moment begins. . ."

I stopped. I wanted to say "from that moment begins poetry," but Zorba would not have understood. I stopped.

"What begins?" asked Zorba's anxious voice. "Why did you stop?"

". . . begins the great danger, Zorba. Some grow dizzy and delirious, others are afraid; they try to find an answer to strengthen their hearts, and they say: 'God!' Others again, from the edge of the leaf, look over the precipice calmly and bravely and say: 'I like it.'"

Zorba reflected for a long time. He was straining to understand.

"You know," he said at last, "I think of death every second. I look at it and I'm not frightened. But never, never, do I say I like it. No, I don't like it at all! I don't agree!"

He was silent, but soon broke out again.

"No, I'm not the sort to hold out my neck to Charon like a sheep and say: 'Cut my throat, Mr. Charon, please: I want to go straight to Paradise!'"

I listened to Zorba in perplexity. Who was the sage who tried to teach his disciples to do voluntarily what the law ordered should be done? To say "yes" to necessity and change the inevitable into something done of their own free will? That is perhaps the only human way to deliverance. It is a pitiable way, but there is no other.

But what of revolt? The proud, quixotic reaction of mankind to conquer Necessity and make external laws conform to the internal laws of the soul, to deny all that is and create a new world according to the laws of one's own heart, which are contrary to the inhuman laws of nature—to create a new world which is purer, better and more moral than the one that exists?

Zorba looked at me, saw that I had no more to say to him, took up the cage carefully so that he should not wake the parrot, placed it by his head and stretched out on the pebbles.

"Good night, boss!" he said, "That's enough."

A strong south wind was blowing from Africa. It was making the vegetables and fruits and Cretan breasts all swell and grow. I felt it on my forehead, lips and neck; and like a fruit my brain cracked and swelled.

I could not and would not sleep. I thought of nothing. I just felt something, someone growing to maturity inside me in the warm night. I lived lucidly through a most surprising experience: I saw myself change. A thing that usually happens only in the most obscure depths of our bowels was this time occurring in the open, before my eyes. Crouched by the sea, I watched this miracle take place.

The stars grew dim, the sky grew light and against this luminous background appeared, as if delicately traced in ink, the mountains, trees and gulls.

Dawn was breaking.

from *The Stranger*

Albert Camus

Meursault, the hero of Camus' penetrating existential novel, is sentenced to death for a murder. His guilt is unimportant at this point. In too many ways, Meursault is being punished for his failure to react, act, feel, think, and grieve in precisely the same fashion as his fellows. His judges remember back to the funeral of his own mother, when he could not, or would not, weep. Perhaps it is this "image" of Meursault that is tried, judged, and convicted.

In this excerpt, Meursault is spending his last night in the cell. At dawn, he will die. He rejects the usual social amenities. This, of course, increases his captors' conviction that he is a cold-blooded villain. Read his words and decide for yourself.

Then all day there was my appeal to think about. I made the most of this idea, studying my effects so as to squeeze out the maximum of consolation. Thus, I always began by assuming the worst; my appeal was dismissed. That meant, of course, I was to die. Sooner than others, obviously. "But," I reminded myself, "it's common knowledge that life isn't worth living, anyhow." And, on a wide view, I could see that it makes little difference whether one dies at the age of thirty or threescore and ten—since, in either case, other men and women will continue living, the world will go on as before. Also, whether I died now or forty years hence, this business of dying had to be got through, inevitably. Still, somehow this line of thought wasn't as consoling as it should have been; the idea of all those years of life in hand was a galling reminder! However, I could argue myself out of it, by picturing what would have been my feelings when my term was up, and death had cornered me. Once you're up against it, the precise manner of your death has obviously small importance. Therefore—but it was hard not to lose the thread of the argument leading up to that "therefore"—I should be prepared to face the dismissal of my appeal.

At this stage, but only at this stage, I had, so to speak, the *right*, and accordingly I gave myself leave, to consider the other alternative; that my appeal was successful. And then the trouble was to calm down that sudden rush of joy racing through my body and even bringing tears to my eyes. But it was up to me to bring my nerves to heel and steady my mind; for, even in considering this possibility, I had to keep some order in my thoughts, so as to make my consolations, as regards the first alternative, more plausible. When I'd succeeded, I had earned a good hour's peace of mind; and that, anyhow, was something.

It was at one of these moments that I refused once again to see the chaplain. I was lying down and could mark the summer evening coming on by a soft golden glow spreading across the sky. I had just turned down my appeal, and felt my blood circulating with slow, steady throbs. No, I didn't want to see the chaplain. . . . Then I did something I hadn't done for quite a while; I fell to thinking about Marie. She hadn't written for ages; probably, I surmised, she had grown tired of being the mistress of a man sentenced to death. Or she might be ill, or dead. After all, such things happen. How could I have known about it, since, apart from our two bodies, separated now, there was no link between us, nothing to remind us of each other? Supposing she were dead, her memory would mean nothing; I couldn't feel an interest in a dead girl. This seemed to me quite normal; just as I realized people would soon forget me once I was dead. I couldn't even say that this was hard to stomach; really, there's no idea to which one doesn't get acclimatized in time.

My thoughts had reached this point when the chaplain walked in, unannounced. I couldn't help giving a start on seeing him. He noticed this evidently, as he promptly told me not to be alarmed. I reminded him that usually his visits were at another hour, and for a pretty grim occasion. This, he replied, was just a friendly visit; it had no concern with my appeal, about which he knew nothing. Then he sat down on my bed, asking me to sit beside him. I refused—not because I had anything against him; he seemed a mild, amiable man.

He remained quite still at first, his arms resting on his knees, his eyes fixed on his hands. They were slender but sinewy hands, which made me think of two nimble little animals. Then he gently rubbed them together. He stayed so long in the same position that for a while I almost forgot he was there.

All of a sudden he jerked his head up and looked me in the eyes.

"Why," he asked, "don't you let me come to see you?"

I explained that I didn't believe in God.

"Are you really so sure of that?"

I said I saw no point in troubling my head about the matter; whether I believed or didn't was, to my mind, a question of so little importance.

He then leaned back against the wall, laying his hands flat on his thighs. Almost without seeming to address me, he remarked that he'd often noticed one fancies one is quite sure about something, when in point of fact, one isn't. When I said nothing, he looked at me again, and asked:

"Don't you agree?"

I said that seemed quite possible. But, though I mightn't be so sure about what interested me, I was absolutely sure about what didn't interest me. And the question he had raised didn't interest me at all.

He looked away and, without altering his posture, asked if it was because I felt utterly desperate that I spoke like this. I explained that it wasn't despair I felt, but fear—which was natural enough.

"In that case," he said firmly, "God can help you. All the men I've seen in your position turned to Him in their time of trouble."

Obviously, I replied, they were at liberty to do so, if they felt like it. I, however, didn't want to be helped, and I hadn't time to work up interest for something that didn't interest me.

He fluttered his hands fretfully; then, sitting up, smoothed out his cassock. When this was done he began talking again, addressing me as "my friend." It wasn't because I'd been condemned to death, he said, that he spoke to me in this way. In his opinion every man on the earth was under sentence of death.

There, I interrupted him; that wasn't the same thing, I pointed out, and, what's more, could be no consolation.

He nodded. "Maybe. Still, if you don't die soon, you'll die one day. And then the same question will arise. How will you face that terrible, final hour?"

I replied that I'd face it exactly as I was facing it now.

Thereat he stood up, and looked me straight in the eyes. It was a trick I knew well. I used to amuse myself trying it on Emmanuel and Celeste, and nine times out of ten they'd look away uncomfortably. I could see the chaplain was an old hand at it, as his gaze never faltered. And his voice was quite steady when he said: "Have you no hope at all? Do you really think that when you die you die outright, and nothing remains?"

I said: "Yes."

He dropped his eyes and sat down again. He was truly sorry for me, he said. It must make life unbearable for a man, to think as I did.

The priest was beginning to bore me, and, resting a shoulder on the wall, just beneath the little skylight, I looked away. Though I didn't trouble much to follow what he said, I gathered he was questioning me again. Presently, his tone became agitated, urgent, and as I realized that he was genuinely distressed, I began to pay more attention.

He said he felt convinced my appeal would succeed, but I was saddled with a load of guilt, of which I must get rid. In his view man's justice was a vain thing; only God's justice mattered. I pointed out that the former had condemned me. Yes, he agreed, but it hadn't absolved me from my sin. I told him that I wasn't conscious of any "sin"; all I knew was that I'd been guilty of a criminal offense. Well, I was paying the penalty of that offense, and no one had the right to expect anything more of me.

Just then he got up again, and it struck me that if he wanted to move in this tiny cell, almost the only choice lay between standing up and sitting down. I was staring at the floor. He took a single step toward me, and halted, as if he didn't dare to come nearer. Then he looked up through the bars at the sky.

"You're mistaken, my son," he said gravely. "There's more that might be required of you. And perhaps it *will* be required of you."

"What do you mean?"

"You might be asked to see. . ."

"To see what?"

Slowly the priest gazed round my cell, and I was struck by the sadness of his voice when he replied:

"These stone walls, I know it only too well, are steeped in human suffering. I've never been able to look at them without a shudder. And yet—believe me, I am speaking from the depths of my heart—I *know* that even the wretchedest amongst you have sometimes seen, taking form against that grayness, a divine face. It's that face you are asked to see."

This roused me a little. I informed him that I'd been staring at those walls for months; there was nobody, nothing in the world, I knew better than I knew them. And once upon a time, perhaps, I used to try to see a face. But it was a sun-gold face, lit up with desire—Marie's face. I had no luck; I'd never seen it, and now I'd given up trying. Indeed, I'd never seen anything "taking form" as he called it, against those gray walls.

The chaplain gazed at me with a sort of sadness. I now had my back to the wall and light was flowing over my forehead. He muttered some words I didn't catch; then abruptly asked if he might kiss me. I said, "No." Then he turned, came up to the wall, and slowly drew his hand along it.

"Do you really love these earthly things so very much?" he asked in a low voice.

I made no reply.

For quite a while he kept his eyes averted. His presence was getting more and more irksome, and I was on the point of telling him to go, and leave me in peace, when all of a sudden he swung round on me, and burst out passionately:

"No! No! I refuse to believe it. I'm sure you've often wished there was an afterlife."

Of course I had, I told him. Everybody has that wish at times. But that had no more importance than wishing to be rich, or to swim very fast, or to have a better-shaped mouth. It was in the same vein, when he cut in with a question. How did I picture the life after the grave?

I fairly bawled out at him: "A life in which I can remember this life on earth. That's all I want of it." And in the same breath I told him I'd had enough of his company.

But, apparently, he had more to say on the subject of God. I went close up to him and made a last attempt to explain that I'd very little time left, and I wasn't going to waste it on God.

Then he tried to change the subject by asking me why I hadn't once addressed him as "Father," seeing that he was a priest. That irritated me still more, and I told him he wasn't my father; quite the contrary, he was on the others' side.

"No, no, my son," he said, laying his hand on my shoulder, "I'm on *your* side, though you don't realize it—because your heart is hardened. But I shall pray for you."

Then, I don't know how it was, but something seemed to break inside me, and I started yelling at the top of my voice. I hurled insults at him, I told him not to waste his rotten prayers on me; it was better to burn than to disappear. I'd taken him by the neckband of his cassock, and, in a sort of ecstasy of joy and rage, I poured out on him all the thoughts that had been simmering in my brain. He seemed so cocksure, you see. And yet none of his certainties was worth one strand of a woman's hair. Living as he did, like a corpse, he couldn't even be sure of being alive. It might look as if my hands were empty. Actually I was sure of myself, sure about everything, far surer than he; sure of my present life and of the death that was coming. That, no doubt, was all I had; but at least that certainty was something I could get my teeth into—just as it had got its teeth into me. I'd been right, I was still right, I was always right. I'd passed my life in a certain way, and I might have passed it in a different way, if I'd felt like it. I'd acted thus, and I hadn't acted otherwise; I hadn't done x whereas I had done y or z. And what did that mean? That, all the time, I'd been waiting for this present moment, for that dawn, tomorrow's or another day's, which was to justify me. Nothing, nothing had the least importance, and I knew quite well why. He, too, knew why. From the dark horizon of my future a sort of slow, persistent breeze had been blowing toward me, all my life long, from the years that were to come. And on its way that breeze had leveled out all the ideas that people tried to foist on me in the equally unreal years I then was living through. What difference could they make to me, the deaths of others, or a mother's love, or his God; or the way a man decides to live, the fate he thinks he chooses, since one and the same fate was bound to "choose" not only me but thousands of millions of privileged people who, like him, called themselves my brothers. Surely, surely he must see that? Every man alive was privileged; there was only one class of men, the privileged class. All alike would be condemned to die one day; his turn, too, would come like the others'. And what difference could it make if, after being charged with murder, he were executed because he didn't weep at his mother's funeral, since it all came to the same thing in the end? . . .

. . . Almost for the first time in many months I thought of my mother. And now, it seemed to me, I understand why at her life's end she had taken on a "fiance"; why she'd played at making a fresh start. There, too, in that Home where lives were flickering out, the dusk came as a mournful solace. With death so near, Mother must have felt like someone on the brink of freedom, ready to start life all over again. No one, no one in the world had any right to weep for her. And I, too, felt ready to start life all over again. It was as if that great rush of anger had washed me clean, emptied me of hope, and, gazing up at the dark sky spangled with its signs and stars, for the first time, the first, I laid my heart open to the benign indifference of the universe. To feel it so like myself, indeed, so brotherly, made me realize that I'd been happy, and that I was happy still.

from "Soon There Will Be No More Me"

Lyn Helton

*Death is inevitable. It is the culmination of the process we call
life. Perhaps you have experienced the death of a grandparent,
aunt, uncle, or a close friend, or even that of a parent, brother, or
sister, and had a great deal of difficulty dealing with that death.
Imagine, then, how much more difficulty you might have in dealing
with your own death, if you knew it was coming soon.*

*In this reading excerpted from her book, a young girl shares
with us the experience of anticipating her own death. At the age of
nineteen, she has been informed that she has a terminal illness.
Her words here reflect her reactions—despair, fear, loneliness,
strength, acceptance of the need to cope with the inevitable.*

Dying is beautiful—even the first time around, at the ripe old age of
twenty. It's not easy most of the time, but there is a real beauty to be found in
knowing that your end is going to catch up with you faster than you
expected, and that you have to get all your loving and laughing and crying
done as soon as you can.

You know that you don't have a lot of time to play games. You don't
want to spend the time wasting precious moments doing nothing or feeling
nothing.

I have so many things to write about, so many things to pour out to
someone who will listen. But it's hard to write about things that hurt, and
things that need to be thought out privately, when you know someone else
will be reading them.

In the beginning I always tried to keep comforting thoughts flowing in
my mind, things like "don't worry, it's a wrong diagnosis," or "surely they
have a cure for this somewhere!"

But as I slowly realized the seriousness of having cancer, my attitude
changed. I got scared, sometimes I couldn't even sleep at night. I'd sit up,
wrapped in a blanket, in my old green rocker until I'd be sick to my
stomach—and I'd vomit, alone, in the darkness, while my husband and
baby slept, and I'd just be scared.

What's it like to die? If someone could just tell me maybe I'd feel better.

There are lots of little things I want to do. Fill this book, knit Tom a
sweater. Grow my hair long. I pray for time.

Excerpted from "Soon There Will Be No More Me," by Lyn Helton, as it appeared in *West
Magazine*, January 16, 1972.

I pray that I live long enough to see Jenny become a human independent of Tom and me. At least old enough to reason some on her own. Old enough so she'll remember me.

Well, last night's wishes will probably go undone. Especially the last one. I know I won't live long enough for Jenny to remember me.

I went up to Children's Hospital today and they did some chest X rays. Bad news, bad news. I have a lung lesion, or spread of my disease, osteogenic sarcoma—one of the rare and very deadly types of cancer.

I first thought, well, you knew what was going to happen. Then I wanted to cry, then I changed the subject. Now I want to know why. Why, Why, Why?

I had some pretty strong thoughts on dying, last night. When I'm lying in bed, it is so hard not to think about it. It's so damn unfair. To me, to Jenny, to Tom.

I can't understand it at all. I can't understand the way all of this works into the scheme of things. Why doesn't it at least have some purpose? It has only brought me pain, and my family pain. Why?

Tom is right, though—I've still got a lot of living to do, before it's time to die. Guess I should do some. I should make a list of all the things I want to do. There are so many things!

I want to write this book for Jenny. I don't know exactly about what. I just want to leave her a part of me. I want to tell her about how I feel. About how I did things. About how important she is to me.

I want to make things good between Tom and me. I know the best thing I could do would be to make love the way we used to—but I just can't, it hurts so, and I don't know why else. I want to give him so much—I wish I could give him, of all things, a motorcycle. But more than material things, I want to give him all of myself.

> I feel myself fade
> in your hands
> my head droops a little
> always in sadness

I probably told the story of how I first noticed the lump on my leg a thousand times. . . .

It all started shortly before I gave birth to Jennifer. It was in November, 1969, when I first noticed a lump, or sore spot, growing on my knee. I was only nineteen, and pregnant for the first time, and wonderfully in love with my husband. We were happy—that's all I need to say. If you've ever had just one really happy moment in your life—that's how we were all the time. With a new baby on the way and Christmas just around the corner, I just wasn't going to be concerned with the matter.

Finally a doctor came and told me that I had cancer, and that they would have to amputate my leg in order to stop the growth. I didn't cry, tried not to anyway, and asked when it would have to be done. He said he would do the operation the next day. That really floored me! I told him that I would have to think about it and talk to my husband. He agreed, so I called Tom to come and get me and take me home. I cried—God, this can't be real, can it?

> Look around
> grass is high
> it's the springtime
> of my life
> I'm gonna die

In June, 1970, we made the decision to go to Children's Hospital in Denver for the treatment I needed. I was told that I would be receiving drugs and radiation, that I wouldn't be able to have more children, that the radiation would cause skin discoloration and possibly a burn, and that there was little pain involved in the actual radiation treatment.

I'm so tired and nervous tonight. I wish Tom would try and be more understanding. He doesn't realize what it's like, I don't think. When I get to feeling down, he thinks I'm just feeling sorry for myself. I know I do—but I don't think that's wrong. He could help by being kinder sometimes. I don't know. Maybe it's just me.

> Sitting in your rocking chair
> nonchalant as hell
> reading a book
> of unknown faces
> as I lie here
> waiting
> it'll be midnight
> or later yet
> when your friends
> in that book say goodnight
> and I'll be lying here
> waiting
> and you'll kiss me
> and rub your icy feet up mine
> as I lay here comfy
> in the bed
> I warmed myself

and I'll turn over
and mumble
yes, I'm awake
I was just
waiting

What's it like to die? Sometimes I think I know. It's cold and hard, and so lonely. Everybody tries to be so nice. I don't know how to react.

I'm sort of afraid, about dying. I don't regret not taking the drugs. They made me hate to live. I'm just afraid of not knowing what it's like after you die. I don't know how I'll be toward the end. I have to be strong.

I can't seem to break out of myself. For days now, my thought processes have been so dull, and I don't know why. I just can't seem to think intelligently. It's really bothering me. Part of it is, I think, the way Tom and I have been living. We are so unaware of what is going on around us. We never read or discuss situations anymore. We just end up arguing about things, because we are both too poorly informed to discuss anything. This is a real problem. I think we should do something about it. A trip to the library is definitely in order. I've wanted to go for several days now, but like so many things we want to do, it hasn't been done. I wish I could get a job, so that I could be out with people. Seclusion is not good at all. I need fresh ideas and new thoughts. My mind has simply used up all of its resources, and I have failed to feed it. I think I will get some books, and put myself on a new diet!

Last night Tom cried during the night for me. It is the first time he has let his emotions show so strongly. I felt close, like we used to be, before that all happened.

The dilemmas of dying are many. Can't figure out if you want to be buried, or cremated, embalmed or not—what clothes you want to be buried in, what you want on your gravestone.

To Jenny,

If you ever feel the need of someone to talk to, honey, don't be afraid to come to this book. I know I can't help with all my written words, but please take comfort in knowing that whatever is wrong, or whatever has made you hurt, I would have deeply cared, and tried my best to understand. I love you so much, baby.

There are so many things I always wanted to tell my daughter. Perhaps one very important thing I wanted most to say, was, no matter what, always do what you feel is right, or best for you. Treat your body and mind right, and they in turn will give you health and beauty.

If you want to sleep with a boy before you are married, please remember that sex is a function, but love is an emotion, and through it you can be deeply hurt, or given a happiness you will never forget. Don't just sleep with any man, for sex. At least feel an affection, a bond of giving and receiving, with him. This is so important, Jennifer. And for pete's sake, don't get pregnant. Tell your father you need something. If you know your own mind well enough, when and if this time comes, he'll feel it in the way you ask, and will understand. Remember though, he is a very sensitive man. Don't hurt him.

Wow! How's that for a bit of advice? Remember, I was only nineteen when I wrote it. But I do believe it—and know that it is good, and right.

I guess I'm bitter. I feel bitter when I look at pictures of Jennifer and realize that soon I won't even be able to see pictures of her. I won't get to touch her or be with her or remember her.

Oh, how I wish that at least in death you could remember! I wonder if you can. I doubt it. Death being not proud. What does that mean, I wonder, in the book—I don't think I read it. It means to me that death isn't afraid to come and take you away no matter who you are, which is upsetting. I have so much to give, so many things to do, so many people to be—and I'm not going to get to do it.

It's July now. I haven't written in my book for a very long time. I think I'm going to die soon.

At this point all I can do is wait, and be scared. I wonder what I have to expect, what sort of pain I have to go through. From what I understand, the whole thing isn't too pleasant. I just hope it goes fast.

The other night, when I wrote that I thought I was going to die, I had the most incredible melancholy feeling. I think that with the thought that I was dying, and all, I began speeding a little, but I still felt this incredible calm. All the thoughts of what I should be up doing were going so fast through my mind that I couldn't keep up with them. I kept thinking let me wake up just one more morning, to get all those things done. I think I was almost pleading. I haven't yet written all I wanted to say to Jenny, and that is so important. I have to get it done. And soon.

I think I have accepted death as well as anyone can. But what makes it hard is when I try to talk to people close to me, and tell them what I'd like done—with Jenny and Tom and my things—they refuse to listen. Then it makes me feel funny. It's such a hassle.

. . . So I don't know how I'll feel later when it gets even worse than this. Maybe I won't feel this way at all.

Sometimes high
sometimes low
feelin' mean
and dirty
I see my face
reflected there
now scarred
what once was pretty

A commercial about lung cancer is on TV. My chest hurts. Tom is smoking in the front room. What does it take to make people realize that they are killing themselves?

It's so hard. People have been so nice but there isn't anybody I can cry with. Nobody to touch me. Nobody to say it's okay. Nobody to comfort me and to listen to my self-pity. I'm so tied up inside it hurts so bad. Oh God, why does it work this way? Jenny hears me crying and wonders what's wrong.

I feel peaceful. Summer is over and fall is my time, my poetry. I love it. Virgo in September, and changing leaves, falling, cluttering, drifting to the ground. The smell of the sun, the dying grass, the light filtering through the branches. In the autumn the sun is in the peace position. It is the time for warm sweaters and football and soft music and touching and loving. Oh I love it all so much!

Tomorrow is a new day and if I don't die by then I will be twenty years old. The mystery of my life has begun to unfold.

Autumn is the time for loneliness
the time to write unfinished poems
and sing unfinished songs
before winter freezes them forever

I'm getting so close to death. I look at Jenny and it hurts so bad knowing that we will be soon losing each other. I think of Tom. I think of his face. I think of his losing me. And of me losing him. . . . I'm going to miss you, honey. The way you touch me and comfort me when I'm sad. The way you love and smile. . . . I'm confused, honey, not scared. What's happening to us? Where am I going?

Thinking about dying and about me and feeling rage at the fact that there will soon be no me.

I'm thinking about the man I love. I like what we have between us. It's been scratchy lately because of my sickness but it is growing back. We live together, just him and me and our little baby and no one gets in unless we want them. We only need each other.

I don't ever want to leave my man. Now I'm thinking how unfair it is. A tear wells up and creeps down my cheek. Love is not something you can live or die without.

> I lie here so melancholy death can come
> let it touch me now and I won't fight
> my body is drugged with pain pills
> I feel so warm and safe
> something is happening to me
> am I getting close to death?
> I feel afraid that I am
> I feel beautiful though
> even though I haven't done my book yet
> I know I have at least touched people
> I'm happy and sad
> I'm human and dying
> I'm a lot of things
> but mostly I'm Lyn
> wife and lover to Tom
> mother and friend to Jennifer
> also a writer of hope to my people

Dying

Robert S. Morison

Should people have the right to choose the time and circumstances of their own death? When is a person legally dead? When the heart stops beating? When the brain ceases to function? Can a person stop a doctor from keeping him or her alive? Should a doctor have the right to decide on a "mercy killing" when the patient is in excruciating and unending pain? Robert S. Morison explores this and other problems associated with death in our time.

The medical and legal professions have no clearcut definitions for death. That lack is becoming an increasingly important aspect of the moral, legal, and medical discussions of doctors, lawyers, and religious leaders. Nearly two-thirds of all deaths in industrialized countries are associated with the infirmities of old age, but medicine and technology can be used to keep old people alive long after their brains cease to function meaningfully. Many are maintained as vegetables in hospitals. Should they be allowed to die naturally? Read this article and decide for yourself.

The contemplation of death in the twentieth century can tell us a good deal about what is right and what is wrong with modern medicine. At the beginning of the century death came to about 15 percent of all newborn babies in their first year and to perhaps another 15 percent before adolescence. Nowadays fewer than 2 percent die in their first year and the great majority will live to be over 70.

Most of the improvement can be explained by changes in the numbers of deaths from infectious disease, brought about in large part by a combination of better sanitation, routine immunization and specific treatment with chemotherapeutic drugs or antibiotics. Also important, although difficult to quantify, are improvements in the individual's non-specific resistance that are attributable to improved nutrition and general hygiene.

Infectious diseases typically attack younger people. Equally typically, although not uniformly, they either cause death in a relatively short time or disappear completely, leaving the individual much as he was before. That is what makes death from infection particularly poignant. The large number of people who used to die of infection died untimely deaths; they had not lived long enough to enjoy the normal human experiences of love, marriage, supporting a family, painting a picture, or discovering a scientific truth.

The medical profession and the individual physician clearly had every incentive to struggle endlessly against deaths of this kind. Every triumph over an untimely death was rewarded by the high probability of complete recovery and a long, happy, and productive life. No wonder the profession developed an ethic that placed a preponderant emphasis on preserving life at all costs. No wonder also that it became preoccupied with the spectacular advances in science and technology that made such triumphs possible.

Nevertheless, it is still clear that we must all die sometime. As a matter of fact, the age at which the last member of a cohort, or age class, dies is now much the same as it was in biblical times. Whereas life expectancy at birth has improved by perhaps two and a half times, life expectancy at 70 has changed very little. (It is now approximately 12 years.) The difference is that in earlier times relatively few people managed to reach 70, whereas under present conditions nearly two-thirds of the population reach that age. As a result most people no longer die of some quick, acute illness but of the chronic deteriorations of old age. Only very recently has the general public or even the medical profession begun to realize that the attitudes and techniques developed in the battle against untimely death may not be entirely appropriate in helping the aged patient adapt to changed physiological and psychological circumstances.

The progress of technology puts in the physician's hands a constantly increasing number of things he can do for and to his aging patients. In the jargon of modern policy, the "options" have been greatly increased and the problem of therapy has become largely a problem of choice. Modern students of decision theory point out that all methods of choice making reduce ultimately to the making of value judgments. When a pediatrician encounters an otherwise normal child with a life-threatening sore throat, the value judgment is simple and immediate. The life is obviously worth saving at all costs and the only choice to be made is what antibiotic to use. At the other end of life, however, most patients present a varied mosaic of diminished and disordered function. For a man or woman over a certain age there is no such thing as complete recovery. Treatment directed at supporting one vital system may simply bring into greater prominence a more awkward or more painful disorder. Furthermore, many of the treatment options, unlike the treatment of acute infections that may threaten premature death, are far from simple and inexpensive. Instead they are often cumbersome, painful, and costly. The art, moreover, is constantly changing, so that it is hard to estimate the probable results of some of the most elaborate procedures.

I have approached the problem of terminal illness, or the dying patient, in this somewhat circuitous fashion in order to show that the problems surrounding the deathbed are not quite so unprecedented or so unconnected with the rest of medicine as to require the development of entirely new attitudes or perhaps even a new profession of "thanatologists." Dying is continuous with living, and the questions that are now asked with such insistence at the bedside of the dying should also be at least in the back of the mind of those who attend the living in earlier stages. The physician must consider the quality of the life he is struggling to preserve and the probable effects of his therapy on this quality, whatever the age of the patient. He should also know how to help a patient of any age to accept circumstances that cannot be changed. The so-called terminally ill patient simply represents the limiting case. In this instance the value questions have become paramount.

For reasons that are not all easy to identify the past few years have seen an astonishing increase in public attention to death and dying. A recent bibliography listing the titles of both books and papers in scholarly journals on the subject is several pages long. It is a rare daily newspaper or popular periodical that has not published one such article or several.

Approaches to the topic may be roughly separated into two classes: those that deal with making the patient's last days as physically and psychologically comfortable as possible and those that discuss the propriety of allowing or helping the patient to die at an appropriate time. Let us turn first to the care of the terminally ill.

Students of the process of dying have long emphasized the loneliness of the dying person. Not only is he destined to go where no one wants to follow but also the people around him prefer to pretend that the journey is really not going to take place. The practice of placing familiar articles and even animals, servants, and wives in the tomb or on the funeral pyre of the departed is testimony to man's desire to assuage the loneliness beyond. In *The Death of Ivan Ilych* Leo Tolstoy has given the classic description of the conspiracy of denial that so often surrounds the dying. The situation has certainly been made worse by the technological changes since Tolstoy's day. Then, at least, most people died at home, many of them surrounded by family and friends. Even if these attendants were primarily concerned with what would happen to themselves, as were those awaiting the death of the old Count Bezhukoi that Tolstoy also portrayed, they not only kept the patient from being physically alone but also made him quite conscious of being the center of attention.

Nowadays only a minority of people die at home, and the number is decreasing. Precise figures are hard to obtain, but the scattered studies that have been made agree that about half of all deaths occur in large general hospitals and a smaller but increasing number in nursing homes. Probably fewer than a third die at home, at work or in public places.

The past few years have seen a growing awareness that the big general hospital is not a very good place to die. Even though such hospitals have large staffs, most of these professionals are preoccupied with administrative matters and with the increasingly complicated technical aspects of keeping people alive. Surrounded by these busybodies, the dying patient is more often than not psychologically isolated. Recognizing that such an atmosphere is bad both for patients and for younger physicians in training, a few inspired physicians have developed special programs to instruct members of the hospital staff in the needs of the dying patient. Such efforts have been received with enthusiasm by the still quite limited numbers of physicians and students who have been exposed to them.

The usefulness of training hospital staff members to deal with the dying patient is a concept that is now spreading throughout the country. There is substantial hope that the next generation of physicians, nurses, and administrators will be much more understanding and helpful in meeting the special needs of the dying than their predecessors were. One of the leaders in this movement is an Illinois psychiatrist, Elisabeth K. Ross. In an effort to inject something approaching methodological rigor into her understanding and teaching of the needs of the dying, she has distinguished five stages exhibited by dying patients: denial, anger, bargaining (usually with God), depression, and acceptance. This effort toward intellectualization of the problem is admirable; at the same time it is probably true that what has been most influential in alleviating the loneliness of the dying is the warmth of Dr. Ross's sympathy and the intensity of her dedication to the effort.

A high proportion of the patients in nursing homes are destined to die there or to be removed only at the very last minute for intensive hospital care, yet few of these institutions appear to have given much thought to the special problems of the dying. The most striking exceptions are provided by what in England are called "hospices." The best known of them is St. Christopher's, outside London. It was started by a physician who was also trained as a nurse. She appears to have combined the best of both professions in developing arrangements for taking care of seriously ill patients and providing a warm and understanding atmosphere for them. Because many of the patients at St. Christopher's suffer from malignant disease, special emphasis is put on the alleviation of pain. It has been found that success depends not only on providing the right drugs at the right time but also on developing an attitude of understanding, confidence, and hope. Psychological support involves, among other things, deinstitutionalizing the atmosphere by encouraging members of the family, including children and grandchildren, both to "visit the patient" in a formal sense and to carry on such activities as may be usual for their age, so that the patient feels surrounded by ongoing normal life. Everyone who has observed the program or has been privileged to participate in it speaks appreciatively and even enthusiastically about its achievements.

Hospices also serve as centers for an active home-care program that is demonstrating the practicality of tending to many dying patients in the home, provided that the physical arrangements are satisfactory and that specialized help from outside is available for a few hours a day. Unfortunately most insurance plans, including the otherwise enlightened National Health Service in Britain, have tended to emphasize hospital care to the detriment of adequate support for proper care in the home.

Recent studies of home care for seriously ill patients suggest that in many cases it can be not only more satisfactory emotionally than hospital care but also considerably less costly. Much more information is needed before administrators of health plans can determine precisely how many and what kinds of personnel should be available for how long to deal with various kinds of home situations. Similarly, a few preliminary surveys of the technological ways of adapting the American home for the care of the chronically ill have been made. Here again there is enough information to suggest the importance of funds for special types of beds and wheelchairs, the installation of plumbing within easy range of the sickbed, and so on. The data, however, are not yet precise enough to allow adequate planning or the calculation of insurance premiums adequate to cover such services.

In spite of the potential emotional and economic benefits of home care one cannot overlook the fact that many social and technological changes have made illness and death at home very different from what they were in the days of Ivan Ilych and Count Bezhukoi. It is not appropriate here to try to cast up an account of the costs and benefits of such factors as rising social and geographic mobility and the transition from the extended family to the nuclear family. When these costs are counted, however, it may be well to include mention of the increasing difficulty in finding a good place to grow old and die.

Let us next examine the question of when it becomes appropriate to die. No matter how considerate the physician, how supportive the institutional atmosphere, how affectionately concerned the family and friends or how well-adjusted the patient himself, there comes a time when all those involved must ask themselves just how much sense it makes to continue vigorously trying to postpone the inevitable. Regrettably, the literature addressed to the topics of death and dying often seems preoccupied more with dissecting the various ethical and legal niceties surrounding the moment and manner of death than with what one can do to make the last few months or years of life as rewarding as possible. No doubt this preoccupation is prompted by an apparent conflict between ancient taboos on the one hand and certain obvious commonsense considerations on the other.

Now, virtually no one who has thought about the matter at all, from John Doe to the Pope, feels that any absolute moral or legal obligation requires one to do everything one knows how to do in order to preserve the life of a severely deteriorated patient beyond hope of recovery. Indeed, in actual practice it now seems probable that only a small minority of patients have everything possible done for them right up to the moment of death. The difficulties, then, are not with the general principle but with how to arrange the details. First and foremost in presenting themselves are the theoretical and even metaphysical problems involved in the ways that men of goodwill attempt to justify actions that appear to violate the taboo against killing. Second, there are practical questions to be answered. How can the individual make sure that his wishes are carried out? Who is to make the decision if the patient is no longer competent to do so? What are the physician's responsibilities? What, for that matter, are his possible liabilities? How far should society go in attempting to protect the rights and regulate the behavior of the various parties?

No more than an outline of the theoretical problems can be presented here. Current discussion centers principally on three issues. First is the definition of death. Next is the difference, if any, between negative and positive euthanasia and last is the definition of "extraordinary means."

The possibility of redefining death came into prominence a few years ago when a group of Boston physicians grew concerned about precisely when it was appropriate to remove a prospective donor's organs for transplantation. It rapidly became clear that "defining" death, for whatever purpose, is a complicated philosophical matter that admits of no easy resolution. What the members of the Boston group actually did was to devise an operational redefinition of the criteria to be applied in declaring that a person has died. The major difficulty they faced arose from the purely technical fact that it is now possible to maintain the function of the heart and the lungs by artificial means. The failure of these two vital functions can therefore no longer be regarded in all cases as the paramount criteria for pronouncing death, as was once set forth in all conventional medical-legal texts.

The Boston group instead recommended the use of a set of signs testifying to an essentially complete failure of a third set of functions: those of the nervous system. This proposal has been received with approval by a large number of physicians, theologians, and lawyers, and has now been included in the law of several states. The criteria as they stand are extremely rigid and involve the death of essentially all levels of the nervous system. They thus seem entirely adequate both to protect the patient against premature assaults in order to retrieve viable organs and at the same time to guard him against unduly zealous attempts to maintain elementary vital signs in the name of therapy.

There is another class of patients, however, in whom elementary vital signs have not failed, although the higher brain functions—thinking, communicating with others, and even consciousness itself—have departed. Such a patient constitutes a most distressing problem to families and physicians, and it has been suggested that a further revision of the criteria for a pronouncement of death might be used to justify the termination of active treatment in such cases. The idea is that what is really human and important about the individual resides in the upper levels of the nervous system, and that these attributes indeed die with the death of the forebrain.

The presumed merit of such a revision grows out of the way it avoids the basic ethical problem; obviously it makes no sense to go on treating what can rationally be defined as a corpse. The weight of opinion, however, seems to be against dealing with the question of cerebral incapacity in this oblique way. From several standpoints it seems preferable to face up to the fact that under these circumstances a patient may still be living in some sense, but that the obligation to treat the living is neither absolute nor inexorable.

No less a moral authority than the Pope appears to have lent his weight to this view and even to have spoken for most Christians when he announced a few years ago that the physician is not required to use "extraordinary means" to maintain the spark of life in a deteriorated patient with no evident possibility of recovery. Nevertheless, serious ambiguities still remain. At first the Vatican's phraseology appears to have been designed to allow the withdrawal of "heroic" and relatively novel procedures such as defibrillation, cardiac massage, and artificial respiration. More subtle analysts point out that there is no absolute scale of extraordinariness, and that what is or is not extraordinary can only be judged in relation to the condition of a given individual. Hence there is nothing extraordinary about using all possible means to keep alive a young mother who has suffered multiple fractures, severe hemorrhages, and temporary unconsciousness. Conversely, the term extraordinary may well be applied to relatively routine procedures such as intravenous feeding if the patient is elderly, has deteriorated, and has little hope of improvement. Thus the most active proponents of the doctrine of extraordinary means clearly interpret "extraordinary" to mean "inappropriate in the circumstances." Although many people who hold this position would disagree, it is not easy for an outsider to distinguish their interpretation from advocacy of what is sometimes called "negative euthanasia."

Negative euthanasia refers to withdrawal of treatment from a patient who as a result is likely to die somewhat earlier than he otherwise would. Many thoughtful and sensitive people who favor the principle dislike the term because it suggests that treatment is being withdrawn with an actual, if unspoken, intent to shorten the patient's life. These critics, who place a high value on the taboo against taking life, prefer to regard the withdrawal of active therapy as simply a matter of changing from a therapeutic regime that is inappropriate to one that is more appropriate under the circumstances. If death then supervenes, it is not regarded as the result of anything the physician has or has not done but simply as a consequence of the underlying illness. Thus the physician and those who have perhaps participated in his decision are protected from the fear that they are "playing God" or from similar feelings of guilt.

To My Family, My Physician, My Lawyer
and All Others Whom It May Concern

Death is as much a reality as birth, growth, maturity, and old age—it is the one certainty of life. If the time comes when I can no longer take part in decisions for my own future, let this statement stand as an expression of my wishes and directions, while I am still of sound mind.

If at such a time the situation should arise in which there is no reasonable expectation of my recovery from extreme physical or mental disability, I direct that I be allowed to die and not be kept alive by medications, artificial means, or "heroic measures". I do, however, ask that medication be mercifully administered to me to alleviate suffering even though this may shorten my remaining life.

This statement is made after careful consideration and is in accordance with my strong convictions and beliefs. I want the wishes and directions here expressed carried out to the extent permitted by law. Insofar as they are not legally enforceable, I hope that those to whom this Will is addressed will regard themselves as morally bound by these provisions.

Signed _____

Date _____

Witness _____

Witness _____

Copies of this request have been given to _____

_____

_____

_____

"LIVING WILL" is a formal request prepared by Concern for Dying. It informs the signer's family or others who may be concerned of the signer's wish to avoid the use of "heroic measures" to maintain life in the event of irreversible illness. Reprinted with permission of Concern for Dying, 250 West 57th Street, New York, New York 10019.

Many of those who favor negative euthanasia also recognize that appropriate care of the terminally ill may include "positive" procedures, such as giving morphine (which, among other effects, may advance the moment of death). Invoking what is known in Catholic circles as the doctrine, or law, of double effect, they regard such positive actions as permissible as long as the conscious intent is to achieve some licit purpose such as the relief of pain. This view in turn requires the drawing of an important moral distinction between "awareness of probable result" and "intent."

Other moralists, such as the blunter and more forthright proponents of what is called situational ethics, may discuss such subtleties as irrelevant logic-chopping. In their view it is a mistake to extend the generalized taboos and abstract principles of the past to encompass the peculiarities of the twentieth-century death scene. They prefer to focus attention on the scene itself and to do what seems best in terms of the probable results for all concerned. Perhaps not surprisingly, the situational ethicist, who derives much of his philosophical base from classical utilitarian, or consequential, ethics, sees relatively little difference between negative and positive euthanasia, that is, between allowing to die and causing to die.

For the sake of completeness let me inject my own opinion that although there may be only a trivial intellectual distinction between negative and positive euthanasia, it seems unwise and in any event useless at this time to enter into an elaborate defense of positive euthanasia. Although the principle has its enthusiastic advocates, their number is strictly limited. The overwhelming majority of physicians and certainly a substantial majority of laymen instinctively recoil from such active measures as prescribing a known poison or injecting a large bubble into a vein. There seems to be a point where simple human reactions supersede both legal sanction and rational analysis. As an example, very few New York physicians or nurses are anxious to exercise the right given them by the laws of the state to perform abortions as late as the twenty-fourth week of pregnancy. Furthermore, it appears that as a practical matter negative euthanasia, or the withdrawal of all active therapy except the provision of narcotics to subdue restlessness and pain, will in any case be followed in a reasonable length of time by the coming of what Osler termed near the turn of the century the "old man's friend": a peaceful death from bronchial pneumonia. Thus, in the terminology of the law courts, we need not reach the most difficult question.

In view of the prevailing theoretical uncertainties, it is not surprising that what is done to or for the dying patient varies widely from place to place and from physician to physician. It is impossible to be precise because very few scientific observations have been made. Perhaps the most careful study is one conducted by Diana Crane of the University of Pennsylvania, who asked a large number of physicians and surgeons what they would probably do in a series of precisely outlined clinical situations. From this and more anecdotal evidence it seems clear that very few do everything possible to prolong the lives of all their patients. At the other extreme, even fewer physicians would appear to employ active measures with the avowed intent of shortening life. In between there is an enormous range of decisions: to give or not to give a transfusion, to prescribe an antibiotic or a sulfa drug, to attach or disconnect a respirator or an artificial kidney, to install a cardiac pacemaker or to let the battery of one that is already installed run down. The overall impression gained both by the informed observer and by the sometimes despairing layman is that the median of all these activities lies rather far toward officiously keeping alive.

The reasons are obvious enough: the momentum of a professional tradition of preserving life at all costs, the reluctance of the physician and the layman to ignore ancient taboos or to impair the value of such positive concepts as the sanctity of life, and the ambiguities of the love-hate relationship between parents and children or husbands and wives. Finally, there is the continuing uncertainty about the legal position of a physician who might be charged with hastening the death of a patient by acts of either omission or commission.

Up to now, at least, the legal deterrent appears to have been something of a chimera. A conscientious search of the available literature in English has uncovered not one criminal action charging that a physician omitted treatment with the intent to shorten life. Indeed, there are surprisingly few actions that charge positive euthanasia. Even in the few actions that have been lodged, juries have shown a reluctance to convict when there is evidence that the action was undertaken in good faith to put the patient on the far side of suffering.

Approaching the problem from a somewhat different angle, although the definitive examples are few, there appears to be general agreement that the adult patient in full possession of his senses has every right to refuse treatment. It is somewhat less certain that such refusal is binding after a patient loses legal competence. Even less clear is the status of the expressed wish of a potential patient with respect to what he would want done in certain hypothetical future circumstances. Efforts to clarify the status of such communications, sometimes called "living wills," with physicians and relatives are being actively pursued.

Important though it may be to establish the rights and privileges of those foresighted enough to want to participate in the design of their own death, it must be admitted that such individuals now constitute only a trivial part of the population. The great majority prefer not to think about their own death in any way. Indeed, most people do not even leave a will directing what to do with their material possessions.

What, then, can be done for that large number of people likely to slip into an unanticipated position of indignity on a deathbed surrounded by busybodies with tubes and needles in their hands, ready to substitute a chemical or mechanical device for every item in the human inventory except those that make human life significant? In such instances, under ideal, or perhaps I should say idyllic, circumstances the attending physician would have known the patient and his family for a long time. Further, he would have sensed their conscious and unconscious wishes and needs, and drawing on his accumulated skills and wisdom, he would conduct the last illness so as to maximize the welfare of all concerned. Unfortunately under modern conditions few families have a regular physician of any kind and even fewer physicians possess the hypothetical virtues I have outlined.

However that may be, at least three approaches to the problem are being actively pursued at present. Foremost among them is the active discussion I have referred to. Not only the professional journals but also the monthly, weekly, and daily press are publishing numerous articles on death and dying. Radio and television programs have followed suit, and it must be a rare church discussion group that has not held at least one meeting devoted to death with dignity. At the very least such discussion must remove some of the reluctance to speak of death or even think about it. At best it must improve the possibility of communication and understanding between the patient and the physician. The resulting change in the climate of opinion cannot fail to make it easier to discard outmoded taboos in favor of the common sense of contemporary men.

Second, and equally important, are the formal and informal efforts to improve the education of physicians by redressing the imbalance between technical skill and human wisdom that has grown up during the century. In addition to the kind of clinical concern for the dying exemplified by Dr. Ross, many medical schools are converting their courses in medical ethics from a guild-oriented preoccupation with fee splitting and other offenses against the in-group to a genuine concern for ethical values in the treatment of patients.

Third, there are the more formal attempts to clarify rights, responsibilities, and roles by means of legislation. Part of this effort is directed at establishing the obligation of a physician to follow the expressed wishes of his patient or, at the very least, at protecting the physician from liability if he does so. Other legislative proposals stem from a more or less explicit conviction that death is too important a matter to be left to physicians. Difficulty is often encountered, however, in finding a satisfactory alternative, and there is now much discussion of the relative merits of assigning ultimate authority to the next of kin, to an ombudsman or to a committee of social scientists, philosophers, and theologians.

It is too early to predict how such suggestions will turn out, but there are some reasons for feeling that it may be well to go slow in formalizing what is bound to be a difficult situation and instead to redouble efforts toward developing the capacity of medical men and laymen to deal informally with the problem. In actual practice the conduct of a drawn-out terminal illness involves a series of small decisions, based on repeated evaluations of the physical and emotional condition of the patient and the attitudes, hopes, and fears of his family and friends. It is not easy to see how an outsider such as an ombudsman, much less a committee, can be very easily fitted into what is typically an unobtrusive incremental process. Concrete evidence on this point may be found with respect to the beginning of life in the attempts by opponents of contraception to inject either a sheriff or a bureaucrat, so to speak, into the bedroom. These attempts have not proved satisfactory and are more and more being denounced by the courts as invasions of privacy.

As long as progress is being made at the informal, grass-roots level, it may be just as well to refrain from drafting tidy legislative solutions to problems so profound. Whatever else may be said, it is obvious that changing attitudes toward death and dying provide an excellent paradigm of how changing technologies force on us the consideration of equally significant changes in value systems and social institutions.

from *How to Save Your Own Life*

Erica Mann Jong

The death of another person affects us in a variety of ways. How we respond to another person's death depends on our relationship with that person. Erica Jong, in How to Save Your Own Life, describes her reactions to a friend's death.

Before Jeannie left, she took me aside and gave me a slim, oblong package wrapped in tissue paper.

"What is it?"

"Something to remember me by," she said cryptically.

"Remember you? I'll never forget you as long as I live."

"Longer," she said, smiling.

I tore open the package. Inside was a notebook covered in red marble-patterned paper, with a red morocco spine and red morocco corners. On the first endpaper, Jeannie had written (in a hand that seemed to flatten the lowercase letters into submission—but leave the uppercase ones standing taller as a result):

Life can only be understood backwards,
but it must be lived forwards.
  —Kierkegaard, via Jeannie Morton

"A notebook," Jeannie said, "to understand your life—or save it. You could call it, *How to Save Your Own Life.*"

"How did you know that was exactly what I needed?" I asked.

"Because I'm a witch," she laughed, hugging me. "Just make sure you fill up the notebook. Do it for me."

"I'll mail it to you as soon as I'm through."

"You may never be through," Jeannie said.

My friends Louise and Robert Miller drove Jeannie back to the Algonquin at midnight, had a nightcap with her—and then wanted to head home.

She would not let them go, but held them captive in the lobby, ordering drink after drink, swallowing her sleeping pills with vodka, waiting for the pills to take effect, to quiet the panic, keep down the demons.

Jeannie clutched Bob's wrist with hysterical tightness, growing tighter and tighter as her fear of going upstairs to her room increased. She tried to convince them to stay with her—but when, at 3:00 A.M., they pleaded exhaustion, she downed another Valium—and leaned back in the lobby armchair to doze. They finally left her there, not knowing what else they could do short of both getting into bed with her.

In October she was dead. Already she was laid out in the funeral parlor, her children were called home from college, her husband and lovers all remarried her in death, and, the whole world over, schoolgirl poets were using her as the subject of their poems. She was ossifying into myth. Another suicidal lady poet. She, who had been so funny, so outrageous, so pure in her intuition and so warm, was being frozen into cult.

The weekend after her death, I was having my picture taken in Central Park, by a fellow named Rod Thomas, who is a photographer and a poet and also a devoted fan of Jeannie's. Rod took me wandering through the park, where we reminisced about her and took pictures of me under trees, on rocks, in row-boats. They were supposed to be pictures for a new book of poems—but in all of them I looked so haunted that something kept us from using them. I'll never know whether or not the decision was wise. In none of the pictures did I look quite like myself—nor did I look like Jeannie, really—but some transmigration had taken place. Whether of the soul or of some other part is not for me to say.

Photographs, anyway, are the most curious indicators of reality. They are said to convey the exact nature of the material world, but actually, what they convey is spiritual and only partly the result of the masses of light and shadow in the world of rocks and trees and flesh. Things happen in photographs that do not happen in life. Or else we perceive in photographs what we cannot perceive in life. Is perception equivalent to existence? That is the premise on which we base our lives, yet it may well be a false premise.

In these photographs, something new had entered my face: a special sort of daring, the courage to be a fool.

All this is retrospect, hindsight. "Life can only be understood backwards, but it must be lived forwards" it said in the notebook which, in the months after Jeannie gave it to me, I had found too beautiful (and had been too depressed) to use. Of course I was not completely without the fool's daring before Jeannie's death. I had done plenty of dumb things, and suffered for them, and learned from them. But with her death, some new element entered my chronic, anguishing indecision. "Live or die," she seemed to be saying to me from the grave, "but for god's sake don't poison yourself with indecision."

Throughout our lives, we are brought in contact with spiritual advisors; the trick is not in meeting them, but in recognizing them when we do. I recognized Jeannie from the start, but if she had not died, would I have acted upon the recognition? I wonder.

2 The Nature of Humanity

What is humanity? This is the age-old question. The Psalmist asked it of his God, wondering how the deity could pay so much attention to such an insignificant part of the universe. Shakespeare extolled humanity throughout his poetic career, but colored his entire catalog of works with a touch of irony that betrayed his curiosity and bemusement at this "piece of work."

The question of human nature is essentially a philosophical problem, but psychologists are discovering that they cannot do a good job of understanding human nature without coming to grips with it. We will try to explore the question to a limited degree here, turning to thinkers who have a sympathetic but reality-oriented approach to the matter, for the beginnings of an answer.

Hadley Cantril is a psychologist who has pioneered in the study of perception, the processes by which we "make sense" out of our sense experiences. In the first selection, "A Fresh Look at the Human Design," he tries to point out that human motivation—what makes us tick—is much more complicated than people who work exclusively with rats and guinea pigs might lead us to believe.

The nature-of-humanity question brings us squarely to the fact of our interpersonal dimensions and relations. Are humans only animals? Only souls? Only brains? Does the way we view our own nature have anything to say about the way in which we relate to each other? Dr. Erich Fromm senses that industrial society tends to transform humans into things. In an excerpt from The Revolution of Hope, he discusses what he feels we must do to recapture our feeling of human identity.

Many women are discovering a new identity. In "The Women's Room" by Marilyn French, the author discusses the problems she has in trying to give up her old identity for a new one.

Few thinkers attempt to tackle the question of humanity's future on the levels of science, philosophy, and theology. Teilhard de Chardin, who wrote the third selection in this chapter, is one of the few. Our selection is from his book, The Future of Man.

A Fresh Look at the Human Design

Hadley Cantril

Humankind, as Dr. James Bugental tells us, is the challenge to humankind. But most studies of human experience are dull and uninteresting because students can't find themselves in the literature. They read about the "organism" or the "subject," but fail to find the flesh and blood being with whom they can identify. Cantril tells us that we are far more than a combination of stimulus-response patterns. In this excerpt, he describes the complex matter of human nature in terms of the things that really motivate people.

The human being seems at last to be entering the main body of psychology with a vengeance. For years he has all too often been shorn of his most characteristic attributes, until he has been scarcely recognizable. Variables such as appetites, wants, values, and temperament have been neglected because they are not easily manipulated in the laboratory and can so disturb otherwise neat experimentation. As Henry A. Murray pointed out nearly two decades ago, "The main body of psychology started its career by putting the wrong foot forward, and it has been out of step with the march of science much of the time. Instead of beginning with studies of the whole person adjusting to a natural environment, it began with studies of a segment of a person responding to a physical stimulus in an unnatural laboratory environment."[1] One consequence of this false start has been a

Reprinted with permission from the *Journal of Individual Psychology* 19 (1963): 3-16.
1. H.A. Murray et al., *The Assessment of Men* (New York: Holt, Rinehart & Winston, 1948), p. 466.

proliferation of model building which often takes on the aspect of playing games. Another consequence has been an overemphasis by some investigators on a single variable which proves at best tentative and partial after the fad for it has run its course.

It is therefore no wonder that so many students of psychology have found it an insufferably dull subject and that many social scientists and inquiring laymen feel that most of the psychology they read provides them unconvincing, unrewarding concepts from which to choose as they try to give plausible accounts of the behavior of men and women in real-life situations. They sense that somewhere along the line too much of human experience has been left out of account.

It is appropriate, then, for those of us concerned with human experience and behavior in all its subtle ramifications to spell out what seems to us to ring true and what appear to be the demands that the genetically built-in design of the human being imposes on any society, political culture, or enduring social relationship. It is all too easy to neglect the basic functional uniformities which take diverse forms and to leave the accounting or explanation at that level. Differences are often dramatic and simpler to detect than the similarities they may obscure. Here I shall try to orchestrate into some systematic unity the diversities of mankind found in different societies and contexts. . . .

Man requires the satisfaction of his survival needs.

Any listing of the characteristics of any living organism must begin here. Neurophysiologists have located and described in a most general way two built-in appetitive systems found in higher animals: one system propelling them to seek satisfying and pleasurable experiences, and the other protecting them from threatening or unpleasant experiences.[2] These two systems together can be thought of as the basic forces contained within all human beings, which not only keep them and the species alive as their simple survival needs for food, shelter, and sex are gratified but also are involved in the desire for life itself.

These appetitive systems, of course, become enormously developed, refined, and conditioned—especially in man—as new ways are learned to achieve satisfactions and avoid dangers and discomforts. It has often been noted that unless the survival needs are satisfied, a person devotes himself almost exclusively to a continued attempt to fulfill them, a preoccupation which preempts his energies and repels any concern for other activities.

2. H. Cantril and W.K. Livingston, "The Concept of Transaction in Psychology and Neurology," *Journal of Individual Psychology* **19** (1963):3–16.

Most people in the world today are still concerned with living a type of life that constitutes well-being on a relatively simple level with what amenities their cultures can provide.

Man wants security in both its physical and its psychological meaning to protect gains already made and to assure a beachhead from which further advances may be staged.

Man wants some surety that one action can lead to another, some definite foothold which provides an orientation and integration through time. People invariably become embittered if they nurse a dream for what they regard as a long time with no signs of it becoming a reality. . . .

Man craves sufficient order and certainty in his life to enable him to judge with fair accuracy what will or will not occur if he does or does not act in certain ways.

People want sufficient form and pattern in life to be sure that certain satisfactions already enjoyed will be repeatable and will provide a secure springboard for takeoffs in new directions.

The conflict of old loyalties with emerging new loyalties in the case of developing people is bound to create uncertainties, doubts, and hesitations. If people become frustrated and anxious enough, they will do almost anything in a desperate attempt to put some order into apparent chaos or rally around new symbols and abstractions that enable them to identify with a new order that promises to alleviate the uncertainties experienced in the here and now.

In stressing process and change, the desire of people to preserve the *status quo* when it has proved satisfying and rewarding and to protect existing forms against alteration must never be overlooked. This craving for certainty would include the satisfactions that come from the sense of stability provided by our habitual behavior—including much of our social and political behavior.

Human beings continuously seek to enlarge the range and enrich the quality of their satisfactions.

Man is engaged in a ceaseless quest to extend the range and improve the quality of his satisfactions through the exercise of his creative and inventive capacities. This is, of course, a basic reason why order of any kind is constantly being upset. Whitehead expressed the point eloquently and repeatedly, for example, in his statements that "the essence of life is to be found in the frustrations of established order"[3] and that "the art of progress is to preserve order amid change, and to preserve change amid order."[4]

The distinguished British philosopher John Macmurray has used the phrase "the self as agent" as the title of his book analyzing the role of action in man's constant search for value satisfactions.[5] In a companion volume, he has noted that "... human behavior cannot be understood, but only caricatured, if it is represented as an adaptation to environment.[6] The search for an enlargement of satisfactions in the transactions of living can also be phrased as the *desire for development in a direction*, the desire to do something which will bring a sense of accomplishment as we experience the consequences of successfully carrying out some intention and which will thus give us an occasional feeling that our lives are continuous creations in which we can take an active part. During a conversation in Beirut, a wise man once remarked to me that "people are hungry for new and good experiences." ...

The particular value satisfactions man acquires are the result of learning. Some of the values learned will serve as the operative ideals of a people; others will be chiefly instrumental. People in rich countries have learned to want and to expect many aspects of a good life that less favored people have not yet learned are possibilities. From this point of view, one might say that the competition between social and political systems is a competition in teaching people what to want and what is potentially available to them, and then in proving to them in their own private experience that these wants are best attainable under the system described.

Human beings are creatures of hope and are not genetically designed to resign themselves.

This characteristic of man stems from the characteristic just described: that man is always likely to be dissatisfied and never fully "adapts" to his environment.

Man seems continually to hope that the world he encounters will correspond more and more to his vision of it as he acts within it to carry out his purposes, while the vision itself continuously unfolds in an irreversible direction. The whole process is a never-ending one. It is characteristic of

3. A.N. Whitehead, *Modes of Thought* (New York: Macmillan, 1938).
4. A.N. Whitehead, *Symbolism: Its Meaning and Effect* (New York: Macmillan, 1929), p. 515.
5. J. Macmurray, *The Self as Agent* (New York: Harper & Row, 1957).
6. J. Macmurray, *Persons in Relation* (London: Faber, 1961), p. 46.

man in his ongoing experience to ask himself, "Where do I go from here?" Only in his more reflective moods does a person ask, "Where did I come from?" or "How did I get this way?" Most of the time, most people who are "plugged into" the changing world around them are future-oriented in their concerns.

Human beings have the capacity to make choices and the desire to exercise this capacity.

Any mechanical model of man constructed by a psychologist or by anyone else is bound to leave out the crucially important characteristic of man as an "appetite-perceptive agency." Perceptions are learned and utilized by people to provide prognoses or bets of a variety of kinds to weigh alternative courses of action to achieve purposes. Consciously or without conscious awareness, people are trying to perceive the probable relation between their potential acts and the consequences of these acts to the intentions that constitute their goals.

The human nervous system, including the brain, has the capacity to police its input, to determine what is and what is not significant for it, and to pay attention to and to reinforce or otherwise modify its behavior as it transacts in the occasions of living.[7] In this sense, the human being is a participant in, and producer of, his own value satisfactions: People perceive only what is relevant to their purposes and make their choices accordingly.

Human beings require freedom to exercise the choices they are capable of making.

This characteristic of man related to freedom is deliberately worded as it is, rather than as a blanket statement that "human beings require freedom," since the freedom people want is so relative to their desires and the stage of development they have attained. Human beings, incidentally, apparently require more freedom than other species of animals because of their much greater capacity to move about and to engage in a much wider variety of behavior.

It seems true that maximum freedom is a necessary condition if a highly developed individual is to obtain maximum value satisfaction. It is equally true, as many people have pointed out, that too much freedom too

7. H. Cantril and W.K. Livington, "The Concept of Transaction in Psychology and Neurology," pp. 3–16.

soon can be an unbearable burden and a source of bondage if people, like children, are insufficiently developed to know what to do with it. For freedom clearly involves a learning of responsibility and an ability to take advantage of it wisely.

The concept of freedom is essentially a psychological and not a political concept. It describes an individual's opportunity to make his own choices and to act in accord with them. Psychologically, freedom refers to the freedom to experience more of what is potentially available, the freedom to move about and ahead, to be and to become. Freedom is thus less and less determined and more of a reality as man evolves and develops; it emerges and flowers as people learn what it can mean to them in terms of resolving some frustrations under which they are living. . . .

Human beings want to experience their own identity and integrity (more popularly referred to as the "need for personal dignity").

Every human being craves a sense of his own self-constancy, an assurance of the repeatability of experience in which he is a determining participant. He obtains this from the transactions he has with other individuals.

People develop significances they share with others in their membership and reference groups. If the satisfaction derived from and the significance of participation with others cease to confirm assumptions or to enrich values, then a person's sense of self-constancy becomes shaken or insecure, and his loyalties become formalized and empty or are given up altogether. He becomes alienated or seeks new significances, new loyalties that are more operationally real.

People want to experience a sense of their own worthwhileness.

This differentiation is made from the desire for personal identity and integrity to bring out the important relationship between this search for identity and the behavior and attitudes of others toward us. A human being wants to know he is valued by others and that others will somehow show through their behavior that his own behavior and its consequences make some sort of difference to them in ways that give him a sense of satisfaction. When this occurs, not only is a person's sense of identity confirmed, but he also experiences a sense of personal worth and self-respect. The process of extending the sense of self both in space and in time appears also to involve the desire that one's "presence" not be limited merely to the here and now of existence, but extend into larger dimensions. These human cravings seem to be at the root of man's social relationships.

People acquire, maintain, and enrich their sense of worthwhileness only if they at least vaguely recognize the sources of what personal identity they have: their family, their friends and neighbors, their associates or fellow workers, their group ties, or their nation. The social, religious, intellectual, regional, or national loyalties formed play the important role of making it possible for individuals to extend themselves backward into the past and forward into the future and to identify themselves with others who live at more or less remote distances from them. This means the compounding of shared experiences into a bundle that can be conceptualized, felt, or somehow referred to in the here and now of daily living, thus making a person feel a functional part of a more enduring alliance. Man accomplishes such feats of self-extension largely through his capacity to create symbols, images, and myths which provide focal points for identification and self-expansion. After reviewing the lessons from history, Muller noted as one of the "forgotten simplicities" the fact that "men have always been willing to sacrifice themselves for some larger cause, fighting and dying for their family, tribe, or community, with or without hope of eternal reward."[8]

Human beings seek some value or system of beliefs to which they can commit themselves.

In the midst of the probabilities and uncertainties that surround them, people want some anchoring points, some certainties, some faith that will serve either as a beacon light to guide them or as a balm to assuage them during the inevitable frustrations and anxieties that living engenders.

People who have long been frustrated and who have searched for means to alleviate their situations are, of course, particularly susceptible to a commitment to a new system of beliefs or an ideology that they feel holds promise of effective action.

Beliefs are confirmed insofar as action based on them brings satisfying consequences, and they are denied with growing skepticism if disastrous results consistently occur because they are followed.

8. H.J. Muller, *The Uses of the Past* (New York: Mentor Books, 1954), p. 392.

Commitment to a value or belief system becomes more difficult among well-informed and sophisticated people who self-consciously try to reconcile what they believe with what they know and what they know with what they believe. In such circumstances, beliefs become more secular and less important as personal identifications.

Human beings want a sense of surety and confidence that the society of which they are a part holds out a fair degree of hope that their aspirations will be fulfilled.

If people cannot experience the effectiveness of social mechanisms to accomplish some of the potential goals they aspire to, then obviously their frustrations and anxieties mount, and they search for new means to accomplish aims. On the other hand, they make any sacrifice required to protect a society which they feel is fulfilling their needs but which appears seriously threatened. . . .

. . . If the gap between what society actually provides in terms of effective mechanisms for living and what it purports to provide becomes too great, the vacuum created will sooner or later engender the frustrations that urge people on to seek new social patterns and symbols. Whitehead wrote:

> The major advances in civilization are processes which all but wreck the societies in which they occur—like unto an arrow in the hand of a child. The art of free society consists first in the maintenance of the symbolic code; and secondly in fearlessness of revision, to secure that the code serves those purposes which satisfy an enlightened reason. Those societies which cannot combine reverence to their symbols with freedom of revision, must ultimately decay either from anarchy, or from the slow atrophy of a life stifled by useless shadows.[9]

Every social and political system can be regarded as an experiment in the broad perspective of time. Whatever the experiment, the human design will in the long run force any experiment to accommodate to it. This has been the case throughout human history. Few would deny that the varied patterns of experiments going on today hold out more promise of satisfying the human condition for a greater number of people than ever before.

9. A.N. Whitehead, *Symbolism: Its Meaning and Effect*, p. 88.

What Does It Mean to Be Human?

Erich Fromm

According to Erich Fromm, an "identity crisis" comes from one's inability to relate to him- or herself in a human way. In the industrial age in which we live, people have been alienated, dehumanized to a stimulus-response mechanistic entity. In his book The Revolution of Hope, *Fromm gives us some worthwhile insights into what it means to be human.* I am *is a complete concept, yet it is usually a prelude to something else that identifies us—student, teacher, engineer; Catholic, Jew, Buddhist; Democrat or Republican, and so on. In this excerpt, Fromm tries to help his readers sense the* I am *in the complete meaning of being human, rather than signifying that a position, possessions, or other exterior factors give us significance.*

In recent years, the problem of identity has been much in the foregound of psychological discussion, especially stimulated by the excellent work of Erik Erikson. He has spoken of the "identity crisis" and, undoubtedly, he has touched upon one of the major psychological problems of industrial society. But in my opinion, he has not gone as far or penetrated as deeply as is necessary for the full understanding of the phenomena of identity and identity crisis. In industrial society men are transformed into things, and things have no identity. Or do they? Is not every Ford car of a certain year and a certain model identical with every other Ford car of the same model and different from other models and vintages? Has not any dollar bill its identity; like any other dollar bill inasmuch as it has the same design, value, exchangeability, but different from any other dollar bill in terms of the differences in the quality of the paper brought about by the length of use? *Things* can be the same or different. However, if we speak of identity, we speak of a quality which does not pertain to things, but only to man.

What then is identity in a *human* sense? Among the many approaches to this question, I want to stress only the concept that identity is the experience which permits a person to say legitimately "I"—"I" as an organizing active center of the structure of all my actual or potential activities. This experience of "I" exists only in the state of spontaneous activity, but it does not exist in the state of passiveness and half-awakeness, a state in which people are sufficiently awake to go about their business but not awake enough to sense an "I" as the active center within themselves. This concept of "I" is different from the concept of ego (I do not use this term in the Freudian sense but in the popular sense of a person who, for example, has a "big ego.") The experience of my "ego" is the experience of myself as a thing, of the body I have, the memory I have—the money, the house, the social position, the power, the children, the problems I *have*. I look at myself as a thing and my social role is another attribute of thingness. Many people easily confuse the identity of ego with the identity of "I" or self. The difference is fundamental and unmistakable. The experience of ego, and of ego-identity, is based on the concept of having. I *have* "me" as I have all other things which this "me" owns. Identity of "I" or self refers to the category of being and not of having. I am "I" only to the extent to which I am alive, interested, related, active, and to which I have achieved an integration between my appearance—to others and/or to myself—and the core of my personality. The identity crisis of our time is based essentially on the increasing alienation and reification [thing-ing] of man, and it can be solved only to the extent to which man comes to life again, becomes active again. There are no psychological shortcuts to the solution to the identity crisis except the fundamental transformation of alienated man into living man.

The increasing emphasis on ego versus self, on having versus being, finds a glaring expression in the development of our language. It has become customary for people to say, "I have insomnia," instead of saying, "I cannot sleep"; or, "I have a problem," instead of, "I feel sad, confused" or whatever it may be; or, "I have a happy marriage" (sometimes successful marriage), instead of saying, "My wife and I love each other." All categories of the process of being are transformed into categories of having. The ego, static and unmoved, relates to the world in terms of having objects, while the self is related to the world in the process of participation. Modern man *has* everything: a car, a house, a job, "kids," a marriage, problems, troubles, satisfactions—and if all that is not enough, he has his psychoanalyst. He *is* nothing.

A concept which presupposes that of identity is that of integrity. It can be dealt with briefly because integrity simply means a willingness not to violate one's identity, in the many ways in which such violation is possible. Today the main temptations for violation of one's identity are the opportunities for advancement in industrial society. Since the life within the society tends to make man experience himself as a thing anyway, a sense of identity is a rare phenomenon. But the problem is complicated by the fact that aside from identity as a conscious phenomenon as described above, there is a kind of unconscious identity. By that I mean that some people, while consciously they have turned into things, carry unconsciously a sense of their identity precisely because the social process has not suc-ceeded in transforming them completely into things. These people, when yielding to the temptation of violating their integrity, may have a sense of guilt which is unconscious and which gives them a feeling of uneasiness, although they are not aware of its cause. It is all too easy for orthodox psychoanalytic procedure to explain a sense of guilt as the result of one's incestuous wishes or one's "unconscious homosexuality." The truth is that inasmuch as a person is not entirely dead—in a psychological sense—he feels guilty for living without integrity.

Our discussion of identity and integrity needs to be supplemented by at least briefly mentioning another attitude for which Monsignor W. Fox has coined an excellent word: *vulnerability.* The person who experiences himself as an ego and whose sense of identity is that of ego-identity naturally wants to protect this thing—him, his body, memory, property, and so on, but also his opinions and emotional investments which have become part of his ego. He is constantly on the defensive against anyone or any experience which could disturb the permanence and solidity of his mum-mified existence. In contrast, the person who experiences himself not as having but as being permits himself to be vulnerable. Nothing belongs to him except that he *is* by being alive. But at every moment in which he loses his sense of activity, in which he is unconcentrated, he is in danger of neither having anything nor being anybody. This danger he can meet only by constant alertness, awakeness, and aliveness, and he is vulnerable compared with the ego-man, who is safe because he *has* without *being.*

from *The Women's Room*

Marilyn French

The previous article, written by Erich Fromm, stresses the importance of the concept of "I am". Historically, women have been taught to establish their identities by living for others. They developed a "you are" type of existence, especially in the roles of mother and wife. In this selection, the author discusses the difficulties she encounters in trying to be who she feels she is.

Well, you see what I mean. Every new person you meet and really take in violates your psyche to some degree. You have to juggle your categories to fit the person in. Here where I am, people see me some way—I don't know exactly how. Middle-aged matron, rabid feminist, nice lady, mad-woman: I don't know. But they can't see me who I am. So I'm lonely. I guess maybe I wouldn't be able to say who I am myself. One needs some reflection from the outside to get an image of oneself. Sometimes, when I am really low, the words of Pyotr Stephanovich come into my mind: You must love God because He is the only one you can love for Eternity. That sounds very profound to me, and tears come into my eyes whenever I say it. I never heard anyone else say it. But I don't believe in God and if I did I couldn't love Him/Her/It. I couldn't love anyone I thought had created this world.

Oh God. (Metaphorically speaking.) So people handle loneliness by putting themselves into something larger than they are, some framework or purpose. But those big exterior things—I don't know, they just don't seem as important to me as what Norm said to Mira or Bliss to Adele. I mean, do you really care about 1066? Val would scream that it was significant, but my students don't care about 1066. They don't even care about World War II or the Holocaust. They don't even remember Jean Arthur. For them, Elvis Presley is part of the quaint, irrelevant past. No, it's the little things that matter. But when you're dealing with a lot of insignificant lives, how do you put things together? When you look back on your life, are there places where you can put your finger, like crossroads on a map or a scholar's crux in Shakespeare, where you can say, "There! That is the place where every-thing changed, the word upon which everything hinged!"

I find that difficult. I feel like a madwoman. I walk around my apart-ment, which is a shithouse, full of landlord's odds and ends of leftover furniture and a few dying plants on the windowsills. I talk to myself, myself, myself. Now I am smart enough to provide a fairly good running dialogue, but the problem is there's no response, no voice but mine. I want to hear another's truth, but I insist it be a truth. I talk to the plants but they shrivel and die.

I wanted my life to be a work of art, but when I try to look at it, it swells and shrinks like the walls you glean in a delirious daze. My life sprawls and sags, like an old pair of baggy slacks that still, somehow, fits you.

Like Mira, Val, and lots of others, I went back to the university late in life. I went with despair and expectations. It was a new life, it was supposed to revitalize you, to send you radiant to new planes of experience where you would get tight with Beatrice Portinari and be led to an earthly paradise. In literature, new lives, second chances, lead to visions of the City of God. But I have been suspecting for a while now that everything I ever read was lies. You can believe the first four acts, but not the fifth. Lear really turned into a babbling old fool drooling over his oatmeal and happy for a place by the fire in Regan's house in Scarsdale. Hamlet took over the corporation by bribing the board and ousting Claudius, and then took to wearing a black leather jacket and German Army boots and sending out proclamations that everyone would refrain from fornication upon pain of death. He wrote letters to his cousin Angelo and together they decided to purify the whole East Coast, so they have joined with the Mafia, the Marines, and the CIA to outlaw sex. Romeo and Juliet marry and have some kids, then separate when she wants to go back to graduate school and he wants to go live on a commune in New Mexico. She is on welfare now and he has long hair and an Indian headband and says *Oooom* a lot.

Camille lives: she runs a small popular hotel in Bordeaux. I've met her. She has bleached blond hair, thick orange makeup, and a hard mouth, and she knows everything about the price of vermouth, clean sheets, bottled orange drink, and certain available female bodies. She's thicker all around than she used to be, but she still has a shape. She meanders around in a shiny pale blue pantsuit, and sits in her bar laughing with friends and keeping an eye out for Bernard, the married man who is her latest lover. Except for her passion for Bernard, she is tough and fun. Don't ask what it is about Bernard that makes her so adore him. It is not Bernard, but love itself. She believes in love, goes on believing in it against all odds. Therefore, Bernard is a little bored. It is boring to be adored. At thirty-eight, she should be tough and fun, not adoring. When he leaves her, a month or two from now, she will contemplate suicide. Whereas, if she had been able to bring herself to stop believing in love, she would have been tough and fun and he would have adored her forever. Which would have bored her. She then would have had to be the one to tell him to clear out. It is a choice to give one pause.

Tristan and Isolde got married after Issy got a divorce from Mark, who was anyhow turned on to a groupie at that point. And they discovered the joys of comfortable marriage can't hold a candle to the thrill of taboo, so they have placed an ad in the Boston *Phoenix* asking for a third, fourth, or even fifth party of any gender to join them in tasting taboo joys. They will smoke, they will even snort a little coke, just to assure a degree of fear about being intruded upon by the local police. Don't judge: they, at least are trying to hold their marriage together. And you?

The problem with the great literature of the past is that it doesn't tell you how to live with real endings. In the great literature of the past you either get married and live happily ever after, or you die. But the fact is, neither is what actually happens. Oh, you do die, but never at the right time, never with great language floating all around you, and a whole theater full of witnesses to your agony. What actually happens is that you do get married or you don't, and you don't live happily every after, but you do live. And that's the problem. I mean, think about it. Suppose Antigone had lived. An Antigone who goes on being Antigone year after year would be not only ludicrous but a bore. The cave and the rope are essential.

It isn't just the endings. In a real life, how can you tell when you're in Book I or Book III, or Act II or Act V? No stagehands come charging in to haul down the curtain at an appropriate moment. So how do I know whether I'm living in the middle of Act III and heading toward a great climax, or at the end of Act V and finished? I don't even know who I am. I might be Hester Prynne, or Dorothea Brooke, or I might be the heroine of a TV drama of some seasons back—what was her name?—Mrs. Muir! Yes, she walked on the beach and was in love with a ghost and originally she looked like Gene Tierney. I always wanted to look like Gene Tierney. I sit in a chair and I have no one to knit woolen stockings for so it's irrelevant that I don't know how to knit. (Val could, oddly. Nothing works the way it does in books. Can you imagine Penthesilea knitting?) I'm just sitting here living out even to the edge of doom—what? Valerie's vision? Except she forgot to tell me what comes next.

A Note on Progress

Pierre Teilhard de Chardin

Modern humans are in many ways superior to primitive humans and other primates. Their superiority over primitive humans is largely the result of accumulated self-knowledge; their superiority over other primates lies in the human capacity for self-consciousness.

Pierre Teilhard de Chardin feels that each thinking human being expresses the evolutionary progression of human thoughts and acts. In this excerpt from his book, The Future of Man, de Chardin discusses how we have progressed to our present state of consciousness. He sees humanity at a choice point in history, where we can view ourselves as a part of, and not the center of, the universe.

The conflict dates from the day when one man, flying in the face of appearance, perceived that the forces of nature are no more unalterably fixed in their orbits than the stars themselves, but that their serene arrangement around us depicts the flow of a tremendous tide—the day on which a first voice rang out, crying to Mankind peacefully slumbering on the raft of Earth, "We are moving! We are going forward!"...

It is a pleasant and dramatic spectacle, that of Mankind divided to its very depths into two irrevocably opposed camps—one looking towards the horizon and proclaiming with all its new-found faith, "We are moving," and the other, without shifting its position, obstinately maintaining, "Nothing changes. We are not moving at all."

These latter, the "immobilists," though they lack passion (immobility has never inspired anyone with enthusiasm!), have common sense on their side, habit of thought, inertia, pessimism, and also, to some extent, morality and religion. Nothing, they argue, appears to have changed since man began to hand down the memory of the past, not the undulations of the earth, or the forms of life, or the genius of Man, or even his goodness. Thus far practical experimentation has failed to modify the fundamental characteristics of even the most humble plant. Human suffering, vice, and war, although they may momentarily abate, recur from age to age with an increasing virulence. Even the striving after progress contributes to the sum of evil: to effect change is to undermine the painfully established traditional order whereby the distress of living creatures was reduced to a minimum. What innovator has not re-tapped the springs of blood and tears? For the sake of human tranquility, in the name of Fact, and in defense of the sacred Established Order, the immobilists forbid the earth to move. Nothing changes, they say, or can change. The raft must drift purposelessly on a shoreless sea.

But the other half of mankind, startled by the look-out's cry, has left the huddle where the rest of the crew sit with their heads together telling time-honored tales. Gazing out over the dark sea they study for themselves the lapping of waters along the hull of the craft that bears them, breathe the scents borne to them on the breeze, gaze at the shadows cast from pole to pole by a changeless eternity. And for these all things, while remaining separately the same—the ripple of water, the scent of the air, the lights in the sky—become linked together and acquire a new sense: the fixed and random Universe is seen to move.

No one who has seen this vision can be restrained from guarding and proclaiming it. To testify to my faith in it, and to show reasons, is my purpose here.

It is clear in the first place that the world in its present state is the outcome of movement. Whether we consider the rocky layers enveloping the Earth, the arrangement of the forms of life that inhabit it, the variety of civilizations to which it has given birth, or the structure of languages spoken upon it, we are forced to the same conclusion: that everything is the sum of the past and that nothing is comprehensible except through its history. "Nature" is the equivalent of "becoming," self-creation: this is the view to which experience irresistibly leads us. What can it mean except that the Universe must, at least at some stage, have been in movement; that it has been malleable, acquiring by degrees, not only in their accidental details but in their very essence, the perfections which now adorn it? There is nothing, not even the human soul, the highest spiritual manifestation we know of, that does not come within this universal law. The soul, too, has its clearly defined place in the slow ascent of living creatures towards consciousness, and must therefore in one way or another have grown out of the general mobility of things. Those who look reality in the face cannot fail to perceive this progressive genesis of the Universe, and with a clarity which leaves no room for doubt. Whatever the other side may say, clinging to their imaginary world, the Cosmos did once move, the whole of it, not only locally but in its very being. This is undeniable and we shall not discuss it further. But is it still moving? Here we have the real question, the living, burning question of Evolution.

It is the fundamental paradox of Nature as we see it now that its universal plasticity seems suddenly to have hardened. Like an ocean-wave caught in a snapshot, or a torrent of lava stiffened by cooling, the mountains and living things of the earth wear the aspect, to those who study them, of a powerful momentum that has become petrified. Nature seen at a distance appears to be malleable and in motion; but seek to lay hands on it, to deflect by force even the least of Life's directions, and you will encounter nothing but absolute rigidity, an unshakably stubborn refusal to depart from the pre-ordained path.

But let us note that this present rigidity of Nature does not, as some people believe, in any way lessen the certainty of its past mobility. What we regard as the fixity of present organisms may be simply a state of very slow movement, or of rest between spells of movement. It is true that we have not yet succeeded in shaping life to our requirements in the laboratory; but who has shaped or witnessed the shaping of a geological stratum? The rock which we seek to compress crumbles because we work too fast or with over-small fragments. Calcareous matter, if it is to be made malleable, needs to be embedded in a vast mass, and perhaps its reshaping is a process of immense slowness. If we have not seen the upward thrust of mountain ranges it is because their rise was accomplished either in widely spaced jerks or with so slow a rhythm that since the coming of Man nothing of the kind has happened, or at least nothing that has been perceptible to us. Why should not Life, too, be mobile only in great masses, or through the slow action of time, or in brief stages? Who can positively affirm that at this moment, although we perceive nothing, new forms are not taking shape in the contours of the earth and of Life?...

The plasticity of Nature in the past is an undeniable fact; its present rigidity is less capable of scientific proof. If we had to choose between a total process of evolution and a state of complete fixity, that is to say between two absolutes—everything incessantly in motion, or everything for ever immovable—we should be bound to choose the first. But there is a third possible hypothesis, namely that everything was at one time fluid but is now irrevocably fixed. It is this third alternative that I wish to examine and dismiss.

The hypothesis of a definitive halt in terrestrial evolution is, to my mind, suggested less by the apparently unchanging nature of present forms than by a certain general aspect of the world coinciding with this appearance of cessation. It is most striking that the morphological change of living creatures seems to have slowed down at the precise moment when Thought appeared on earth. If we relate this coincidence to the fact that the only general line taken by biological evolution has been in the direction of the largest brain—broadly speaking, of the highest state of consciousness—we are compelled to wonder whether the true fundamental impulse underlying the growth of animal forces has not been the need to know and to think; and whether, when this over-riding impulse eventually found its outlet in the human species, the effect was not to produce an abrupt diminution of "vital pressure" in the other branches of the Tree of Life. This would explain the fact that "evolving Life," from the end of the Tertiary Period, has been confined to the little group of higher primates. We know of many forms that have disappeared since the Oligocene, but of no genuinely new species other than the anthropoids. This again may be explained by the extreme brevity of the Miocene as compared with other geological periods. But does it not lead us to surmise that the "phyla" possessing higher psychic attributes have absorbed all the forces at Life's disposal?

If we are to find a definitive answer to the question of the entitative progress of the Universe we must do so by adopting the least favorable position—that is to say, by envisaging a world whose evolutionary capacity is *concentrated upon* and *confined to* the human soul. The question of whether the Universe is still developing then becomes a matter of deciding whether the human spirit is still in process of evolution. To this I reply unhesitatingly, "Yes, it is." The nature of Man is in the full flood of entitative change. But to grasp this it is necessary (a) not to overlook the *biological* (morphogenic) value of moral action, and (b) to accept the organic nature of individual relationships. We shall then see that a vast evolutionary process is in ceaseless operation around us, but that it is situated within the *sphere of consciousness* (and collective consciousness).

What is the difference between ourselves, citizens of the twentieth century, and the earliest human beings whose soul is not entirely hidden from us? In what respects may we consider ourselves their superiors and more advanced than they?

Organically speaking, the faculties of those remote forebears were probably the equal of our own. By the middle of the last Ice Age, at the latest, human groups had attained to the expression of aesthetic powers calling for intelligence and sensibility developed to a point which we have not surpassed. To all appearance the ultimate perfection of the human *element* was achieved many thousands of years ago, which is to say that the individual instrument of thought and action may be considered to have been finalized. But there is fortunately another dimension in which variation and growth are still possible, and in which we continue to evolve.

The great superiority over Primitive Man which we have acquired, and which will be enhanced by our descendants in a degree perhaps undreamed-of by ourselves, is in the realm of self-knowledge; in our growing capacity to situate ourselves in space and time, to the point of becoming conscious of our place and responsibility in relation to the Universe.

Surmounting in turn the illusions of terrestrial flatness, immobility and autocentricity, we have taken the unhopeful surface of the earth and "rolled it like a little ball"; we have set it on a course among the stars; we have grasped the fact that it is no more than a grain of cosmic dust; and we have discovered that a process without limit has brought into being the realms of substance and essence. Our fathers supposed themselves to go back no further than yesterday, each man containing within himself the ultimate value of his existence. They held themselves to be confined within the limits of their years on earth and their corporeal frame. We have blown asunder this narrow compass and those beliefs. At once humbled and ennobled by our discoveries, we are gradually coming to see ourselves as a part of vast and continuing processes; as though awakening from a dream, we are beginning to realize that our nobility consists in serving, like intelligent atoms, the work proceeding in the Universe. We have discovered that there is a Whole, of which we are the elements. We have found the world in our own souls.

What does this conquest signify? Does it merely denote the establishment, in worldly terms, of an idealized system of logical, extrinsic relationships? Is it no more than an intellectual luxury, as is commonly supposed—the mere satisfaction of curiosity? No. The consciousness which we are gradually acquiring of our physical relationship with all parts of the Universe represents a genuine enlarging of our separate personalities. It is truly a progressive realization of the universality of the things surrounding each of us. And it means that in the domain external to our flesh our *real and whole body* is continuing to take shape.

That is in no way a "sentimental" affirmation.

The proof that the growing co-extension of our soul and the world, through the consciousness of our relationship with all things, is not simply a matter of logic or idealization, but is part of an organic process, the natural outcome of the impulse which caused the germination of life and the growth of the brain—the proof is that it expresses itself in a *specific evolution of the moral value of our actions* (that is to say, by the modification of what is most living within us.)

No doubt it is true that the scope of individual human action, as commonly envisaged in the abstract theory of moral and meritorious acts, is not greatly enhanced by the growth of human knowledge. Inasmuch as the will-power of contemporary man is not in itself more vigorous or unswerving than that of a Plato or an Augustine, and individual moral perfection is still to be measured by steadfastness in pursuance of the known good (and therefore relative) we cannot claim as *individuals* to be more moral or saintly than our fathers.

Yet this must be said, to our own honor and that of those who have toiled to make us what we are: that between the behavior of men in the first century A.D. and our own, the difference is as great, or greater, than that between the behavior of a fifteen-year-old boy and a man of forty. Why is this so? Because, owing to the progress of science and of thought, our actions today, whether for good or ill, proceed from an incomparably higher point of departure than those of the men who paved the way for us towards enlightenment. When Plato acted it was probably in the belief that his freedom to act could only affect a small fragment of the world, narrowly circumscribed in space and time; but the man of today acts in the knowledge that the choice he makes will have its repercussions through countless centuries and upon countless human beings. He feels in himself the responsibilities and the power of an entire Universe. Progress has not caused the *action of Man* (Man himself) to change in each separate individual; but because of it the action of *human nature* (Mankind) has acquired, in every thinking man, a fullness that is wholly new. Moreover, how are we to compare or contrast our acts with those of Plato or Augustine? All such acts are linked, and Plato and Augustine are still expressing, through me, the whole extent of their personalities. There is a kind of human action that gradually matures through a multitude of human acts. The human monad has long been constituted. What is now proceeding is the animation (assimilation) of the Universe by that monad; that is to say, the realization of a *consummated human Thought*.

There are philosophers who, accepting this progressive animation of the concrete by the power of thought, of Matter by Spirit, seek to build upon it the hope of a terrestrial liberation, as though the soul, become mistress of all determinisms and inertias, may someday be capable of overcoming harsh probability and vanquishing suffering and evil here on earth. Alas, it is a forlorn hope; for it seems certain that any outward upheaval or internal renovation which might suffice to transform the Universe as it is could only be a kind of death—death of the individual, death of the race, death of the Cosmos. A more realistic and more Christian view shows us Earth evolving towards a state in which Man, having come into the full possession of his sphere of action, his strength, his maturity, and his unity, will at last have become an adult being; and having reached this apogee of his responsibility and freedom, holding in his hands all his future and all his past, will make the choice between arrogant autonomy and loving excentration.

This will be the final choice: revolt or adoration of a world. And then, by an act which will summarize the toil of centuries, by this act (finally and for the first time completely human) justice will ensue and all things be renewed.

3 The Biosocial Experience

Humans are more than animals, but they are animals. This is the paradox and the source of much of our confusion about human nature. Those who make of Homo sapiens nothing more than a bundle of reflexes, instincts, and sensations do humanity a disservice. Others, who make humanity a deity or a disembodied spirit, ignore the very real evidence of our physical nature.

The complexity of human nature, in addition to confusing our simplistic schemes, also provides us with rich ground for research and exploration. People are neither apes nor angels. People are human. They are part of the animal kingdom, but respond differently than any other animals to various kinds of situations and stimuli. They are creators of stimulation as well as organisms that respond to it. In addition, people are social. They are born into social groupings and never cease to have some involvement with other people.

The first selection of this chapter, written by Robert G. Amick, one of the editors of this anthology, is a short story entitled "Optimal Jones and His Wife Belle." Amick attempts to explore the interaction of people, society, and the physical environment in some "ideal world" of the future, when most of the problems we now consider to be the most pressing will have been solved.

Abraham Maslow, one of the pioneers in humanistic psychology, integrates recent biological research with humanistic concepts. In his article he presents a model for a humanistic philosophy of biology.

The next article of the chapter is a research study that shows the impact of the environment on the

*biological development and functioning of human
beings. Mary H. Cadwalader reports the findings of a
study following the life pattern of medical students at
Johns Hopkins.*

*In the last article, Lois Timnick reports on how the
biochemical reactions of our bodies can affect our
emotions and personalities.*

Optimal Jones and His Wife Belle

Robert G. Amick

*It is often said that only the realization that biological life is
limited enables people to become fully involved in their own
humanness and that of other persons. Technology, however, strives
to create an "ideal society" through quite different means, and
according to quite different criteria.*

*We may someday be able to create a society that is
technologically perfect, with perfectly functioning people. What
new problems of involvement may this create? This short story by
Robert Amick attempts to explore the question through a look at a
society of the future.*

The small electrical current brought immediate alertness to Optimal
Jones' conscious mind. He unplugged his electrodes from the headboard,
and looked down at his still-sleeping wife. Optimal enjoyed his wife's new
face, thinking to himself that it was an improvement over the previous two.
He thought, however, that the doctor had made her breasts a little too large.

The three-dimensional television set was giving the temperature for
the day. The announcer asked everyone to vote for the date he wished it to
rain, in order to replenish the water supply. The Weather Control Specialists had done an outstanding job in regulating climatic conditions,
Optimal thought. Now Belle would rather lie out in the sun than take her
tanning pills. Optimal still preferred the pills because of the more even
distribution of coloring all over the body.

Optimal put on his insulated plastic body covering, and walked to the
far end of the room. He opened a cabinet and took his energy pills, noticing
that the supply was running low.

Written especially for this anthology by Robert G. Amick.

He sat down at his desk and key-punched a message to his wife:

1) *Pick up more energy pills.*
2) *Buy a new plastic body covering.*
3) *Vote for rain on Monday.*
4) *Thanks for the nice evening.*
5) *I love you.*

Walking back to the bed, he fed the card into his wife's computer, hearing the soft *whirr* that signified that the message was being fed into her brain through the electrodes.

Optimal picked up his Black Box and strapped it onto his belt. He connected his electrodes to the box and stimulated his hypothalamus. The feeling of pleasure and well-being that washed over him assured him that it was working.

He recalled once reading an old psychology textbook's description of feelings of "depression." He wondered how it felt, and laughed to himself about the primitive notions humans had once had. These days, the psychophysiobiologist, through brain implantation at birth, had virtually eliminated all such archaic, animalistic feelings as fear and anger, so that one experienced a constant euphoric state of well-being. During his adolescence, he remembered, some of the more daring boys had on occasion cross-wired their Black Boxes. They talked about how the feelings produced made them more aware of their bodies, something Optimal never quite understood. He recognized the mechanistic functions of the body for carrying one's thought processes throughout his life. But when the body wore out, the brain was transplanted to the Human Resource Computer Bank, to be kept stimulated for perpetual life. What particular value, then, to being more aware of it?

He took a last look at his wife, again appreciating the new face. He bent over her, patted her on the bottom, and kissed her goodbye.

Optimal left the apartment and walked down the hall to the air shaft. He stepped inside the bullet-shaped elevator room, fastened his safety belt, and then pressed the button for the transportation room. The sudden acceleration gave a pleasant tingle to his stomach. He remembered one time as a small boy getting sick to his stomach, because he had not yet learned how to press the Black Box to inhibit the sensation. He had regurgitated all over the inside of the elevator.

The door opened automatically. A pleasant female voice said, "Transportation room. Have a nice day." During Optimal's last body alteration, the doctor had mentioned research being done in the area of altering the vocal chords, so one could have any voice he desired. He thought this would be a great step forward. He wanted a voice with more authority—one that sounded like that of the president of his Area Commune.

The transportation room was busy. Most of the electric cars were being used. He walked over to one, but some small child had dripped his ice cream all over the seat. He chose another, drove it to the electrical magnetic track, and pushed the lever to Automatic. It would take him to the end of the area for Blue Electric Cars, where he would transfer to a Red to get to his meeting at the Area Commune Meeting Hall. Supposedly, there was to be a critical announcement at today's meeting.

As he sat back in the car, he pressed his Short-Term Memory Button until he recalled the previous evening's events. His wife had taken the Baby Boy Pill, and there was a ninety percent probability that they would have a son. They felt extremely fortunate that their application for a child had been accepted, particularly for a male. This had been an unusual year in that more couples had applied for females.

The Blue Electric Car reached its destination. Optimal stepped out of the car and found a red one available. He drove to the electrical magnetic track leading to the Area Commune Meeting Hall. It would take about a half-hour to make the trip; he set the timer on the Black Box for twenty-five minutes. He was learning his fourth language in a program sponsored by the Area Commune. He plugged one of his electrodes into the car radio and turned it on. He then stimulated the Reticular Activating System, immediately falling asleep.

As he awoke, he became conscious of the radio-teacher finishing the day's vocabulary "... déjeuner, breakfast, déjouer, to baffle, délà, beyond, délabré, ruined or dilapidated."

The electric car swung onto the pick-up lot. Optimal removed his electrodes. He observed that more scientists than usual seemed to be present today. Probably because of the special announcement, he thought.

He joined the group of scientists from his section. They walked to the building together, sharing bits of information. Optimal told the others that his Parenthood Application had been accepted. Everyone congratulated him. His sense of well-being was accelerated by the reaction from the others; he pressed the Inhibitory Button on the Black Box to control the over-stimulation.

Taking his seat in the Meeting Hall along with the other members of the committee, he stimulated his Optimal Level of Awareness button. The World Social Environmentalist Specialist walked to the podium and began to speak:

"Fellow scientists, I am pleased to report that this is the twenty-seventh month without a crime of violence and the seventy-second month without a murder. The only disease that has been recorded in the last thirty-two months is the 'scourge of mankind,' the common cold."

This brought laughter from the audience.

"We are still overproducing food and material wealth for the entire world. There are a few problems with the Berbers from the High Atlas refusing to accept the three-dimensional television sets. The Environmental Control Specialists are trying to give them an awareness of the usefulness and pleasure of the sets through reinforcing radio programs."

As he continued to report, those present began to notice an increasingly anguished look on the face of the Physical Environmentalist Specialist, seated to the left of the speaker. He began tapping his fingers on the desk and sitting forward in his chair as the Environmentalist Control Specialist concluded his speech and returned to his seat.

There was clapping from the audience as the Physical Environmentalist Specialist took the stand. His voice cracked as he looked downward and began to speak slowly: "We have confirmed that as of 10:43 tonight, the sun's energy will reach the point of negative energy output. After that time, it will no longer be capable of supporting human life."

The Mind-Body Correlation

Abraham H. Maslow

Abraham Maslow is one of the most respected names among humanistic psychologists. In a recent book, The Farther Reaches of Human Nature, *he applies his ideas to the development of a humanistic philosophy of biology. He presents a convincing argument that the human organism has an innate "biological wisdom"—that most people, especially children, have a tendency to choose what is good and healthy for them, and that therapists need to recognize and pay attention to these tendencies. To capitalize on the impetus to health, Maslow suggests that a "loving knowledge" of the patient may be most useful, rather than the extremely detached, objective study characteristic of other sciences.*

It seems to me that we are on the edge of a new leap into correlating our subjective lives with external objective indicators. I expect a tremendous leap forward in the study of the nervous system because of these new indications.

. . . Apparently it is now possible to say that the healthy organism itself gives clear and loud signals about what it, the organism, prefers or chooses,

From A.H. Maslow, "Toward a Humanistic Biology," *American Psychologist,* 24 (1969): 724-735.

or considers to be desirable states of affairs. Is it too big a jump to call these "values"? Biologically intrinsic values? Instinct-like values? If we make the descriptive statement, "The laboratory rat, given a choice between pressing two auto-stimulus-producing buttons, presses the pleasure center button practically 100 percent of the time in preference to any other stimulus-producing or self-stimulus-producing button," is this different in any important way from saying, "The rat prefers self-stimulation of his pleasure center"?

I must say that it makes little difference to me whether I use the word "values" or not. It is certainly possible to describe everything I have described without ever using this word. Perhaps as a matter of scientific strategy, or at least the strategy of communications between scientists and the general public, it might be more diplomatic if we not confuse the issue by speaking of values. It does not really matter, I suppose. However, what does matter is that we take quite seriously these new developments in the psychology and biology of choices, preferences, reinforcements, rewards, etc.

I should point out also that we will have to face the dilemma of a certain circularity that is built into this kind of research and theorizing. It is most clear with human beings, but my guess is that it will also be a problem with other animals. It is the circularity that is implied in saying that "the good specimen or the healthy animal chooses or prefers such and such." How shall we handle the fact that sadists, perverts, masochists, homosexuals, neurotics, psychotics, suicidals make different choices than do "healthy human beings"? Is it fair to parallel this dilemma with that of adrenalectomized animals[1] in the laboratory making different choices from so-called "normal" animals? I should make it clear that I do not consider this an insoluble problem, merely one that has to be faced and handled, rather than avoided and overlooked. It is quite easy with the human subject to select "healthy" persons by psychiatric and psychological testing techniques and *then* to point out that people who make such and such a score, let us say in the Rorschach test, or in an intelligence test, are the same people who will be good choosers in cafeteria (food) experiments. The selection criterion then is quite different from the behavior criterion. It is also quite possible, and as a matter of fact in my own opinion quite probable, that we are within sight of the possibility of demonstrating by neurological self-stimulation that the so-called "pleasures" of perversion or murder or sadism or fetishism are not "pleasures" in the same sense that is indicated in the Olds or Kamiya experiments. Certainly this is what we already know from our subjective psychiatric techniques. Any experienced

1. Those from which the adrenal gland has been removed, so that their systems no longer produce adrenalin.

psychotherapist learns sooner or later that underlying the neurotic "pleasures" or perversions is actually a great deal of anguish, pain, and fear. Within the subjective realm itself, we know this from people who have experienced both unhealthy and healthy pleasures. They practically always report preference for the latter and learn to shudder at the former. Colin Wilson has demonstrated clearly that sexual criminals have very feeble sexual reactions, not strong ones. Kirkendall also shows the subjective superiority of loving sex over unloving sex.

I am now working with one set of implications that are generated by a humanistic-psychological point of view of the sort I have sketched out above. It may serve to show the radical consequences and implications for a humanistic philosophy of biology. It is certainly fair to say that these data are on the side of self-regulation, self-government, self-choice of the organism. The organism has more tendency toward choosing health, growth, biological success than we would have thought a century ago. This is in general anti-authoritarian, anti-controlling. For me it brings back into serious focus the whole *Taoistic* point of view, not only as expressed in contemporary ecological and ethological studies, where we have learned not to intrude and to control, but for the human being it also means trusting more the child's own impulses toward growth and self-actualization. This means a greater stress on spontaneity and on autonomy rather than on prediction and external control. To paraphrase a main thesis from my *Psychology of Science:*

> In the light of such facts, can we seriously continue to define the goals of science as prediction and control? Almost one could say the exact opposite—at any rate, for human beings. Do we ourselves want to be predicted and predictable? Controlled and controllable? I won't go so far as to say that the question of free will must necessarily be involved here in its old and classical philosophical form. But I *will* say that questions come up here and clamor for treatment which do have something to do with the subjective feeling of being free rather than determined, of choosing for oneself rather than being externally controlled, etc. In any case, I can certainly say that descriptively healthy human beings do not like to be controlled. They prefer to feel free and to be free.

Another very general "atmospheric" consequence of this whole way of thinking is that it must inevitably transform the image of the scientist, not only in his own eyes but in the eyes of the general population. There are already data which indicate that, for instance, high school girls think of scientists as monsters and horrors, and are afraid of them. They do not think of them as good potential husbands, for instance. I must express my own opinion that this is not merely a consequence of Hollywood "Mad Scientist" movies; there is something real and justified in this picture, even if it is terribly exaggerated. The fact is that the classical conception of science is the man who controls, the man who is in charge, the man who does things to people, to animals, or to things. He is the master of what he surveys. This picture is even more clear in surveys of the "image of the physician." He is generally seen at the semiconscious or unconscious level as a master, a controller, a cutter, a dealer out of pain, etc. He is definitely the boss, the authority, the expert, the one who takes charge and tells people what to do. I think this "image" is now worst of all for psychologists; college students now consider them to be, very frequently, manipulators, liars, concealers, and controllers.

What if the organism is seen as having "biological wisdom"? If we learn to give it greater trust as autonomous, self-governing, and self-choosing, then clearly we as scientists, not to mention physicians, teachers, or even parents, must shift our image over to a more Taoistic one. This is the one word that I can think of that summarizes succinctly the many elements of the image of the more humanistic scientist. Taoistic means asking rather than telling. It means nonintruding, noncontrolling. It stresses noninterfering observation rather than a controlling manipulation. It is receptive and passive rather than active and forceful. It is like saying that if you want to learn about ducks, then you had better ask the ducks instead of telling them. So also for human children. In prescribing "what is best for them" it looks as if the best technique for finding out what is best for them is to develop techniques for getting *them* to tell us what is best for them.

In point of fact, we already have such a model in the good psychotherapist. This is about the way he functions. His conscious effort is not to impose his will upon the patient, but rather to help the patient— inarticulate, unconscious, semiconscious—to discover what is inside *him*, the patient. The psychotherapist helps him to discover what he himself wants or desires, what is good for him, the patient, rather than what is good for the therapist. This is the opposite of controlling, propagandizing, molding, teaching in the old sense. It definitely rests upon the implications and assumptions that I have already mentioned, although I must say that they are very rarely made, for example, such implications as trust in the health-moving direction of most individuals; of expecting them to prefer health to illness; of believing that a state of subjective well-being is a pretty good guide to what is "best for the person." This attitude implies a preference for spontaneity rather than for control, for trust in the organism rather than mistrust. It assumes that the person wants to be fully human rather than that he wants to be sick, pained, or dead. Where we do find, as psychotherapists, death wishes, masochistic wishes, self-defeating behavior, self-infliction of pain, we have learned to assume that this is "sick" in the sense that the person himself, if he ever experiences another healthier state of affairs, would far rather have that healthier state of affairs than his pain. As a matter of fact, some of us go so far as to consider masochism, suicidal impulses, self-punishment, and the like as stupid, ineffective, clumsy gropings toward health.

Something very similar is true for the new model of the Taoistic teacher, the Taoistic parent, the Taoistic friend, the Taoistic lover, and finally the more Taoistic scientist.

The classical conception of objectivity came from the earliest days of scientific dealing with things and objects, with lifeless objects of study. We were objective when our own wishes and fears and hopes were excluded from the observation, and when the purported wishes and designs of a supernatural god were also excluded. This of course was a great step forward and made modern science possible. We must, however, not overlook the fact that this was true for dealing with nonhuman objects or things. Here this kind of objectivity and detachment works pretty well. It even works well with lower organisms. Here too we are detached enough, noninvolved enough so that we can be relatively noninterfering spectators. It does not *matter* to us to any great degree which way an amoeba goes or what a hydra prefers to ingest. This detachment gets more and more difficult as we go on up the phyletic scale. We know very well how easy it is to anthropomorphize, to project into the animal the observer's human wishes, fears, hopes, prejudices if we are dealing with dogs or cats, and more easily with monkeys or apes. When we get to the study of the human beings, we can now take it for granted that it is practically impossible to be the cool, calm, detached, uninvolved, noninterfering spectator. Psychological data have piled up to such a point that no one could conceivably defend this position.

Any social scientist who is at all sophisticated knows that he must examine his own prejudices and preconceptions *before* going in to work with any society or a subcultural group. This is one way of getting around prejudgments—to know about them in advance.

But I propose that there is another path to objectivity, that is, in the sense of greater perspicuity, of greater accuracy of perception of the reality out there outside ourselves, outside the observer. It comes originally from the observation that loving perception, whether as between sweethearts or as between parents and children, produced kinds of knowledge that were not available to nonlovers. Something of the sort seems to me to be true for the ethological literature. My work with monkeys, I am sure, is more "true," more "accurate," in a certain sense, more *objectively* true than it would have been if I had disliked monkeys. The fact was that I was fascinated with them. I became fond of my individual monkeys in a way that was not possible with my rats. I believe that the kind of work reported by Lorenz, Tinbergen, Goodall, and Schaller is as good as it is, as instructive, illuminating, true, because these investigators "loved" the animals they were investigating. At the very least this kind of love produces interest and even fascination, and therefore great patience with long hours of observation. The mother, fascinated with her baby, who examines every square inch of it again and again with the greatest absorption, is certainly going to know more about her baby in the most literal sense than someone who is not interested in that particular baby. Something of the sort, I have found, is true between sweethearts. They are so fascinated with each other that examining, looking, listening, and exploring becomes itself a fascinating activity upon which they can spend endless hours. With a nonloved person this would hardly be the case. Boredom would set in too rapidly.

But "love knowledge," if I may call it that, has other advantages as well. Love for a person permits him to unfold, to open up, to drop his defenses, to let himself be naked not only physically but psychologically and spiritually as well. In a word, he lets himself be seen instead of hiding himself. In ordinary interpersonal relations, we are to some extent inscrutable to each other. In the love relationships, we become "scrutable."

But finally, and perhaps most important of all, if we love or are fascinated or are profoundly interested, we are less tempted to interfere, to control, to change, to improve. My finding is that, that which you love, you are prepared to leave alone. In the extreme instance of romantic love, and of grandparental love, the beloved person may even be seen as already perfect so that any kind of change, let alone improvement, is regarded as impossible or even impious.

In other words, we are content to leave it alone. We make no demands upon it. We do not wish it to be other than it is. We can be passive and receptive before it. Which is all to say that we can see it more truly as it is in its own nature rather than as we would like it to be or fear it to be or hope it will be. Approving of its existence, approving of the way it is, *as it is*, permits us to be nonintrusive, nonmanipulating, nonabstracting, noninterfering perceivers. To the extent that it is possible for us to be nonintrusive, nondemanding, nonhoping, nonimproving, to that extent do we achieve this particular kind of objectivity.

This is, I maintain, a method, a particular path to certain kinds of truth, which are better approached and achieved by this path. I do *not* maintain that it is the only path, or that all truths are obtainable in this way. We know very well from this very same kind of situation that it is also possible via love, interest, fascination, absorption, to distort certain *other* truths about the object. I would maintain only that in the full armamentarium of scientific methods, that love knowledge or "Taoistic objectivity" has its particular advantages in particular situations for particular purposes. If we are realistically aware that love for the object of study produces certain kinds of blindness as well as certain kinds of perspicuity, then we are sufficiently forewarned.

Early Warnings of Future Disaster

Mary H. Cadwalader

As the detective looks for clues in solving a crime, modern medicine has been collecting evidence that our daily habits, emotional makeup, and other factors can provide an early warning of probable future health problems. In a unique study following a number of medical students over a period of twenty-eight years, the students' attitudes, habits, and health backgrounds were analyzed, and patterns established. Some tentative but highly interesting correlations have emerged, information that may one day help us to predict the probability of such vital matters as suicidal tendencies and heart attacks.

In 1952 two young men, each well-educated and well-to-do, entered the Johns Hopkins School of Medicine with the brightest of prospects. Both were sons of prominent medical men, had been brought up in cultivated surroundings, had attended Ivy League universities, were handsome and well-liked, and were expected by their instructors to "do excellent work" and to "make outstanding physicians." But in actuality their futures were forlorn. Both died before the age of 40, one of suicide, the other of cancer.

Could these tragedies have been foreseen? Were there clues in the physical or emotional makeups of these young men that could have been spotted and recognized as early-warning signals of disaster?

And do such clues, as yet tenuously glimpsed and little understood, exist in a number of us, hinting of premature illness or death before our time?

A unique study—thought to be the longest continuous analysis of its type in the country—suggests that clues do exist, and moreover that they are as often embedded in one's personality and habits of daily life as in one's bodily frame. Under Dr. Caroline Bedell Thomas, Professor Emeritus of Medicine at Johns Hopkins University, certain details in the profile of an individual are being found to foreshadow the likelihood of disease or death overtaking him or her prematurely. The Precursors of Essential Hypertension and Coronary Artery Disease (to give the study its full name) has been in progress for 28 years and is now beginning to bear fruit. It is finding precursors not only to the diseases named in its title but to cancer and suicide as well. While there have been similar studies, many were retrospective; that is, they selected groups of the already afflicted and searched backward for predictors and causes. Dr. Thomas' study is prospective in that she began with healthy men and women in their early twenties and is following them through their lives. Other prospective studies have usually started with middle-aged populations.

"We all know racehorses don't pull plows and plowhorses don't win races, but perhaps we don't realize how people are also limited by their physiques or their personalities, and that when these limits are ignored severe illness may result. My goal is to identify the danger signals, the earliest indicators of disease," says Dr. Thomas, who received a Mastership from the American College of Physicians last year.

Starting her study in 1946, Dr. Thomas recognized that a pool of valuable test material was arriving each year at Johns Hopkins as medical students. First, they were young and healthy; second, they were readily available and could be thoroughly tested during their medical school years. They could be interviewed in depth. But, most importantly, as future physicians themselves they could appreciate the value of cooperating in the lifelong follow-up program. Seventeen successive classes were tested between 1947 and 1964. In addition to physiological examinations which included electrocardiograms and cholesterol levels, students underwent tests of their reactions to cold, to exercise, to smoking, and to a salt-free diet. The presence of disease and causes of death in parents, grandparents, uncles, and aunts were recorded.

Psychological probings went deeper still. Standard Rorschach and figure-drawing tests were given to bring out characteristics such as aggression, passivity, anxiety, hostility, and depressive trends. Questionnaires covered early childhood, schooling, family life, outside interests, emotional outlook, and personal aims and objectives. There were eleven pages of questions concerning habits of life: smoking, drinking (coffee and tea as well as alcohol), diet, medication, hobbies, and pastimes, even laxative-taking and sleepwalking. One test developed by Dr. Thomas which was to prove revealing involved Habits of Nervous Tension, called HNT. Subjects were asked 25 questions on their responses to stress. Some of the most important signs of nervous tension were difficulty in sleeping, frequent urination, irritability, loss of appetite, and either an urge to be left alone or to confide in others and seek advice.

The picture of each young man or woman that emerged was so vivid that today staff assistants who have not met any of the subjects feel they know them "like old friends." Changes appear as the annual follow-up questionnaires are dutifully returned. As time goes on, some quit smoking, some get divorced, get promoted, or concede they are tired and overworked. Dr. Thomas and her staff are compiling exhaustive data on a total of 1,337 students, of whom only six have been "lost," that is, have vanished and failed to reply to the follow-ups.

Now, as the earlier subjects ripen into mature medical men, usually prominent in their communities, life (and death) is beginning to catch up with them. Testimony to the excellent health of the majority is that only 41 have died. Thirty-six, however, have reported some type of malignant tumor, 12 have suffered heart attacks and more than 100 have blood-pressure levels signaling early hypertension. As the study population moves into middle age, the study itself is hitting its most productive years and already has some positive statements to make.

The most important is that susceptibility to premature disease and death may, in fact, be predicted in the full bloom of youth. Dr. Thomas hastens to emphasize the word *susceptibility*. By no means is it possible to assert that suicide, cancer, coronary heart disease, stroke, or mental illness—the afflictions under the statistician's microscope—will overtake a specific person. In the great majority of mankind, obviously, there seem to be counterbalancing factors which safeguard the internal equilibrium. Nevertheless, adding up the many little indicators which, over the years, have revealed themselves as red flags, Dr. Thomas feels the *potential* for suicide or for certain types of illness can definitely be shown.

Dr. A., for example, of the pair mentioned at the start of this article, embodied many of the traits the suicides in the Hopkins study had in common. He was underweight and ectomorphic (slender in body form), his father was older than average (44) when he was born and, during his childhood, he had felt a sort of chilly aloofness within his family. He was a heavy coffee drinker, but consumed little alcohol. He had scored significantly on the Habits of Nervous Tension test, indicating that, even as a young man, he was sensitive to stress. (A retrospective study of University of Pennsylvania and Harvard students also linked nervous tension in youth with suicide in later life.)

Dr. A. had mentioned occasional depressed moods, and these developed later into two extended periods of gloom, the first requiring hospitalization and the second ending fatally with his taking an overdose of barbiturates when he was 35.

Dr. B., on the other hand, was different. He fitted what Dr. Thomas sees as the slowly emerging picture of the cancer victim—often a "low-gear" person, with low blood pressure and low cholesterol levels, who is self-contained under stress. Like the suicide, however, the precancer individual appeared less close to his parents than "unaffected" individuals in the study. Dr. B. said his family was undemonstrative. And he gave largely negative responses to the HNT questionnaire, apparently seldom prey to bursts of anger, anxiety, or exhilaration. Or was, at least, unaware of such moods. These findings fit with those of other studies suggesting that cancer victims tend to repress their emotions and have feelings of isolation dating to childhood.

Dr. B. had a sudden seizure one day, was found to have an inoperable malignant tumor, and succumbed within six months, just before his fortieth birthday.

Susceptibility to hypertension and coronary heart disease can also be assayed, Dr. Thomas thinks, and in this area her findings corroborate other research on older groups. For instance, the well-known Framingham heart study, begun in 1949 in Massachusetts under the sponsorship of the U.S. Public Health Service, found that in a large group of middle-aged people, high cholesterol levels, high blood pressure, and cigarette smoking marked those who were bordering on or already had coronary heart disease. What the Johns Hopkins study indicates is the presence of these same precoronary characteristics when individuals were still in their early twenties. Dr. Thomas has also shown that hypertension develops far more frequently in the offspring of hypertensive parents than in others. She now finds that hypertension, too, manifests itself long before it becomes an overt menace.

The aspect of the study that most fascinates Dr. Thomas at present, however, is the link between personality and subsequent illness, and because the roster of deaths to date records suicide as the major cause—16 of the 41 deaths have been self-inflicted—this group has come under the closest scrutiny.

Taking the Rorschach test answers, in which subjects state what the famous series of inkblots resemble, Dr. Thomas and her staff found a list of key words that were used by suicides, while nonsuicides employed them rarely. The list included words like: alcoholic, bleeding, fractured, ulcerated, dwarfed, toothless, cancerous, drowning, and so on—words of pathological or morbid content. More than 42,000 Rorschach responses were sorted and computerized by the staff.

Among the suicides, key words denoting cancer appeared 14 *times* as often as in the answers of the rest. "Two women with carcinoma of the breast," was how a suicide described one of the inkblots, where nonsuicides more often saw something like "two fat women lugging a ragged pillow." "Drowning" is another sinister key word. Five years before he killed himself, one student said an inkblot looked like "a man with hands upraised, crying for help, drowning." Among the nonsuicides, only four used that word, two of whom have since suffered emotional disturbances.

Equally intriguing, such words appeared a good deal more often in the Rorschachs of those who were later to develop coronaries, hypertension, malignancies, and mental illness than in those of the "unaffected" population—those who so far remain healthy. Where the unaffected group tended to see clouds, insects, or "a piece of fried chicken" in the inkblots, a typically morbid response (from a student who later developed cancer) was: "an embryonic monster with a tail, large feet, decaying stumps for arms."

"The meaning of these findings concerning pathological content is still highly speculative," wrote Dr. Thomas in a paper published last June. "Are such responses . . . a reflection of unconscious dreads and morbid fears which, in some individuals, are ever-present stresses undermining the biological guardians of general resistance?" If dark thoughts are furtively gnawing at the health of presumably normal youngsters, in short, will such answers, given in a routine testing situation, serve as predictors of premature illness?

It is too soon to say with certainty, but results from the ongoing Precursors Study indicate the warnings are there, and long before life has worked its hardships and strains upon us. Pondering ways to enlarge such knowledge, Dr. Thomas reflects that "if all hundred-or-so medical schools in the country applied a strictly uniform series of tests like these to the roughly one hundred students admitted to each school each year, we'd be testing 10,000 people annually, and I think the patterns would emerge quickly and convincingly."

Body Rhythms May Be Linked to Illness

Lois Timnick

Manic-depressive disorder has sometimes flippantly been called "easy-glum, easy-glow." However, it is a serious disease that affects 1 percent of the population and whose effect on the family and community is much wider. Current research seems to indicate that depression and mania could be caused by a biological "clock" within us that controls the rhythms of our bodies and which appears to affect most of the body's activities. The following article describes some of the recent research into circadian rhythms and the chemical substances that affect them.

The notion that severe psychiatric illnesses are somehow related to the body's circadian or daily rhythms and seasonal changes has never drawn much serious scientific attention. It is usually lumped in—however mistakenly—with ads for biorhythm charts and police theories about the effects of tides, barometric pressure and the full moon on criminal behavior.

But now researchers from the prestigious National Institute of Mental Health report that some forms of depression may be triggered by disturbances in the body's "biological clock"—those mechanisms that synchronize internal rhythms with the outside environment.

And a team from Harvard University has found an annual rhythm in schizophrenia: Some types of this disorder may be linked to what time of year the patient was born.

Dr. Frederick K. Goodwin, chief of the NIMH's clinical psychobiology branch, told a recent American Psychiatric Association seminar in Snowmass, Colorado, that these findings about depression may open the door to nondrug treatments for the disorder, to the development of new drugs specifically aimed at altering biological rhythms or at least to ways of accelerating patient response to antidepressants currently in use.

Animal studies indicate, he said, that both of the drugs used to control depression and mania work partly through their unique ability to speed up or slow down the "clock" in the brain.

The role of circadian rhythms in mental illness, he said, is "no longer just a wild idea."

Depression affects an estimated one in five women, one in 10 men. About 1 percent of the population suffer a form known as manic-depressive illness, characterized by periodic and often predictable swings from extreme highs to severe lows—and it is this type Goodwin's team is most concerned with.

Most of the body's activities—the secretion of regulatory hormones, enzymes, chemical messengers of all sorts—have a daily or circadian (from the Latin words for "about" and a "day") rhythm that falls a bit short of or runs a bit over 24 hours. Normally, environmental cues such as light provide signals to the brain's pineal gland and hypothalamus that synchronize these rhythms or lock them in at a certain time of day to make sure they stay in phase with each other.

Without such cues, studies have shown, animals and humans begin to "free run"—that is, each of their internal rhythms goes at its own pace, and they fall asleep and wake up later and later until whole days are lost or gained. With no "clock" to reset the various rhythms as necessary, those that are supposed to dip when others peak eventually begin to peak at the same time. This is the same kind of thing that can happen when one flies across time zones, and is called a "beat phenomenon."

As far back as the mid-1960s, the University of Minnesota's Franz Halberg suggested that this beat phenomenon might explain both the circadian rhythm disturbances in manic-depressive illness—as reflected in sleep difficulties, for example—and the long-range cyclical nature of the disorder as well.

But until recently there was no way of testing that theory.

Two technological advances at the NIMH changed all that: a miniature computerized monitor a patient can wear that records and stores information about his movements, and a sensitive and specific test that measures levels of the hormone melatonin.

Melatonin is a hormone secreted only by the pineal gland at the base of the brain. Light signals that give the body cues as to the time of day pass through this gland—often called "the third eye"—and thus it is very involved in the regulation of 24-hour rhythms. The release of melatonin, which appears to be lowered in depression and elevated in mania, is controlled by an important brain chemical messenger called norepinephrine, so that knowing the amount of this hormone in the blood gives researchers a window on what is happening in the brain.

By using the activity monitor, temperature levels and the melatonin test, Goodwin's team noticed what he calls "a curious thing" in some of its manic-depressive patients:

"They were 'desynchronized' even though they were not cut off from light, even though they were not in isolation. These were patients on the ward, with clocks and daylight around. But they behaved as if they were cut off, as if they were in caves. They seemed to evidence some defect in their capacity to process environmental light and time cues.

"We're very interested in this because this diurnal [24-hour] change may contribute to the long-term cyclical disturbance which manic-depressive illness represents."

Working independently at UCSD, Dr. Dan Kripke found much the same thing, Goodwin noted.

Finding that the degree to which a patient's rhythms drifted out of phase could be used to predict when he or she would "switch" from depression into mania. Goodwin and his colleague, Dr. Thomas Wehr, chief of the clinical research unit, tried shortening one patient's day artificially, thus accelerating her rhythms and bringing on her mild mania faster.

"Our working hypothesis is that the long-term rhythm in manic-depressive illness may be the final outcome of this short-term rhythm disturbance—the circadian or diurnal variation," Goodwin explained. "Circadian rhythms appear slowed during depression and accelerated in mania."

Earlier studies by Goodwin, Dr. Robert Post and several European investigators had shown that depression can be dramatically improved—briefly—by sleep deprivation.

So the next step, taking into account all they were learning about melatonin, temperature and activity rhythms, was to try to sustain that kind of improvement by altering a manic-depressive patient's biological rhythms. The NIMH team kept a 41-year-old woman patient up all night (by having someone stay up talking with her), then put her to bed at 6 P.M. and woke her at midnight. Her depression lifted.

She stayed "well" on this advanced schedule for two weeks, then relapsed again. The researchers moved her back another six hours. Again a remission.

The third time they tried, the ploy failed, leading them to think that they had moved too far around the clock.

Her temperature peak—the time of day, usually late afternoon, when our temperatures are highest and we feel the best—shifted along with her earlier sleep schedule at first, but began to drift back to where it had been after about 10 days or two weeks.

"It seemed as if something had happened biologically in her brain, which after all is where temperature regulation goes on, that caused her not to be able to sustain this improvement," Goodwin said. "Now one reason we're interested in this is that there's something about that two-week period that comes up very frequently in psychobiology: It takes on the average of two weeks for tricyclics (one type of antidepressant drug) to begin to exert their beneficial effects on depression. It takes lithium (used for mania) about that time. This data is trying to tell us something, but what that something is, I think, it's too early to say."

Already, however, the concept of altered biological rhythms is leading to new approaches to treating depression. The NIMH team is trying to speed up drug response by combining drugs with sleep deprivation. They are exploring whether sleep deprivation alone, done, say, twice a week for three weeks, can have a sustained antidepressant effect without drugs—which would be particularly valuable for those patients who do not respond to current drugs or who suffer undesirable side effects. And they are working on ways of screening new drugs that are specific for certain forms of mental illness in which these biological rhythms are disturbed.

In that regard, much interest is being focused on a drug called D.D.A.V.P., a derivative of a natural compound in the brain called vasopressin. Studies by Dr. Philip Gold and Goodwin suggest the drug might be useful in treating depression.

Vasopressin is a chemical messenger that comes from a clump of cells in the hypothalamus called the "suprachiasmatic nucleus," thought to be the seat of the major biological clock responsible for synchronizing all those body rhythms as well as controlling water and electrolyte metabolism and memory and thought, all of which are disturbed in depression.

The annual rhythms of schizophrenia, also reported at the APA seminar in Colorado, were observed by Harvard University's Dr. Seymour Kety and Dennis Kinney in an ongoing study of the genetics of schizophrenia begun in Denmark (a country chosen for its careful record-keeping) in the early 1960s.

The researchers studied schizophrenic patients who had been adopted as children in order to sort out genetic and environmental influences.

Eight percent of those with no schizophrenic relatives in their natural families to suggest a genetic factor were found to have been born in the cold winter months.

Kety said it is not yet known why the schizophrenic birth rate was high during the first four months of the year.

It could be due to annual rhythms in certain brain chemicals.

Or to a greater likelihood of birth injuries during more severe weather.

But "a more interesting possibility," he said, is that one form of schizophrenia may be caused by a virus that peaks during the winter or in the warm summer months, coinciding with the first trimester of such pregnancies.

The prevalence of schizophrenia among the lower socioeconomic classes of large cities has been attributed to stress, but Kety notes that it would be just as likely to result from a "virus whose propagation is favored by congestion, poor living conditions and less than optimal hygiene."

4 The Emotional Self

Words are such limiting creatures! We are insisting on the holistic approach to the study of humans and their emerging selves, yet our words force us to act as if humans were partitioned up, separated into parts. We don't believe there is a real division between mind, body, emotion, or any other aspects of human experience. Yet, our words, our entire culture and what it does to our thinking, force us to deal with experiences as if they really were separate.

Here we're interested in exploring that integrated side of human selfhood that consists in, begins with, causes, and is expressed by emotions. Emotions are just as much a part of people as their intellect, muscles, digestion, and reproduction.

Many people fail to experience themselves as significant persons because of emotional conflicts. Some, fearful of too many things, live sheltered half-lives. Others, afraid of fear itself, prance about playing brave, bluffing, wearing a John Wayne mask that intends to fool everybody. Still others, told that anger is "bad," pretend to love and like everyone. Or they react to genuinely anger-provoking situations with a shrug and a complacent smile. They play at being "cool," a much-admired attitude in a certain part of our society.

The first article in this chapter, by Barbara Kevles, attempts to establish patterns by which we can deal with our own anger and tendencies toward violence. These are not in the oversimplified how-to-do-it fashion of Dale Carnegie's books, but are relatively simple principles which we hope will invite your contemplation and application to your own life.

Despite newspaper accounts of violent street crimes, research indicates that a huge percentage of all *beatings and murders occur between family members in the home. In our second reading, Kitty Hanson analyzes why this should be so, describes police tactics being used to curb such violence, and provides suggestions for "fighting fair" in your own family.*

In the third selection, Eleanor Brown discusses depression, a feeling nearly all of us experience at one time or another, sometimes with devastating results.

The last selection, by Willard Gaylin, presents the other side of being human, our overwhelming capacity for caring and loving each other.

Make Love Not War in Your Own Life

Barbara Kevles

Few feelings in the human armamentarium of emotions cause us so much trouble as anger. The earliest writings tell us that ancient peoples wrestled with this problem as well.

Anger is not bad. It can and often does lead to bad (unproductive, hurtful, or destructive) behaviors. But it can also lead to good (healthy and positive) behaviors, as those who enjoy making up after a quarrel will testify. Here, Barbara Kevles presents her ideas about the place of anger and violence in our lives.

When America watched the violence televised from the Democratic Convention, most of the affluent made no connection between Chicago and their own lives. How absurd! Acts of violence happen not only beyond the hedges, the picket fences, the front doors of the middle class, but smack in their own homes. In perfectly proper families, parents beat children to a pulp; teen-agers wreck the family car on purpose; sons and daughters are evicted from their homes.

"Proper" families breed violence by substituting status symbols for love. Hugs, approval, encouragement are earned by children for doing things: keeping a stylish appearance at the family affair, scoring high grades—and are earned by parents for giving things: a Corvair for Christmas, a fun fur for the college campus. When *things* are substituted for expressing feelings, families bottle up what they want to say. Talk bottled long enough explodes into violence.

Violence: Last Resort at Communication

Violence is expressed in many ways. *The Oxford Dictionary* defines it: "Physical force to inflict injury or damage upon persons or property." How can a nice girl from a nice home destroy her mother's kitchen? How can a well-brought-up boy knife a brother?

Nice girls and boys are better trained at keeping up appearances than at expressing their feelings. To most of us the language of pain is as foreign as Ubangi. Bankrupt of words to defend feelings, those hurt seem to have only one alternative to get their point across—violence. Violence is a message that often is not understood.

Some authorities extend the definition of violence beyond the physical to include the psychological impact: A white boy brings home a Negro girl and is disowned.

A girl caught sleeping with a married man is commanded by her parents to shoot her dog and, instead, shoots herself.

There are infinite ways of inflicting pain without touching. This covert violence avoids the issue. We don't have to confront the people we depend upon with our grievances. This is underground guerrilla warfare in the recreation room.

Rickie can't wait for next fall because then she moves out of the posh Manhattan apartment shared with mother (a divorcée) and into the dormitory at New York University. She and her mother battle daily. After one particularly brutal argument, mother explodes emotionally and sends Rickie to an aunt in Long Island for the summer. Long Island is Squaresville. Rickie is boxed in, frustrated, abandoned. One afternoon, she stood before the bathroom mirror and gulped down a quinine pill, then another, then several. But when the pain became excruciating, she called the doctor. Why had she tried suicide?

Rickie tried to get through to her mother, but mother discouraged the criticism with "Because . . . " or "I'm your mother, that's why. . . " or "As long as you live under my roof . . . " We are not taught how to criticize our family or, for that matter, ourselves. The rage that had bottled up for years inside Rickie finally turned on her.

Rickie receives help now from a psychiatrist twice a week. Through these sessions she is coming to understand how much she needs her mother and, what she didn't know, *how much her mother needs her.*

The first time Rickie's mother visited her in the hospital when she was recovering from her suicide attempt, she confessed failure as a parent. They both cried. She asked her mother to trust her even when she is making mistakes, on the faith she'll outgrow her hangups. Rickie says, "Our meeting was like a scene from a soap opera, but we've never been the same since."

Is talking about a problem a solution or a stopgap? Are we born with innate violence? Dr. Frederick Wertham, an authority on human violence, says, "No. Violence is learned behavior. It is not an instinct like sex or hunger. Animals do not kill for hate, spite, revenge, sadism or greed. Most important of all, they never systematically kill large numbers of the same species. So when we speak of massacres, extermination camps, mass bombings . . . we should not refer to the 'bestial' in man. It isn't the beast, it is man itself. . . ."

Most animals have an inborn mechanism that prevents such beasts of prey as wolves or lions from killing members of their pack. Man has such an instinctive drive, too. Unfortunately, this instinct against killing his kind has been smothered by his deluxe weapon arsenal. Man's power to kill man has grown beyond his control.

But, we are not *inherently* violent. Wertham states that when a person prepares to threaten or carry out a violent act, a part of his lower brain is stimulated. But the violent urge, Wertham stresses, "can be inhibited by higher centers in the brain, the cerebral cortex."

How can we control violence in America when television, magazines, newspapers continually tell us violence is masculine?

And what is a man? Everywhere a boy looks, in most of the mass media, to be a man is to be cool, show no emotions, use physical violence. If a boy learns he-men solve problems with fists, why shouldn't he? Yet when John Glenn returned after the first man-flight in space, he cried when he saw his wife. One may catch the John Glenns of our society in a two-minute news clip, at best, while the groovy night-time serials feature the hand-to-holster heroes in saturation. Those are society's models—men who, when they kill, never grimace or cry. So, boys try to be men with their fists.

Anthony Storr, one of Britain's most articulate psychiatrists and a man steeped in the studies of ethology—animal instinct under natural conditions—defines aggression as "a drive as innate, as natural and as powerful as sex." Freud branded the aggressive drive as what led man toward destruction and death. Today Storr and others disagree with Freud. They emphasize aggression is essential for survival and mastery of the environment. Storr writes in his book, *Human Aggression*, "In adult life, the aggressive drive which in childhood enables the individual to break free of parental domination serves to preserve and define identity." On constructive control of aggression's destructive impulses, Storr guardedly warns, "There is no clear dividing line between those forms of aggression which we all deplore and those which we must not disown if we are to survive."

It's startling to speak of love in the same breath with aggression, but the facts prove aggression is essential to lovemaking. The "passive woman in sex" myth is very unsatisfactory if followed. The best possible outlet for the ever-increasing stockpile of aggression is love. Konrad Lorenz, father of modern ethology, thinks only animals capable of intense aggression are capable of intense personal ties and love since the aggressive instinct can be the energy for violence, or, redirected, the same energy can be transformed into acts of love.

In the course of writing this article, I participated involuntarily in a revealing act of violence. A friend, Barbara Connell, her husband and I were watching President Johnson announce his latest bid for peace in Vietnam and his decline to run again for the Presidency. I persisted in making asides.

When it was all over, Barbara, who is a Democrat's Democrat, verbally attacked me, "You weren't listening from the top. You're the kind of person who approaches a situation with preconceived notions. You're one of millions of negative people who see nothing good about this country."

Rather than give vent to my anger at her, I stalked out of the house and spent the next half hour walking. When I returned, I refused to talk about Johnson, the war, or my cousins in Vietnam. Barbara tried to force me to say what was bothering me. I wouldn't. I had to be polite. Barbara grabbed my shoulders and shook me, shouting, "Do you want to be my friend, do you? Then tell me what you feel."

Then, though fearful of losing the friendship, I came out and accused Barbara of maligning me. She apologized and I apologized, too, for being supersensitive. Once we said what we *really felt*, once we aired hostilities, the tension eased. After arguing, we both felt a deeper communication, a sense of ultra-frequency contact—a real high.

From this, an epiphany: It's not enough to cool it, to not act violently. The way to love other people is to express what we feel—anger and love—without aiming to hurt feelings. Open but reverent communication is how to make love in our lives.

How to Deal with Violence in Your Own Life

1. Stop playing the role of victim in your family. Step out of the role of child-student and take the role of guru-adult. Start a rap going with your parents over mutual pain points. If they've criticized your appearance, for example, compliment them on their concern for your well-being, then

criticize them by opening with "I know you didn't mean to, but . . . " "You might have said . . . " "Did you consider my feelings when you . . . ?" As long as you both show respect for each other, very difficult areas can be discussed rationally.

2. When someone hurts you, express what you feel immediately. Say:

"I was embarrassed by"

"You put me down when"

"I was jealous of"

"I was hurt by"

"I tried to . . . but you wouldn't listen."

3. When you criticize someone else, be prepared to take some artillery fire in return. It is frightening, sometimes terrifying, to have it out because when you attack, you must also expose your vulnerabilities. Don't hold back. As poet Kahlil Gibran said: "Pain breaks the shell of understanding."

4. When you become so enraged you cannot speak in normal conversational terms, YELL!

5. If you are always put down at home, find an outlet elsewhere that will give you an intake of self-esteem. Educated people are desperately needed to help the ghetto poor. Inquire into projects where you could make a real contribution and boost your ego.

6. If you hear the same criticisms time and again, don't tune out on your critic. Confront and try to discover the real reasons. You may learn you have a fault, or that it is a sign of insecurity in the other person projected on you.

7. Read Dr. Frederick Wertham's book, *A Sign for Cain: An Exploration of Human Violence; Joy* by William C. Schutz; and *Human Aggression* by Anthony Storr.

Violence in the Family: A Secret U.S. Tragedy

Kitty Hanson

It may be difficult to accept, but there is a greater chance that you may be assaulted or murdered by a member of your own family than that a stranger may attack you. There are a number of reasons why this is so, but prime among them is probably the fact that few family members ever learn how to communicate their anxieties, fears, and resentments before they reach the explosive stage. Police spend a huge amount of their time making "house calls" to stop family fights. In this article, Kitty Hanson describes new methods they are using to try to cope with such violence, and gives some useful suggestions on how to fight fairly in your own family.

They quarreled a lot, the neighbors said. This time, it started at dinner in the kitchen of their third-floor walkup in a working-class section of Queens. Five hours later, the dirty dishes and barely touched food still sat on the kitchen table as old hurts, old angers, old frustrations spilled out into the drab apartment while their voices grew louder and angrier.

Suddenly the man started toward her and for a moment they circled one another, the table between them. Then he lunged and her fingers found the knife lying on the table. She started to scream.

"You coulda heard 'em a mile away," said a man who lived across the street. "When she started screamin' I called the cops."

By the time the police arrived, the woman had already written a bloody ending to what has become today's secret American tragedy—the family fight.

Family fights have become one of the most common and most dangerous expressions of violence in the country today. In virtually every block, in every borough, town, and suburb, couples are kicking, elbowing, slapping, and punching. The rich and well-bred fight just as much as the poor and uneducated, and the choice of weapons ranges from beer cans, bottles, and bread knives to frying pans and pieces of furniture.

Violence in the streets may be more visible, but the violence that takes place in the home is more widespread—and just as lethal.

All too frequently, the hostilities end in assault and death. Husbands and wives, it has been found, are more likely to hurt one another seriously than a criminal is when attacking total strangers.

Most of the aggravated assaults listed in the FBI's annual Uniform Crime Reports stem from family fights. And people who kill their spouses account for about one in 12 homicides in the nation. In New York City, during the first six months of this year, 55 homicides were committed by married and common-law spouses—exactly half of all the intrafamily killings.

To many behavioral scientists and psychologists, the family fight bears the seeds of racial fighting and eventually wars. To marriage counselors and other specialists, it is a call for help by desperately frustrated men and women. To police, it is the most hazardous, most unpredictable situation they have to face.

"It's the worst kind of call you can go on," said a police veteran of the family wars. "You never know what you have. You might get anything from a hello and a cuppa coffee to a shotgun blast through the door."

Police have been beaten, bitten, and scratched, doused with paint, shoved downstairs, shot at, and knifed. Many have been hospitalized. Some have been buried.

A "Code 1062—family dispute" as it comes over the city police radio, is the cause of 40% of all lost-time injuries. And one of five police officers killed in the line of duty in this country is slain while responding to a family dispute call.

Now a special program has been instituted in the New York City Training Division (better known as the Police Academy) to change this grim picture. Since May, all recruits have been taking a special course in family crisis intervention. The idea is to give police some of the technical skills and psychological savvy they need to deal with these highly explosive situations without getting hurt or killed and, it is hoped, without resort to force or arrest.

"In most family disputes," says Patrolman John Sullivan, who conducts the course at the academy, "you really do not need to make an arrest. The most you have is a violation."

The new program includes the use of plays—simulated family disputes in which some of the recruits take part. This play-acting is serious business at the academy, for it can mean preventing injuries and saving lives.

"Let's face it," Sullivan says. "The police are the only rescue service available 24 hours a day every day of the week. And we're the only professionals today who make house calls."

All the family fights staged at the academy are dramatizations of actual events. But even after what they have been told in the classroom, most of the recruits are jolted by the language, the violence, the shifting, seething action.

"Prepares them a little for what they're gonna run into in the street," said an officer in the audience, watching as two recruits—a young man and woman—moved uncertainly but bravely onto the stage and into a screaming, shouting, husband-wife free-for-all. The officers had been kept outside the auditorium until they were "called" by one of the combatants and did not know what was going on until they walked on stage. They did their best to do what they had learned in class.

"Try to separate the disputants," Sullivan had instructed the recruits. "Get them to talk. Get their mind off the fight. Ask the guy his name."

The woman recruit approached the wife while the male officer tried to calm the husband. At the same time they tried to survey the scene for possible weapons (a knife on the table, an iron, bottles of liquor) and tried to keep within one another's view.

That is not easy when people are moving, ducking, and dodging around the room, intent on bashing each other's brains out.

The temptation to restrain the battlers forcibly is overwhelming. But force and restraint almost invariably lead to new violence and possible injury. Husbands and wives who have been battling one another suddenly unite and turn the full force of their anger against the police officer.

"A wife calls the cops on her old man," the officers say, "and then if you try to arrest him or use any kind of force against him, she turns and jumps on you."

"Besides," says Lt. Alton Waldon Jr., commanding officer of the Housing Authority Police Training Center, "when you make an arrest, you are creating a family crisis. Maybe through no fault of your own, but you lock up a breadwinner, you stigmatize a family in the eyes of the neighbors, you force a mother to try to support the family."

In the last few years, more and more police departments are introducing special training and special units for family crisis into their systems. But all of these programs are the outgrowth of one demonstration project conceived and developed by a New York psychologist and given a trial by fire in New York's busy thirtieth precinct from 1967 to 1969.

The psychologist is Dr. Morton Bard, professor of psychology at the Graduate Center of the City University of New York, a former street gang worker and onetime (one year) policeman.

"One reason cops come off poorly in the public's eyes," he says, "is that police are confronted with the most highly complex human dilemmas possible, but have not been given the competence to deal with them.

"The solution is not to turn them into psychologists or social workers, but just to give them all the tools they need to do their job. A gun and a nightstick don't solve most problems."

A demonstration of how trained intervention works is this account by one of the thirtieth precinct's policemen in Bard's original project.

"It was up on 145th Street, and the couple was from the South. We went in there, and I could see right off that this guy was tight, very tight. He was ready to do combat. He's tense and he's looking at my stick, so I hung it up on a nearby chair, purposely, to show there's no intent here. So he calms down a little. Then I took my hat off and I said, 'Do you mind if I smoke?' You could see he was shocked and he says 'Oh, sure, sure.'

"Then the guy sat down and he and his wife proceed to tell us what it was all about. When we explain to her why she's upset, she smiles. You see, she thinks we're on her side. Then we tell him why he's mad and he smiles. Now we're on his side. Well, they eventually shake our hands, they were happy, and we never had another call from them."

As Sullivan tells police recruits these days, "If a family is no worse off when you leave than when you came, you've done a good job."

HERE ARE THE RULES FOR FAMILY FIGHTING

There is a growing trend among marriage counselors and psychiatrists to prevent marital violence by teaching couples how to fight. Here are some of the guidelines recommended by "fight counselors" for couples who want to fight for a happy marriage:

—*Pick the right time and place.* Don't fight at the dinner table or in the bedroom but choose a place that is "neutral" for both partners. . . . Choose a time when both partners feel able to cope with anger and disagreement. (The day a husband [or wife] has a run-in with [a] boss is not conducive to fruitful fighting.)

—*Leave time to reach some conclusion.* Don't start a fight just as [you go] out the door to work or you're both about to leave for an evening with friends.

—*Don't save up complaints over long periods of time.* Talking about angers and frustrations as often and openly as possible prevents "gunnysacking" hurts that can later explode into physical violence.

—*Learn the difference between complaining and blaming.* A complaint deserves a hearing. Blaming, on the other hand, simply forces a partner to defend himself.

—*Listen to your own voice during a quarrel.* Never mind the words. If you hear a whine—you are blaming. Once a person stops blaming and starts assuming responsibility for his own condition, the situation starts to improve.

—*Listen "behind the words."* "You don't love me," can really mean, "I'm scared and lonely and want to be closer."

—*Listen.* Many marital disputes accomplish nothing because neither partner is really listening, each cuts the other off, each is engaged in a solo recitation of grievances.

—*And finally, remember you don't have to be a winner.* Any argument has two goals. One is to win. The other is to arrive at understanding. Pick your goals carefully.

And while the police are learning to deal with domestic violence, psychologists and marriage counselors are trying to help prevent it.

There is a growing trend among counseling professionals today to prevent marital violence by teaching couples how to fight. How to fight verbally, that is, before they have to resort to what one psychologist describes as "fists, fangs, and fingernails."

"Fight is a sign of health," says Dr. Jerome A. Travers, assistant director of parish counseling centers of Manhattan. "It shows there is still some ongoing energy in the relationship. We can use that energy to help solve the problems creating the conflict."

Where there is no fighting, Travers says, there is no concern. Couples at that level just drift. They may drift into separation and divorce.

Psychologist Dr. George R. Bach, whose book, *The Intimate Enemy*, is a textbook for lovers and married couples on fighting fair, believes that verbal conflict is not only acceptable—it is vital in preventing violence.

"When marital complaints are carried along quietly in a gunnysack for any length of time," he says, "they make a dreadful mess when the sack finally bursts."

Even though violence is widespread, most behaviorists insist that it is not "normal." Usually, it results from the inability of partners to handle anger. Americans, they say, are taught that anger is bad or sinful instead of a normal part of the personality. It can be channeled, redirected, or sat on—but it won't go away. Marriages would be a lot healthier, they say, if couples let off steam once in a while.

"Irritation, anger, even moments of mutual hate are bound to appear in such a close relationship as marriage," one counselor pointed out.

Another said he reminds couples of the lyrics of a popular song: "Sometimes I love you, sometimes I hate you, but when I hate you, it's 'cause I love you."

"They figure if someone wrote a song about it, it must be true."

Depression—a Painful Pall over Lives of Millions

Eleanor Brown

We have all, at one time or another, been "down"—sometimes severely so. Depression is a human malady which has been recognized since the ancient Greeks. In this article, Eleanor Brown brings together several theories about depression, suggests ways of managing it, and presents research showing that certain situations are likely to lead to depression. Using these insights, you may be able

to recognize situations that will lead to depression for you and know
how to use or overcome the feeling.

A gray cloak of depression weighs heavily on the lives of millions. It is costly garb, whether measured in terms of human misery or in terms of dollars.

Depressed people suffer and so do those closest to them. Business suffers. Estimates run as high as 15% loss of efficiency because of personal worry in which depression likely plays a large part.

In addition, thousands of others—more disrupted by depression or by psychosis heavily colored with depression—will be hospitalized during the year.

Causes may appear small, even meaningless. In fact, large issues of Watergate, energy crisis, war, and national economic problems are not "depressing." The times may be cheerless, but they render only a handful depressed in daily life.

Intensely personal and identifiable, depression nonetheless is not a single, well-defined entity. Rather, it is a family of loosely associated painful feelings that cluster into varying shades of gray ranging from being in the dumps to being excruciatingly different from one's usual self.

The Freudian view of depression, simply stated, is that depression is anger redirected back on the self. However, knowledge has grown and many professionals either have refined Sigmund Freud's notion or have conceptualized depression from other frames of reference. Psychologically, the warp of depression is a distinct lack of self-respect and the woof is the expectation that things never will be better.

Nobody knows just why, but most depressions wear out, many within weeks or months, almost all within eighteen months.

For the person in depression—named melancholia by Hippocrates around 400 B.C.—help is possible, although not a sure thing. Psychotherapy works for many people. And antidepressant medicines are sometimes used to help severe depressions, electroshock to relieve the most intractable. Without help, however, most people do not cope very well—they simply wait it out.

But three experts say: Don't waste this chance to learn more about yourself.

Dr. Harold Greenwald, a psychoanalyst and teacher who compiled a study of call girls (they typically suffer from severe bouts of depression), says: "Enjoy your depression. Get into it and find out what good things it does for you. If people could accept that it is useful to experience depression occasionally and not think they're terrible because of it, they'd be depressed much less."

Dr. Helen Block Lewis, a psychoanalyst whose research explores the intricate relationship between shame and depression, as well as other factors in personality, says: "If you know the basis of your depression, it will lift pretty quickly. And even if you don't discover the basis, knowing why depression is so difficult to cope with may lessen the intensity."

Dr. Martin Seligman, an experimental psychologist who produces "test-tube depression" in laboratory animals in order to study its cure, prevention, and physiology, says: "Depression is a belief in helplessness. So the single best antidepressant I know is successful action—doing something and watching the results."

Greenwald is upbeat about depression, describing it as useful, even valuable. "Look," he says, "depression is an adult form of a child's crying. Crying was rewarded because it was necessary for survival. As adults we ordinarily don't cry, and many people have to be depressed in order to ask people to come closer and to take care of them for awhile."

In contrast, he also sees depression as allowing withdrawal from too much stimulation or too much demand. "Our society says we must be good mixers, that isolation is only for screwballs. But nobody will question your privacy if you're depressed."

And if someone is successful, depression can alleviate the hostility against him. "We have all been failures, and we know how envious we were of friends who were successful, and how we hated them," Greenwald says. "Depression is like saying, 'Don't be mad at me just because I'm successful—look how bad I feel.'"

Depression can also serve as a point of identity. "Most of us don't know who we are, but when someone's depressed, he knows that much—'Hello, I'm a depressed person.'"

Further, depression is a high-class state. "It has great snob appeal for all of us. Can you imagine a cheerful Schopenhauer or Lincoln?"

A bonus of depression can be creativity, Greenwald continued. "A person on his way out of depression can be extremely creative—I've seen people do wonderful things, sitting down and painting, for example. Or shopping. It can be creative, putting things together to look good."

He points out that everyone has the seeds of depression and of elation within him at any one moment. Which he develops depends on what he wants right then. "Everyone should remember that he has a perfect right to be depressed."

Greenwald views depression as having "nothing to do with anger turned inward or outward—or sideways, for that matter. We know from experimental psychologists that anger and depression are incompatible emotions and cannot be experienced at the same time," he says. "But depression and humor are incompatible, too, and we don't call depression laughter turned inward."

What Greenwald thinks happens is that people put such unrealistic demands on themselves that they get depressed when they fail to live up to those self-imposed demands. "People don't decide to be depressed, but they decide other things which cause depression." The decision might be to be lovable at all times. Or independent and self-sufficient at all times. Or patient, kind, and understanding at all times. "Then one is sure to get depressed," Greenwald points out, "because no one can live up to those expectations without lapse."

The decision might be to be difficult and unloving toward particular people—characteristic of delinquent youth—and depression eventually follows. "No one can live down to those expectations all of the time, either."

Shame which goes unrecognized is the seed which later grows into depression, according to Dr. Lewis. She discovered the importance of shame some years ago in studying a small segment of people for whom psychotherapy did not work—they organized what they learned in therapy in ways that made them feel worse, not better. The common thread among them was shame which had remained undealt with.

From her research in personality factors which incline people either toward shame or toward guilt (both forms of impulse control that are often confused), she became convinced that shame is an important—and much neglected—phenomenon both in theory and in therapeutic practice.

Guilt, on the other hand, is prominent both in theory and in application.

The way to avoid depression, she suggests, is to "red-flag" thoughts that may be screening embarrassment out of awareness. Just what does Dr. Lewis suggest to look for? An incident experienced as a blow or a jolt. A time of feeling blank or tense or lousy. An internal conversation that includes calling oneself silly. These probably represent unrecognized shame.

If a person can think through—gently—what forbidden feelings brought on the feeling, then he unravels the makings of depression. The feeling might be hate, love, sexiness, superiority, or gloating—any feeling which is unacceptable to the person.

"If he can see that he cannot help hating or loving or feeling sexy or superior, or whatever the feeling is, he'll start feeling better almost right away," she said. "Even some acceptance of one's own depression minimizes the pathological implications of it. It helps to keep depression to manageable proportions."

The paralyzing aspect of shame—no such paralysis accompanies guilt—comes with being self-conscious from two points of view, from one's own and from another's. "It's like being two places at once," Dr. Lewis says. "A person split in two is unable to view a situation very accurately and certainly is unable to cope very well."

The psychological aspects of shame are compounded by one's body seeming to go "out of control"—blushing and sweating, for instance—in ways usually experienced as childish and "illogical," she adds.

Shame is such a painful state—more difficult than guilt—that people will do almost anything to keep from feeling it. Thus people develop ways of hiding their embarrassment from themselves.

"People can learn, however, that although it's painful, embarrassment is not the end of the world. And it's better than massive depression."

Seligman is studying a purer culture and more severe forms of depression in laboratory-produced symptoms. "We can arrange for an animal to learn that what he does has absolutely no effect on what happens to him," Seligman says, "and thereby produce what we call 'learned helplessness.'"

All it takes is putting a rat or a dog in a situation where it cannot escape a small but clearly unpleasant electrical shock. Because there is nothing the animal can do to escape—or to stop the shock—after several such experiences he gives up. "Then, surprisingly, put in a box from which he could escape easily, he doesn't even try," he reports. "In fact, the animal doesn't do anything—previous learning that his action does not matter holds."

The core of Seligman's hypothesis is this: Lack of control over trauma, not trauma itself, is responsible for learned helplessness. "Learned helplessness has six prominent features in common with depression: passivity, for one, and difficulty in learning that responding is effective," he says. The other four are: helplessness dissipates in time, it brings a notable lack of aggression, it is accompanied by norepinephrine (a biochemical) depletion, and it brings loss of interest in eating and in social and sexual activity.

That the animals cannot tell how they feel leaves one of several gaps relating his research to depression in human beings, Seligman notes.

His "helpless" animals can be cured. Forced time and again to escape, they learn—very slowly—to seek a way out. In time it takes only a nudge instead of forceful pulling and prodding, and finally the animals act on their own. "It always works, and it is lasting," Seligman says. "It's a 100% cure."

Animals also can be immunized against helplessness.

Letting them learn to master situations—before putting them in those that cannot be mastered—keeps the animals from showing depressive symptoms. They stay active in their responses.

A history of mastery might inoculate a person against the most severe depressions, Seligman conjectures. "But too much mastery might mean that a person would not develop ways of coping with failure, anxiety, and frustration," he cautions. "I'm thinking of the golden young people for whom everything goes well until they reach college and they have to cope with these stresses for the first time. They fall apart."

People who were not golden children have learned strategies for dealing with minor depression. "Mine is to force myself to work—then I can see that my responses are still effective," he says. "If I start and then give up, it only makes the depression worse. So I choose something I know I can complete and the problem is only getting started."

Caring Makes the Difference

Willard Gaylin

The author states, "We survive only by and with caring." If each of us had one good, caring relationship, we would not have the violence and depression that we do in our society. People have an extraordinary capacity for loving and caring, but it is a side of human nature that many people feel uncomfortable with. For some men, caring and loving are unmanly and silly behaviors. What a hardship this is for their children, and what a waste of human potential.

We live in a time of self-doubt. Unhappy about the world and unsure about our capacities to change it, we are losing faith, not only in our institutions but in ourselves. Frustrated and insecure, we fix responsibility on our very nature. We are failures in our own eyes, a perilous situation for the individual or for the species. Since self-love and self-respect are such essential ingredients of human functioning, their absence threatens our survival. When individuals feel unloved, unwanted, and unworthy they may slip into depression, that most dangerous of psychological states. We seem to be approaching a time of national despair.

When I talk about national despair, I am not talking about social institutions as a political scientist would. It is always hazardous to project from individuals to institutions or to states; I am talking here about the increasing number of individuals who have lost hope and confidence, at least in the political area. In that sense, it seems to me legitimate to talk about a kind of national despair or depression.

Depression does not mean merely "feeling down," or "being depressed," everyday feelings often confused with it by laymen. Clinical depression is a form of mental illness with relatively clear symptoms: a devastating loss of self-confidence and self-esteem; a deep sense of personal failure; and a feeling of despair severe enough to be nearly paralyzing, or to cause suicide attempts.

Early psychoanalytic theories of depression described the illness as caused by the loss of a "love object." And indeed, intense grief over the loss of a loved one can easily lead to depression, particularly among women whose husbands have died, or whose lovers have rejected or abandoned them. But clinical experience has shown that depression can have other causes. In my first encounters with the illness, among male patients at a veterans' hospital, none of those I examined made suicide attempts because of the break-up of a love affair, or the death of a loved one. For them depression was usually brought on by some professional or financial setback, or some social humiliation.

How can such dissimilar events as the loss of a loved one and the loss of a job cause the same illness? In 1849 the philosopher Kierkegaard answered this question in an essay entitled, *The Sickness unto Death:*

> Despair is never ultimately over the external object but always over ourselves. A girl loses her sweetheart and she despairs. It is not over the lost sweetheart, but over herself-without-the-sweetheart. And so it is with all cases of loss, whether it be money, power, or social rank.

As Kierkegaard suggests, we suffer not over the loss of another, but over the depletion of ourselves. If one's self-esteem and ability to cope with life are overly dependent on the support of another person, the loss of that person may precipitate a depression. Similarly, if one is overly dependent on social, financial, or professional status, their loss may also lead to despair and depression.

The loss of a loved one causes depression more commonly among women than men because our culture has traditionally invested security in the masculine roles. In our male-dominated society the husband's position has until recently been the major and often only source of prestige for a woman. The typical widow wonders how she will manage to carry on and make her way alone in the world without the support of her husband.

A man's pride and self-confidence have traditionally been based not on a loved one, but on his professional career and personal attainments. Men tend to jump out of windows more often because of the loss of a business than the loss of a wife or child. This does not mean they love their wives and children less than their business, but that their security, prestige, pride, and self-confidence depend primarily on their careers.

Hopeless and Helpless

The two feelings most characteristic of severe depression are hopelessness and helplessness. The overwhelming sense of hopelessness occurs most often in those who cling to certain adolescent or unrealistic goals and ambitions. The very contrast between those goals and the awareness of one's inability to achieve them can destroy self-confidence and bring on depression. As for helplessness, we tend to use the word so often we forget its terrible literal meaning: without the help of a single caring person, and thus defenseless or impotent. Hopeless and helpless, the depressed individual gives up. This total abandonment and paralysis of will means the depressive has no defense mechanisms or illusions for protection. The illness represents the bankruptcy of survival mechanisms.

Depression can be precipitated by the loss or removal of *anything* that we overvalue in terms of our own security. To the degree that our sense of worth or security is dependent on love, money, social position, power, or drugs—to that extent we will be threatened by its loss. When our reliance is so preponderent, the absence becomes so threatening that we despair of our survival. That is the despair we call depression.

In its most extreme clinical form, depression resembles the sense of despair in everyday life. It is a humiliating, debasing feeling—and a dangerous one. The depressed individual feels abandoned, uncherished, unwanted, alienated, resentful, and angry. Depression breaks down social communication and a sense of identification with others in a way that mere economic deprivation does not. When deprivation is seen as stemming from indifference to us or, worse, contempt for us as individuals, we feel isolated and alienated. When we feel "not acceptable" into the symbolic family of a majority society, when we are made to feel like some alien "other," we tend to see those privileged and secure representatives of that society, if not the society itself, as alien and hostile.

This deprivation may be tolerable if there is some pathway to privilege and approval, regardless of how tortuous and difficult. When the path is barred, however, or so obscured that it seems not present, despair can ensue. It can lead to the destruction of self via drugs or the destruction of others through the rage of impotence and frustration.

To be totally unaccepted and unloved requires either the rejection of one's self—an intolerable situation—or a total dissociation from society. Such total dissociation is dangerous, however, when we are required to live in that social community. Surely the kind of adolescent brutality evidenced in the newspaper every day, in which a street mugger hits a random woman over the head with a lead pipe as a convenient means of gaining the six dollars in her purse, implies more than just the need for six dollars. It suggests that the concept of identity with society has been destroyed, or never developed. It is analogous to the squashing of a bug approaching your picnic table.

If we are not cared for by others, we cannot care for ourselves. To give up on one's self is to give up on one's own personal value, and ultimately to give up a sense of values. A society that treats any serious segment of its population, whether blacks, women, or youth, with distaste or disrespect, runs the risk of convincing that group of its own inadequacy, and thus alienating it from identification with society and allegiance to its moral codes.

Like the mistreated minority, the advantaged middle class is also becoming alienated from our culture. If our disillusionment with our institutions and our way of life is allowed to drift into the hopelessness of despair, we will passively embrace self-hatred and self-pity—the only elements of human potential strong enough to threaten our very survival.

The Self as Tar Baby

A denigrated self-image is a tar baby. The more we play with it, embrace it, the more bound we are to it. Attacks on ourselves and our nature are the last whimpering maneuvers before the catatonic acceptance of defeat. In depression *Homo sapiens*, the most resourceful of all creatures, abandons hope in his own capacity to cope and survive. Without struggle or desire, he is helpless.

A sense of failure is always defined in relationship to our aspirations. And no man hoped for more, or expected more, of himself than the 19th-century man. The 19th century was indeed the century of great expectations. Compare this with the 20th-century counterpart. No longer the arrogant and self-confident creator, potential rival of God, we now perceive ourselves as trapped in a world that we know is necessary for our survival and yet that we nonetheless seem to be compulsively and uncontrollably destroying.

Among the possible reasons for the decline in our self-esteem is the very success of modern science. The explosion of the first atomic bomb lent credibility to the image of the guilt-ridden scientist frightened by his own creations. In recent years the anxiety has mounted with the giant strides of the new biology: the promise of genetic engineering, *in vitro* fertilization, artificial body parts, and rented womb space from surrogate mothers.

Ironically, the very technologies that offered answers to some problems created other problems to compound them. The ecology disaster is only the most recent shattering blow, forcing us into a new sense of humiliation. The vehicles and discarded wrappings of our conveniences are killing us. We are used to throwing things out, but now, just as our garbage is becoming progressively more poisonous, we find ourselves running out of "out." Out is where we live, or where our children may be condemned to live.

If the success of technology has created problems, so has our sense of its failure. Too many promises were realized in the specific only to be lost when weighed as part of the total. Where is the promise of the 19th century to remove pain, hunger, suffering?

The abandonment of religious faith that accompanied the rise of science created its own problems. The accomplishments were man's—not God's. This being the case, when the fall came, where could we look for the authorship of our defeat? On whom could we project the burden and responsibility of the failures? To whom could we turn for succor and salvation?

Self-doubt and confusion also arise on a personal scale, due in great part to some unanticipated effects of the upwardly mobile society. In the traditional Old World society, a person knew that he could not leave the role, station, or often even the locality defined for him by the accident of his birth. He generally accepted his social class as he accepted his height, a part of him not to be questioned. If his father was a baker, he became a baker. For a woman, the role was the same, whatever her father did.

While certainly constrictive, traditional society had its compensations. To be a success in life, all a man had to do was to be a good baker. In an upwardly mobile society, unlimited opportunities seem to be present. The carpenter's son becomes free to become a cabinetmaker or a manufacturer—and the same now with the carpenter's daughter. To be a success means not "succeeding," but surpassing the parent. In the fixed society, it was not uncommon to compliment a man by telling him he was almost as good as his father. In the upwardly mobile society, the previous generation is generally the symbol not of success, but of failure. The parent in our society will insist that his child work harder, lest "you end up like me." The advance in technology has compounded the problems of upward mobility. In many professions the methods of the father are no longer transferable to the son, since they have in fact become obsolete. In too many fields the methodology of even a few years ago seems archaic today. Technology has often made the past seem irrelevant, and sometimes even foolish.

The myth of upward mobility implies that each generation has not only the opportunity, but the obligation to surpass the previous one. The ever-increasing opportunity demands increasing achievement with the possibility of an increasing sense of one's own inadequacy. If you move up a notch, why not the notch above? If success is always defined by the notch above, then the notch we occupy is always the position of failure.

The Horns of the Elk

If it is true, as many fear, that our technology has run out of its adaptive course and purposes, then it bears comparison with certain analogies in nature. In the Darwinian model of self-improvement, certain elks, over the years, developed larger and grander horns. The larger-horned elks, intimidating their competitors and attracting more females, won the battle for survival by virtue of this self-glorifying and self-enhancing equipment. Eventually, with selective breeding over generations, the horns became still larger and more elaborate until they were so grand that they trapped the elk in the trees of the forest that were his natural habitat, and the species began to die out. What had originated as adaptive, had become destructive.

Like the elk's horns, man's technology no longer seems to serve his needs. Technological society may have estranged us from certain limits of normal functioning. That which formerly was our glory and power has begun to reduce us. We feel progressively impotent in the face of the pleasureless social institutions that we ourselves created but that now seem to control us. Following the holocaust, the atom bomb, the Vietnam War, continuing famines and profound inequalities of living standards, persistent bigotry and battery, it is no wonder that we welcome the prophets of doom who describe all these horrors as the likely, if not inevitable, products of the very nature of man.

The reasons for despair seem obvious; the reasons for hope less so. Look around and the world seems a mess. But it is neither the best of times nor the worst of times. Violence, brutality, hunger, injustice, bigotry, war, personal abuse, and inequity have existed in all the generations in history that preceded us.

If the world does seem in more desperate straits than ever before, this stems from the fact that the only solutions obvious to us now don't seem effective any more. Because of our technology we are moving toward a homogeneous, small world. When Periclean Greece and Imperial Rome talked about the destruction of civilization they narcissistically referred to their small corner of the world. When we now talk about the destruction of the world, it is conceivable in a way that it never was before.

And so we despair, not because we are abandoned by God (after all, it was we who abandoned Him), but because we think we have used our best, and it was not enough. We despair as a group in the same way we despair as individuals, when we feel impotent and unable to cope. To think, however, that we have exhausted the potential of our true technology—our imagination—is preposterous. It is as though we have recognized the limitations of the balloon, and not yet discovered the airplane.

Coming face to face with our increasing capacity to destroy ourselves and our world has led many, particularly among the young, to give up not just on one man, or one group of men, but on man himself. This is why I find the antiperson bias of much of the back-to-nature movement so frightening. For if there is nobility in our world, it is the presence and form of people that conceptualize that nobility, and thereby create it. Of course, the garbage in the rivers, the litter in the streets, the destruction of the forests, and the pollution of the air offend me, because they diminish the environment in which human beings live, and will thereby diminish their humanity. To talk, however, of "what a good place the world would be if it weren't for the vile and destructive nature of man" is foolish, particularly when articulated by a member of that species.

It is not surprising, therefore, that many current students of human nature from the fields of anthropology, sociology, and biology, and particularly from the new field of ethology, have emphasized the hostile, territorial, and aggressive aspects of human behavior. Nor is it surprising that such scholarship has been popular in the common marketplace of ideas. But we accept these ideas at risk, and it is time to reconsider this one-sided evaluation of human nature.

Such a pessimistic view must be balanced by one that has received little attention: the extraordinary capacity of the human being for loving and caring. If there is one fact founded in his biology, essential to his survival, and uniquely his own, it is that *Homo sapiens* is a supremely loving animal and a caring one. If we properly contemplate the evidence which supports these positive aspects of human nature, it may direct us back to the very same behavior from which we have been inferring aggression. The wide acceptance of the positions popularized by Konrad Lorenz and his followers was established at least as much on our readiness to hear their sermon as on the nature of the evidence itself. We must look once again into ourselves, and brace ourselves for good news.

Each child born reaches frantically and hungrily for the caring figure who must be there for his survival, even though he may be unaware of that person's existence. The ludicrously helpless phenomenon of the human infant is testament to the bounds of love innate in people. We survive only by and with caring. This caring nature is a fact of our design, and it is good. It is good not because it is "normal," but because it is necessary for the survival of the human species, and goodness is manifestly the burden of that species.

Our intuitive and instinctive responses were shaped genetically by precultural conditions that no longer exist. We have changed the rules of life, redefined the signals of danger and survival, without having changed the built-in response. Our built-in emotions give us dangerously wrong signals for the civilized world we now occupy, and we are obliged to reeducate our intuitions.

But in redesigning ourselves and our social and political institutions we must exercise care that the new institutions will not diminish the most human of qualities—our loving nature—or extinguish it in the adult organism. The caring nature of human beings is so self-evident as to escape our observation if we are not careful. It has survived many periods of self-doubt and self-abuse. We are now in such a time. Perhaps here, a final look at clinical depression may provide some vision of hope, a pathway through our current despair.

The depressive patient has given up all hope of either fight or flight, but these are not the only survival mechanisms. They are not even the most fundamental. *Dependency* is the basic survival mechanism of the human organism. In the critical early period of life, the human animal is capable of neither fight nor flight—only clutch and cling. In the human being, with his disproportionately long period of helplessness, the very survival of the species is based on the built-in dependency maneuvers of the infant and the biologically determined sympathetic responses they elicit in the adult.

When the adult gives up hope in his ability to cope, and sees himself incapable of either fleeing or fighting, he is reduced to a state of depression. This very reduction, with its parallel to the helplessness of infancy, becomes, ironically, one last unconscious cry for help—a plea for a solution to the problem of survival via dependency, a call for love. The very stripping of one's defenses becomes a form of defensive maneuver. It is part of the wonder of the human being that even the state of hopelessness can be used to generate hope. We must hope, as Shelley said, "till Hope creates from its own wreck the thing it contemplates."

I do not despair at the state of the world; I despair at the current state of passive disenchantment and self-denigration. Part of the uniqueness and the wonder of the human species is our ability to redefine our nature. What we are is in great part up to us. In a medieval Talmudic text, we read that "Man, alone amongst animals, is created incomplete, but with the capacity to complete himself." We are the executors of our future.

But if we are convinced that we are innately evil, we will design the institutions of our culture according to that definition. Psychological definitions of the human state can thus become self-fulfilling prophecies. We may not be what we think we are, but what we think we are will determine in great part what we are to become. We must not design our future in terms of our current disillusionment, for those designs, even if erroneously conceived, will influence the future development of our species.

5 The Social Self

People are complex creatures who are both individual units and functional and integral parts of the social units to which they belong. We are born into groups and we never lose our social feeling. We experience our selfhood most fully when we can effectively integrate our individual existences into our social lives. Adler calls this "social interest" and tells us that this paradoxical realization is the healthiest way of living.

Cooperation and competition are processes that all of us experience. Conflict is a further extension of competition. We are under the necessity of finding ways of integrating all of these processes realistically and effectively into our growing sense of self.

In the past few years, the sensitive and thought-provoking German novelist Hermann Hesse has captured the imagination of many college students, as he did those of the 1930s and 1940s. In the excerpt from Hesse's novel Steppenwolf which is found in this chapter, the hero is torn between his tendency to act in a way that will satisfy him personally, and his desire for human contact and the resultant need to act in a socially approved way.

In the second selection of the chapter, a short story, Anthony Winkler, a young writer from Jamaica, introduces us to a unique man—one who seems to be unaffected by pressures from other people because he has no past and no ties to anyone in the present.

The next selection is a "Call to Action," in which the author, Alan Dahms, shows how various institutions can help to further human growth. At a time when our society seems to be cracking apart, Dahms offers some optimistic and practical suggestions.

*In 1950, Erik Erickson wrote Childhood and
Society, the book from which the last excerpt in this
chapter was taken. In it, he describes the impact of the
machine age on American adolescents in terms that
seem even more compelling today than they did when
first written.*

from *Steppenwolf*

Hermann Hesse

*A Steppenwolf has two natures: one human and one that of a
wolf. Harry Haller, the hero of the Hermann Hesse novel from
which this excerpt is drawn, feels he is a Steppenwolf, and as such
he continually experiences an internal struggle about how to deal
with other people. He knows he must observe some conventions of
behavior in order to meet his needs for human contact. But the
"wolfish" part of him laughs at these efforts and ridicules him for
being dishonest.*

*Many people in today's world feel this duality, although
probably not as strongly as Hesse's hero does. See if you recognize
yourself in Harry's struggles.*

Passing by the library I met a young professor of whom in earlier years I
used occasionally to see a good deal. When I last stayed in the town, some
years before, I had even been several times to his house to talk Oriental
mythology, a study in which I was then very much interested. He came in
my direction walking stiffly and with a shortsighted air and only recognized me at the last moment as I was passing by. In my lamentable state I
was half-thankful for the cordiality with which he threw himself on me. His
pleasure in seeing me became quite lively as he recalled the talks we had
had together and assured me that he owed a great deal to the stimulus they
had given him and that he often thought of me. He had rarely had such
stimulating and productive discussions with any colleague since. He asked
how long I had been in the town (I lied and said "a few days") and why I had
not looked him up. The learned man held me with his friendly eye and,
though I really found it all ridiculous, I could not help enjoying these

crumbs of warmth and kindliness, and was lapping them up like a starved dog. Harry, the Steppenwolf, was moved to a grin. Saliva collected in his parched throat and against his will he bowed down to sentiment. Yes, zealously piling lie upon lie, I said that I was only here in passing, for the purpose of research, and should of course have paid him a visit but that I had not been feeling very fit. And when he went on to invite me very heartily to spend the evening with him, I accepted with thanks and sent my greetings to his wife, until my cheeks fairly ached with the unaccustomed efforts of all these forced smiles and speeches. And while I, Harry Haller, stood there in the street, flattered and surprised and studiously polite and smiling into the good fellow's kindly, shortsighted face, there stood the other Harry, too, at my elbow and grinned likewise. He stood there and grinned as he thought what a funny, crazy, dishonest fellow I was to show my teeth in rage and curse the whole world one moment and, the next, to be falling all over myself in the eagerness of my response to the first amiable greeting of the first good honest fellow who came my way, to be wallowing like a suckling pig in the luxury of a little pleasant feeling and friendly esteem. Thus stood the two Harrys, neither playing a very pretty part, over against the worthy professor, mocking one another, watching one another, and spitting at one another, while as always in such predicaments, the eternal question presented itself whether all this was simple stupidity and human frailty, a common depravity, or whether this sentimental egoism and perversity, this slovenliness and two-facedness of feeling was merely a personal idiosyncrasy of the Steppenwolves. And if this nastiness was common to men in general, I could rebound from it with renewed energy into hatred of all the world, but if it was a personal frailty, it was good occasion for an orgy of hatred of myself.

While my two selves were thus locked in conflict, the professor was almost forgotten; and when the oppressiveness of his presence came suddenly back to me, I made haste to be relieved of it. I looked after him for a long while as he disappeared into the distance along the leafless avenue with the good-natured and slightly comic gait of an ingenuous idealist. Within me, the battle raged furiously. Mechanically I bent and unbent my stiffened fingers as though to fight the ravages of a secret poison, and at the same time had to realize that I had been nicely framed. Round my neck was the invitation for eight thirty, with all its obligations of politeness, of talking shop and of contemplating another's domestic bliss. And so home—in wrath. Once there, I poured myself out some brandy and water, swallowed some of my gout pills with it, and, lying on the sofa, tried to read. No sooner had I succeeded in losing myself for a moment in *Sophia's Journey from Memel to Saxony*, a delightful old book of the eighteenth century, than the invitation came over me of a sudden and reminded me that I was neither shaved nor dressed. Why, in heaven's name, had I brought all this on myself? Well, get up, so I told myself, lather yourself, scrape your chin till it bleeds, dress and show an amiable disposition toward your fellow men. And while I lathered my face, I thought of that sordid hole in the clay of the cemetery into which some unknown person had been lowered that day.[1] I thought of the pinched faces of the bored fellow Christians and I could not even laugh. There in that sordid hole in the clay, I thought, to the accompaniment of stupid and insincere ministrations and the no less stupid and insincere demeanor of the group of mourners, in the discomforting sight of all the metal crosses and marble slabs and artificial flowers of wire and glass, ended not only that unknown man, and, tomorrow or the day after, myself as well, buried in the soil with a hypocritical show of sorrow—no, there and so ended everything; all our striving, all our culture, all our beliefs, all our joy and pleasure in life—already sick and soon to be buried there too. Our whole civilization was a cemetery where Jesus Christ and Socrates, Mozart and Haydn, Dante and Goethe, were but the indecipherable names on moldering stones; and the mourners who stood round affecting a pretense of sorrow would give much to believe in these inscriptions which once were holy, or at least to utter one heartfelt word of grief and despair about this world that is no more. And nothing was left them but the embarrassed grimaces of a company round a grave. As I raged on like this I cut my chin in the usual place and had to apply a caustic to the wound; and even so there was my clean collar, scarce put on, to change again, and all this for an invitation that did not give me the slightest pleasure. And yet a part of me began play-acting again, calling the professor a sympathetic fellow, yearning after a little talk and intercourse with my fellow men, reminding me of the professor's pretty wife, prompting me to believe that an evening spent with my pleasant host and hostess would be in reality positively cheering, helping me to clap some court plaster to my chin, to put on my clothes and tie my tie well, and gently putting me, in fact, far from my genuine desire of staying at home. Whereupon it occurred to me—so it is with every one. Just as I dress and go out to visit the professor and exchange a few more or less insincere compliments with him, without really wanting to at all, so it is with the majority of men day by day and hour by hour in their daily lives and affairs. Without really wanting to at all, they pay calls and carry on conversations, sit out their hours at desks and on office chairs; and it is all compulsory, mechanical and against the grain, and it could all be done or left undone just as well by machines; and indeed it is this never-ceasing machinery that prevents their being, like me, the critics of their own lives and recognizing the stupidity and shallowness, the

1. Earlier in the day a funeral procession had passed Harry. On a whim he joined it.

hopeless tragedy and waste of the lives they lead, and the awful ambiguity grinning over it all. And they are right, right a thousand times to live as they do, playing their games and pursuing their business, instead of resisting the dreary machine and staring into the void as I do who have left the track. Let no one think that I blame other men, though now and then in these pages I scorn and even deride them, or that I accuse them of the responsibility of my personal misery. But now that I have come so far, and standing as I do on the extreme verge of life where the ground falls away before me into bottomless darkness, I should do wrong and I should lie if I pretended to myself or to others that that machine still revolves for me and that I was still obedient to the eternal child's play of that charming world.

The Man Who Knew the Price of All Fish

Anthony C. Winkler

Suppose you woke up one morning and found that every tie you had to the past was gone—parents, friends and acquaintances, enemies, loyalties and allegiances, all gone. How would you feel? Would there be any relief in such a situation, or only pain? How do you suppose your behavior would be affected by such a lack of ties?

In this short story, Anthony Winkler writes about such a situation. Baba, the man who knew the price of all fish, may help you realize the importance of your past experiences and present ties in influencing your actions and your perception of reality.

Baba was a black man with no past. He had nothing ahead of him; he had nothing behind him. He had dropped out of oblivion one day, grew up in Montego Bay on the island of Jamaica, growing into manhood with a tremendous lower jaw burgeoning above his windpipe, a jawbone as large as the top jaw of any mastiff, a jaw that jutted out under his face disjointed, unproportioned, stiff, mysteriously heavy, capped with a lower level of green teeth. He was a black man with no past and no future, with a forehead rounded and indented like a goat's, with two thick and hirsute arms that dropped below his waist when he walked.

His eyes, which people would squint to look into, were sunk deep inside his black face, sheltered by two fat lids that dropped thick as cream, squiggled down deep into the mystery blackness of his skin, and black

Published by permission of the author.

themselves, so that except for their shine in the sunlight, they were hidden in the camouflage of his face.

And, on top of all this, he had no past. He had no future; he had no wife; he had no children; he had nothing, except a small black-hulled canoe, and some wire fishpots and mangrove-stained lines he used to catch fish with.

Every night he rowed out in his canoe and set his fishpots and threw down his lines, and every morning he rowed into Giddy Beach with a canoeful of dead fish and sold the dead fish to women as poor as himself who would haggle him furiously, insult his fish, call him a "jinal," meaning that he was intent on robbing them, paw over the corpse of the fish, hold him up to cynical comparison with more successful fishermen, accuse him of having a white mother, call him a Rastafarian—a worshipper of Haile Selassie as the true messiah—then walk away clutching contemptuously at the dead fish wrapped in a newspaper for which they had paid Baba's price. For it was impossible to haggle him down, because he had no past and could not be either insulted or deprecated.

It did not matter what they called his mother, because he had no mother. He had no wife they could say cuckolded him; he had no children who got poor marks at school; he had no grandfather who bubbled over his senility on street corners; he had no cousins who were cat-o-nined in the square for stealing; he had no aunts who painted their faces for tourist men at nights; he had no attachments which made him vulnerable to abuse; he had no one to be called into shame over.

And so, no one had ever haggled him down on the price of his fish. If he said that the green-skinned, beak-teeth parrot fish were a shilling each, it was impossible to shake him. The woman could call the fish gangrened, she could say it had a slimy skin, she could say it was not a fish, she could say anything, it would not matter. She could haggle until her black face was greener than the parrot fish, it would not matter. For once Baba had decided that a fish was worth a shilling, God could not alter its price. The fish was always sold for a shilling.

And because he was so obdurate in his ways, and because he would not be insulted, those women who approached his canoe came to buy, not to haggle. They would gloomily pick out a fish, saying nothing about its complexion, ask him his price, and dip down into their knotted handker-chief for the money tied up in a ball at its corners, and pay him.

Sometimes, for show, because it is obscene for a Jamaican woman to pay an asking price without a show of haggle, one or two would aim a cursory insult at the fish, ask his price once more, say "Rass Clath" in contempt, kiss their teeth with disgust, fidget their fingers over the dead body of the fish with a show of reluctance as if they knew they were to be cheated but had resigned themselves, and pay.

It was impossible to haggle Baba because he had no past. When that jaw locked with a click against the windpipe, it meant that his mind had sprung shut on the price, it meant that a terrible obduracy had fixed its mark on his face, demon stubbornness was ahold of him once again, and nothing, piety, protestation, insult, innuendo, levity, malice, small-talk, nothing could move him.

So the only thing a woman could do, if she meant to keep her Jamaican self-respect, was to insult him or his mother. But she could not even do that because he had no past, and it did not matter. A sphinxlike solemnity would droop over his face, the cream-thick eyelids would float languidly at half-mast, that terrible jawbone would click, and Baba would stand there, imperturbable, unmoved, unmovable.

It was infuriating, it was maddening to the Montego Bay women. Everyone else on the beach could be haggled, except Baba. Any other fisherman would drop his price a half penny if his parrot fish were called slimy, any decent Jamaican pedlar would stir at least a farthing off his fixed price for the sake of show in the face of determined contention from a haggler, any respectable Jamaican would budge a fraction, at least to signal to God and the world a lack of obdurateness, to show others (for the sake of form) that no man can dogmatically know the universal worth of any fish. A mind who would not was holding to infallibility, it was saying that of all the prices that can be made out of numbers, only one was fitted to each fish, and to no other.

And that was what Baba was saying when his jaw clicked in fixity, when he attached a price to a fish, and would not budge it.

He did not understand the philosophy, because he did not think, but that was what he was saying.

There was one woman for whom he nearly shifted his price. She had been new to Montego Bay and had been unversed in the ways of Baba. She had made a frontal assault on the body of a black sam fish, claiming a graveyard stench for it, accusing Baba of selling old bait, pointing to the green glassiness of its eyes as evidence of aging, holding the fish between her fingers by the tail and swinging it lightly over the gunwales of the black-stained canoe to demonstrate from its lack of flex that it had rigor mortis, spitting tobacco through the corners of her mouth near the tail of the fish to show a contempt for its dead body, dropping the fish heavily in the pool of water in the bottom of the boat to show that it would not float and therefore was no longer a fish, calling down biblical imprecations on the fish and the man who would sell it for a shilling, throwing herself on the beach beside the boat and digging her fingers into the sand swearing that she would sooner dig a grave for the fish than pay a shilling for it, and almost moved him. The jaw did not click at first, and then it did and a pyramid hardness settled over his face, and then something miraculous happened! The jaw unclicked and thawed, the eyes came out from under the gelatinous lids, the face sagged and the mouth almost opened. A gasp went up among the hagglers, imprecations were broken off in mid-sentence, a silence descended on the beach as lightly as a butterfly, for it seemed, for a minute, as if Baba were about to relent, as if a melting of the biblical firmness in that jaw was about to begin; it almost seemed, no more than the hint of a seem, that Baba had been moved. He put a thick-fingered hand to the base of the jawbone, he looked down dubiously at the maligned fish, and for the interminableness which tension and danger invest mere seconds with, his mind was slung between two inward peaks, settling firmly neither on one or on another, and he seemed like anyman hung nervously in the gap of indecision.

But it was folly to think so, for no sooner had the flurry among the canoes died down and all eyes swung over to read the symptoms of hesitancy in that massive jawbone, than the hideous click sounded, and the jawbone locked into a siege of adamantine obduracy. This time no one could move him, because he had given a second pause to his decision, and his jaw was doubly cemented in its certainty.

A cry of relief went up from the crowd of hagglers. The woman who had instilled doubt renewed her hysteria with greater fever than before. She said the fish was a "rass cloth fish," a "blood cloth fish," a "bumbo cloth fish"—and, reaching the pinnacle of Jamaican obscenity with that last expression—she turned red with anger for using up all the superlatives available to her without relief. She moaned, she rolled her eyes inside the black sockets in her face showing their fearsome whites, she spat with contempt, she grasped the fish and attempted to mangle it, she said he was an eater of goat turd, his fish were loathesome and diseased, a duppy would lay hands on his mouth as he slept, she ravaged the corners and cupboards of Jamaican folklore for insult, but she could not move him. He was implacable, he was granite, his jawbone had clicked.

For he had no past, and he had no wife, and he had no children, and he had no property, except for the black-stained canoe and the wire fishpots and the lines he used to catch his fish. And once he had caught a fish, he fixed a price to its dead body, and God himself could not dispute it.

His fish were his own. He rowed out over the deep sea at night with a kerosene lamp in the bow of his canoe, and all night he dropped lines and traps to the bottom, floating on the blackness of the deep with only the skin of the cotton-tree canoe between him and its terrors. All night he stayed there pulling up the struggling fish from the bottom of the black sea which licked the sides of his canoe peacefully, heaved him up and down, rolled him on the dreamy somnolence of a night swell, and when he held a fish between his fingers, took the hook out of its gasping jaws, strangled it between his heavy forefinger and thumb, or smashed its head against the bottom of the canoe, it became his, and for the rest of the night he rode in the bottom of the boat with the bodies of the fish, and had time to discover the true price of each. The green parrot fish, the yellow tail snapper, the thick black sam, the red congo tony, they all died in the bottom of the boat sucking dry at the night wind, their gills beating furiously, their eyes stiffening into the glassiness of death, and under the blue starlight Jamaican night an enormous jawbone sat over them brooding. For they were his own, he had dropped his lines into the dreaming sea, and he had pulled them up one by one out of its blackness. When he rowed into Giddy Beach in the morning, the sun would be rising over the Bogue Islands on his left, and the body of every dead fish would have a price.

A Call to Action

Alan M. Dahms

The functioning of society is everyone's responsibility. To accept and carry out that responsibility is not a simple task. Modern humans are complex, partially because technology has affected our behavior in so many ways that we often feel as though we are in a sort of "Alice in Wonderland" tailspin.

In his "Call to Action," Alan Dahms stresses that all of us share the same emotions, regardless of what culture or society we belong to. Dahms offers timely suggestions on how we can solidify world society and how we can maintain our sense of being human in an increasingly technological world. He advocates changes and expansions in our educational and religious institutions, and increased accessibility to psychological help, as primary means in achieving these ends.

The year 1969 marked the start of a new era of human life. When man reached the moon, Earth became an object of his detached scrutiny. This event precipitated an emotional breakthrough for humanity, for it ensured man's consciousness of his tribal intimacy as a species in the cosmos. Each of us can now know we are all in the same boat. We can envision a feeling of emotional solidarity with friend and foe alike. Explicit awareness of this

From *Emotional Intimacy: Overlooked Requirement for Survival,* 1972; Shields Publishing Co., Inc., Ft. Collins, Colorado. Reprinted with permission.

intimacy among men and women of all races and cultures on Earth has become necessary for survival of our species. Technology has created the World Tribe for better or worse. Emotional collaboration is the only constructive possibility for the future development of human society.

This potential for emotional solidarity is both threatening and hopeful. All great changes in human consciousness have caused deep concern and anxiety. Modern technology, symbolized by space exploration, is now in orbit and ready to proceed to some prized destination. To succeed it must be directed by steersmen who are healthy, growth-motivated personalities. This book's thesis is that such personalities can only develop themselves in a constructive climate of emotional intimacy.

In order to achieve this constructive emotional climate, a vast transformation is well under way. This transformation is scientific, cultural technological, social, psychological, religious, philosophical, economic, and political. But the issue is still in doubt. Although promising developments can be found among youth and in educational, psychological, religious, and social welfare programs, many persons resist, often because they are deliberately unaware of human ecological reality. Others resist because they are too intensely preoccupied with physical and economic survival. Still others because they are too profoundly conditioned by competitive existence to redirect their energies toward a collaboration consistent with the new human reality. This book is an attempt to facilitate constructive transformations in persons who seek emotional self-realization for themselves and other men and women. The essential nature of emotional intimacy seems clear.

Since this work is intended to be optimistic, pragmatic, critical, inspiring, and challenging to our closely held assumptions about human relationships, it is time to point out some of the work to be done as we fashion approaches to our individual and collective survival.

Youth Culture

As a result of the lowered voting age, young people may participate more fully in directing our future course, and grow increasingly active in exerting influence on future developments. Since they have less unlearning to do they may be an invaluable source of survival advice.

The rapid assimilation of youth styles into mainstream culture will no doubt continue. As young people realize their voices are heard and their advice is attended to they will need to earnestly set about helping us get together.

Increased involvement in the formal and informal helping relationships through volunteer programs is extremely important. The establishment of outreach programs apart from institutional settings is also needed. The youth-sponsored day care centers and free universities meet a real need in our society. More such programs should be organized.

Young people must stop "throwing themselves on the gears" and accept their share of the responsibility of insuring the physical and emotional survival of all men.

Education

Educators are uncomfortable now. Those choosing to cling tenaciously to traditional views about the educational process are going to become much more uncomfortable.

Our society is taking a hard look at education, and healthy demands for accountability are being hurled at organized education. These demands will continue and increase in volume.

The once sacred bachelor's degree as a pass to certain employment is now suspect. With an oversupply of teachers, scientists, and Ph.D.'s, we are forced into a re-examination of education. What are its goals? What good is it? Should we follow the advice of the devil's advocate, Ivan Illich, and scrap the whole educational system and start over?

My feeling is that a serious attention to these questions will result in meaningful answers. Education may prove its usefulness by increasing the survival prospects of its students in the pretwenty-first-century World Tribe.

As old assumptions are discarded, schools and colleges will probably move toward more open and less mysterious postures. No longer will the average age of college students be twenty. Students of all ages, at all stages in their lives, from adolescence through old age, will enroll in educational programs to gain capacities for survival in a perplexing world. Ideas about evaluation, credit hours, course structures, and teacher-student relationships will change drastically. Educators will come to see themselves as liberators, not controllers. They will help people to be themselves so that students can use intellectual and creative capacities in more productive ways. That is what good teachers have always done.

If we examine the results of recent studies at the University of Florida and the University of Northern Colorado, we can no longer claim that we don't know what good teaching is. Students have always known. These studies have shown that if you ask students to name their best and poorest instructors, that is, those instructors who helped them grow and those who did not, there is surprising agreement among students. Although reasons for naming an instructor as good or poor differ, the agreement on which instructors are positive influences, effective helpers, remains.

Effective helpers are not distinguished from poor ones on the basis of the method or technique they use in classrooms. Whether they use traditional or modern methods is not critical. Whether they lead in their field in terms of vast amounts of knowledge doesn't seem to matter either, although minimal levels of competency are required.

The *perceptions* of the instructor are the crucial thing. His general perceptual organization, his perceptions of other people, of self, and of his professional task are the four variables which are critically important. The effective helper's characteristics are listed below:

General Perceptual Organization

He tends to see people as more important than things. He is not mainly concerned with erasers, pencils, and the physical plant. His highest priorities involve human relationships; he values emotional intimacy.

He tends to see behavior of others as caused by here and now perceptions rather than by historical events in their lives. He focuses on the *now*. In many ways he fits the characteristics of the healthy personality.

Perceptions of Other People

He tends to view other people as basically able rather than as unable to meet the demands of their lives. Others are seen as trustworthy and dependable; more good than evil. He does not believe in the Gospel According to Chicken Little.

Perceptions of Self

The effective helper sees himself as adequate to meet the demands of his own life. He is not experiencing a last one in the box situation, for he feels he belongs in the world. He enjoys a feeling of closeness, for he sees himself as an attractive being.

Perceptions of Professional Task

The effective helper in various settings sees his task as one of freeing people rather than controlling them. He is not suffering from an advanced case of do-gooder syndrome. He encourages those he helps to open; he doesn't perceive his role as pushing people toward predefined goals.

It follows logically that since the effective helper is vitally committed to human values, sees others as able and trustworthy, and sees himself as adequate and valuable, that he would consequently see his task as one of freeing these worthy persons in the process of their own becoming. The growth emerges from the learner and is encouraged by powerful intellectual, physical, and emotional invitations from the effective helper. The Florida studies found this true of counselors, teachers, Episcopal priests, nurses, and college teachers.

It is time educators dropped their lily pad "holy wars" and proceeded with the work to be done. We need to use ourselves fully as innovative learners in education for survival. The development of the total, fully functioning person is the common task of all of us. All disciplines and structures have something to contribute to the task at hand.

Let's cooperatively evolve some new lily pads as we free ourselves from past mislearning. It will be tragic if educators choose to remain in cloistered rooms intellectualizing about trivialities until the society at large thumps them into an awareness about the task before us. Some educators remind me of those threatened crew members who were frantically rearranging the deck chairs on the *Titanic* as it went down. Instead of such an absurd posture, we need to begin construction of a new craft which may be radically different from old structure in ways we cannot fully anticipate.

As Neil Postman and Charles Weingartner suggested in their book *Teaching as a Subversive Activity*, the truly valuable educational process may become the examination of dangerous assumptions that are no longer of survival value. If we are not willing to discard false assumptions, Timothy Leary's dictum "Tune in, turn on, drop out" may describe the course of events for increasing numbers of students. As they become aware of the meaningless nature of some aspects of organized education the students will drop out. After all, if the system is killing them, not to drop out is a form of suicide!

At the moment, many educators are in shock and much of the innovative educational thought is not being done by professional educators but by outsiders such as Erich Fromm, Edgar Friedenberg, Eric Hoffer, Marshall McLuhan, Alvin Toffler, and Buckminster Fuller. Fuller's book, *I Seem to Be a Verb*, coerces us to the realization that we are all in process; that is, if we are *alive*.

Psychology

Within academic and applied psychology we must open ourselves to sharing our lily pads and evolving new ones. We must adopt positive facets of any and all views and create a new survival pad.

More outreach programs in the treatment of the emotionally handicapped are sorely needed. We can no longer overlook the tragic waste of human resources due to psychological problems. Low cost, effective mental health care centers, based perhaps on the best elements of innovations such as Fort Logan and on new ideas, are needed.

Psychotherapy is still a middle- and upper-class luxury. Its availability and accessibility must be extended through increased use of group processes and trained lay helpers who possess qualities of the effective helper.

In our society many people live lives best described by Thoreau: "quiet desperation." Many executives, students, and working people who suffer alcoholism, heart attacks, stomach ulcers, and nervous breakdowns before being forced to stop to re-examine their "oughts" and "shoulds" are paying horrendous prices for their refusal to reassess their priorities. There can be no defense for such a requirement for receiving help. We need a more casual, accepted view of emotional help. It may come to be as accepted as visiting the dentist or physician for physical problems.

What is psychological help? A mere expressed desire to help someone else is not enough. Do-gooders do that. In John Steinbeck's story, *Sweet Thursday*, Hazel, attempting to help a wounded gull, chases it into the sea where it drowns. But Hazel meant well. We must create a well-defined goal for psychological help. That of increasing the needful person's survival prospects is one such important goal advanced by this book.

We will need to *make* all these changes.

Religion

Organized religious organizations need to evolve new lily pads too. They should have more outreach programs. Relationships between the authority figures and the congregations should be more informal. There should be more appreciation for the human qualities we all possess.

This is a religious age. The increasing concern about meaning in life due to the rapid changes all about us is essentially a religious quest in the largest possible sense. Religious organizations need to join the stream and stop screaming, "Come back to our lily pads, you prodigals!"

The new interest in the occult and in Eastern philosophies with their passive emphasis is encouraging to me. Such interests are basically religious also. Religious institutions will need to abandon parts of their structure and organization to be acceptable to their followers. The gap between verbal statements and practice must be narrowed. Important church leaders have been saying this for some time. Martin Buber, Paul Tillich, John A.T. Robinson, and others have joined the human quest by casting aside some of the "oughts" and "shoulds" of past assumptions.

Social Action Programs

More and better social action programs are needed. National resource priorities must be re-oriented. The spending of vast sums of money to defend our foreign policy lily pad must be seriously questioned since our traditional foreign policy position was hammered out prior to the emergence of the World Tribe. It is no longer the United States of America (and some other people) on this planet. It is now a World Tribe that may eventually encompass the United States of Europe, United States of Africa, United States of Russia, United States of China, and United States of India. All will be equal members with us in the world family. What a shift in our view will be required if we are to adjust successfully!

Social action programs will give expression to an emerging emphasis on human values, not things. Youth, educators, psychologists, businessmen, churchmen, and politicians will join forces in pursuits vital to all—a recommitment to people. They may, for the first time, focus on similarities—not differences—in their goals.

Reflections on the American Identity

Erik Erickson

Someday a group of machines may sit around and ponder whether humankind was the missing link in their evolution. In 1950, Erik Erickson talked of some of the dangers of our machine-age society. Among other things, he feared that that society might develop a type of leader who "looks for areas where the law has been deliberately uncharted (in order to leave room for checks, balances and amendments) and tries to use it and abuse it for his own purposes"—a description that seems all too familiar today.

Erickson raises some important points about contemporary socialization and the type of person that socialization tries to produce. Machine-like students, employees, and governmental officials may be efficient in many ways. But, as Erickson points out, the dangers of a whole society of such people are enormous—both for the society and for the individuals concerned.

Reprinted from *Childhood and Society*, 2nd ed., revised, by Erik H. Erikson, with the permission of W. W. Norton & Company, Inc. Copyright 1950, © 1963 by W. W. Norton & Company, Inc.

This American adolescent, then, is faced, as are the adolescents of all countries who have entered or are entering the machine age, with the question: freedom for what, and at what price? The American feels so rich in his opportunities for free expression that he often no longer knows what it is he is free from. Neither does he know where he is not free; he does not recognize his native autocrats when he sees them. He is too immediately occupied with being efficient and being decent.

This adolescent will make an efficient and decent leader in a circumscribed job, a good manager or professional worker, and a good officer, and will most enjoy his recreation with "the boys" in the organizations to which he belongs. As a specimen, he illustrates the fact that in war or in peace, the fruit of American education is to be found in a combination of native mechanical ability, managerial autonomy, personalized leadership, and unobtrusive tolerance. These young men truly are the backbone of the nation.

But are they, as men, not strangely disinterested in the running of the nation? Are these freeborn sons not apt to be remarkably naïve, overly optimistic, and morbidly self-restrained in their dealings with the men who run them? They know how to accept a circumscribed task; they can be boisterous when on a spree; but on the whole, they respectfully shy away from all bigness, whether it is dollars or loud words. They (theoretically) hate autocrats, but they tolerate bossism because they usually cannot differentiate between a boss and "bosses." We have repeatedly mentioned this category of "boss," and it is time to state explicitly that there is a boss and a "boss," just as there is a Mom and a "Mom." We use both words without quotation marks in their more colloquial and more affectionate sense, in the sense of *my Mom*, and *my boss*; while we designate with quotation marks the "Moms" who make for Momism . . . and the "bosses" that constitute the bossism to which we must now make reference.

For the old autocrats have disappeared, and the new ones know how to hide behind the ambiguity of language, which fills the legislatures and the daily press, industrial strife, and organized entertainment. "Bosses" are self-made autocrats and, therefore, consider themselves and one another the crown of democracy. As far as is necessary, a "boss" stays within the law, and as far as is possible he enters boldly into the vacuum left by the emancipated sons in their endeavor to restrict themselves in fairness to others. He looks for areas where the law has been deliberately uncharted (in order to leave room for checks, balances, and amendments) and tries to use it and abuse it for his own purposes. He is the one who—to speak in highway terms—passes and cuts in where others leave a little space for decency's and safety's sake.

Here it is not a matter of taste or mere principle which makes me join those who decry the danger of bossism. I approach the matter from the point of view of psychological economy. "Bosses" and "machines," I have learned, are a danger to the American identity, and thus to the mental health of the nation. For they present to the emancipated generations, to the generations with tentative identities, the ideal of an autocracy of irresponsibility. In them is seen the apparently successful model, "he who measures himself solely by what 'works,' by what he can get away with and by what he can appear to be." They make "functioning" itself a value above all other values. In their positions of autocratic power in legislation, in industry, in the press, and in the entertainment world, they knowingly and unknowingly use superior machinery to put something over on the naïve sons of democracy. They thrive on the complication of "machinery"—a machinery kept deliberately complicated in order that it may remain dependent on the hard-bitten professional and expert of the "inside track." That these men run themselves like machinery is a matter for their doctor, psychiatrist, or undertaker. That they view the world and run the people as machinery becomes a danger to man.

Consider our adolescent boy. In his early childhood he was faced with a training which tended to make him machinelike and clocklike. Thus standardized, he found chances, in his later childhood, to develop autonomy, initiative, and industry, with the implied promise that decency in human relations, skill in technical details, and knowledge of facts would permit him freedom of choice in his pursuits, that the identity of free choice would balance his self-coercion. As an adolescent and man, however, he finds himself confronted with superior machines, complicated, incomprehensible, and impersonally dictatorial in their power to standardize his pursuits and tastes. These machines do their powerful best to convert him into a consumer idiot, a fun egotist, and an efficiency slave—and this by offering him what he seems to demand. Often he remains untouched and keeps his course: this will largely depend on the wife whom he—as the saying goes—chooses. Otherwise, what else can he become but a childish joiner, or a cynical little boss, trying to get in on some big boss' "inside track"—or a neurotic character, a psychosomatic case?

For the sake of its emotional health, then, a democracy cannot afford to let matters develop to a point where intelligent youth, proud in its independence and burning with initiative, must leave matters of legislation, law, and international affairs, not to speak of war and peace, to "insiders" and "bosses." American youth can gain the full measure of its identity and of its vitality only by being fully aware of autocratic trends in this and in any other land as they repeatedly emerge from changing history. And this not only because political conscience cannot regress without catastrophic consequences, but also because political ideals are part and parcel of an evolution in conscience structure which, if ignored, must lead to illness.

As we consider what consequences must arise from the particular dangers threatening the emotional state of the nation, our attention is drawn to Momism and to bossism, the two trends which have usurped the place of paternalism: Momism in alliance with the autocratic rigor of a new continent, and bossism with the autocracy of the machine and the "machines."

Psychiatric enlightenment has begun to debunk the superstition that to manage a machine you must become a machine, and that to raise masters of the machine you must mechanize the impulses of childhood. But let it be clear that the humanization of early childhood—as pioneered by enlightened obstetricians and pediatricians—must have its counterpart in a political rejuvenation. Men and women in power must make a concerted effort to overcome the rooted conception that man, for his own good, must be subject to "machines" either in politics, business, education, or entertainment. American adolescents believe deeply in truly free enterprise; they prefer one big chance in a hundred little ones to an average-sized certainty. The very fact that for this same reason they do not contemplate rebellion (as those seem to fear who would gag their sources of information) obligates us to protect youth against a state of affairs which may make their gestures of free men seem hollow and their faith in man illusory and ineffective.

The question of our time is, How can our [children] preserve their freedom and share it with those whom, on the basis of a new technology and of a more universal identity, they must consider equals? This makes it necessary for men and women in power to give absolute priority over precedent and circumstance, convention and privilege, to the one effort which can keep a democratic country healthy: the effort to "summon forth the potential intelligence of the younger generation."

6 The Working and Creative Self

Often we think of "existence" as apart from our love, marriage, work, fun, or creative activities. Pity. In our society at least, we can both discover and express our significant selfhood in these very areas. It isn't a question of "which came first, the self or the expression."

Many people today are questioning the nature and place of work in our culture. But few will deny that we have all been raised to believe that a person's worth is integrally tied to work ability and productivity.

The Puritan Ethic, or Work-Sin Ethic, makes most of us work in a compulsive way, either out of duty or obligation or else out of fear that idleness is a mark of "sinfulness" or unworthiness. But many people enjoy their labors and find fulfillment and self-expression in them. Some are extremely creative in their laboring, adding to the richness and fullness of their own lives and of their society.

We have selected three readings to illustrate some controversial aspects of work and of creativity. In the first article, Don Fabun illustrates some of the personal and social characteristics of the creative person. Fabun, Director of Publications for Kaiser Aluminum and Chemical Corporation, writes in a crisp and fascinating style and is, in our thinking, one of the best examples of his own subject.

The second selection is a Newsweek article that explores the effect of boredom on production and the worker, and some of the techniques being used to fight that boredom.

The last article, by Wyndham Robertson, follows the class of '73 of Harvard's women M.B.A.'s as they take up careers at executive levels and in fields traditionally the province of men.

The Creative Person:
He Walks Alone upon the Midnight

Don Fabun

What characterizes creative people? Are they necessarily artistic? Do they look or talk or act in a particular way? Do they fit any of our contemporary stereotypes?

Don Fabun feels that several key traits are found in all creative individuals, whether they are artists, machinists, carpenters, teachers, or executives.

In this excerpt from his publication You and Creativity, *we find that the creative traits are well within the range of possibility for any of us, but that for many they have been hidden or limited by upbringing, experiences, and self-imposed doubts.*

Who is this stranger that walks in upon us and upsets our lives? From whence comes the man who "marches to a different drummer," to whom the cherished wisdom of the ages is but chaff upon the wind? Why is he so different? Or is he really so different after all? Is he not perhaps only like ourselves, except that he has kept something we have lost along the way? Who, and what, is the "creative person"?

To begin with, it is not certain there is such a creature; we have a semantic difficulty here. "Ordinary" persons may be highly creative under certain circumstances—as witness the performance of people in concentration or prisoner-of-war camps. On the other hand, quite gifted persons may not do anything essentially creative—i.e., may not form original patterns in a whole lifetime, but will cling to the safe and accepted. History is full of them.

Yet, somehow, the creative person does seem to be different from most other people.

For one thing, of course, he exhibits creativity at a fairly high rate. He is the one society instinctively turns to when it needs "new" ideas. It doesn't matter, of course, whether society asks or not; the creative person will turn them out anyway. If one studies the life stories of highly creative people, it appears obvious that there are certain similarities in their background and in their personalities. But, being creative, they are also quite different from each other. "The full and complete picturing of the creative person will require many images," says Donald W. MacKinnon in "What Makes a Person Creative?" (*Saturday Review,* February 10, 1962).

Here is an outline of one image that emerges—oversimplified, to be sure, more a caricature than a portrait:

1. *Inherited Sensitivity*—a propensity for a greater sensitivity to certain types of experience—mathematical, artistic, musical, mechanical, literary. This appears to be well established by studies of families which exhibit high creativity in certain fields over several generations.

"Possibly," Seidel says, "the artist's apparently odd way of looking at things derives more from the inherited and developed sensitivity which makes him more readily attuned to the subtleties of various sensations and impressions, than from an asymmetrical viewpoint different from the ordinary man in the street. . . . The peculiar way the creative person may look at things derives from a physically based sensitivity toward sensations of a certain type."

2. *Early Training*—the creative person, more likely than not, had his childhood in a home atmosphere that encouraged, rather than discouraged, inquisitiveness (although too rigid a home environment might drive him to seek new and original answers on his own). Creativity is as much a matter of attitude as anything, and most human attitudes may be imprinted before the age of seven.

3. *Liberal Education*—the creative person is more likely to express his creativity if he is exposed to teachers and curricula that place a premium upon questions rather than answers, and which reward curiosity rather than learning by rote and conformity.

4. *Asymmetrical Ways of Thought*—the creative person finds an original kind of order in disorder; it is as if he stared at the reflection of nature in a distorted mirror, where "ordinary" people are able only to see the image in a plain mirror. Most highly intelligent people (as measured by tests) have symmetrical ways of thought, and for them, everything balances out in some logical way.

5. *Personal Courage*—the creative person is not afraid of failure, or being laughed at. He can afford this risk because what is important—to him—is not what others think of him, but what he thinks of himself.

6. *Sustained Curiosity*—the creative person never stops asking questions, even of his most cherished ideas. "Those who have an excessive faith

in their ideas," said Claude Bernard, "are not well fitted to make discoveries." A capacity for childlike wonder, carried into adult life, typifies the creative person.

7. *Not Time-Bound*—morning, noon, and night are all the same to the creative person; he does not work by the clock. Problems may take years to solve, discovery may take decades. With his personal "window of infinity," time has a personal, not a social meaning. Truly creative persons seldom respond well to "deadlines" arbitrarily set by someone else.

8. *Dedication*—unswerving desire to do something, whatever it may be and whatever the obstacles to doing it. The problem will not be left unsolved; the feeling will not remain unexpressed.

9. *Willingness To Work*—it is quite possible that no one in our society works harder than the artist; the same may be said for the creative scientist, inventor, composer, or mathematician. This may not express itself in the number of hours put in on the job, or in obvious physical labor, but in the fact that even in sleep or reverie the creative person is constantly working for a solution. The willingness to spend years simply accumulating data about which a creative question may be asked (Darwin is a good example; so is Edison) is characteristic of the creative person.

It might also be said that the creative person is usually "intelligent" but that the intelligent person is not necessarily creative. For one thing, the tests for determining each measure quite different abilities and so are hard to compare. Intelligence tests mostly ask for the "right" answers; already predetermined. Tests for creativity most frequently ask for original answers and the degree by which they depart from the expected is a measure of their creativity.

Finally, and this seems to be largely true, the creative person is more interested in ideas and things than he is in personal relationships. When B.S. Bloom at the University of Chicago set up two groups—all of whom were chemists or mathematicians—those who were considered creative by their colleagues and those who were not, he could, out of 27 tests given each, find only two differences of any importance. One was that the creative group was made up of extremely hardworking people; and the second was that they tended to be more asocial than social. Other tests have shown that one characteristic of the creative person is that he will almost always, given the prior information, choose an answer that is the opposite to the majority.

So far we have talked about the creative person as if he existed in some sort of vacuum; a creature strange by "normal" standards who stands apart from the herd, thinking his own thoughts and going his own way. But you cannot separate an organism from its environment and expect to understand very much about it. Creativity, as we have said, is an original transaction between an organism and its environment, and for most human beings that environment is the culture in which they find themselves embedded, like an insect in amber.

In some cultures, the creative act may be rewarded by burning at the stake, being hanged or beheaded, or so thoroughly ostracized by the community as to delay the consideration and the acceptance of the creative product by decades or centuries. It may, as some of us remember, lead to crucifixion.

Certainly, there appear to be societies and cultures in which creativity is encouraged or suppressed. One thinks immediately of the difference between the Renaissance and the "Dark Ages," although these are retrospective judgments and it may be that each was, in its own way, equally creative, but that in our times we value the created products of one more than another.

In any event, to return to our original point, "Culture is the matrix and the context for creativity; indeed, it is the context for all creative behavior," says Morton I. Teicher in *Culture and Creativity.* "Culture, elaborated and developed, makes creativity possible, and in turn, is enriched by creativity. The relationship between culture and creativity is a reciprocal relation of interdependence."

"You can never localize creativity as a subjective phenomenon," says Rollo May. "You can never study it in terms simply of what goes on in a person. . . . For what is occurring is always a process, a doing; specifically, a process interrelating the person and his world."

As A.L. Kroeber, in *Configurations of Cultural Growth,* has pointed out, "The nature and number of creative productions shows great variations between cultures and within the same culture at different times."

Is it possible to outline what the characteristics of a culture must be if it is to exhibit a high degree of creativity among the people who live in it at a certain time? We have tried to sketch the creative person; why not the creative society? Let's try. Characteristics of a creative society (or institution within a society, such as business corporations, the church, the government, education, etc.) may be:

(1) Generation of sufficient material wealth to provide time and opportunity for the creative process. Persons involved solely in subsistence are unlikely to exhibit much creativity; their daily lives are focused by the conscious on sheer survival.

(2) A communication system that allows a variety of inputs and free exchange of outputs between members. Societies and institutions that keep things "secret" stifle creativity because the amount of accessible information on which original patterns may be produced has been restricted.

(3) A reward system in which the creative act may be socially and economically rewarded. Much of the creative talent of the world has been wasted because of societies that kept artists in poverty, inventors in ill-equipped laboratories, scientists on bare subsistence.

(4) A climate of acceptability rather than punishment for creative acts; if punishment is too severe, or too certain, creativity may not be thwarted, but the availability of the created product may be long delayed.

(5) Opportunities for privacy; research in non-interruptive surroundings, time for individual meditation, escape from disruption by family, friends, or colleagues are essential to the creative process. Many societies do not provide sanctuaries of any kind.

(6) Ability to form disciple or peer groups, such as art colonies, professional associations, conventions under conditions which favor free association of people with similar interests. These afford intensive environments where individuals may inspire each other.

(7) An educational system that rewards and encourages free inquiry, rather than acting solely as a means for transmitting the already discovered and the already "known."

Societies in which most or all of these conditions are found are, it seems to us, more likely to have a high rate of creativity than those in which they are not found.

The reverse also may be true. "If society sinks into the absolute rut of custom, if it refuses to accept beneficial mutations in the cultural realm," says Loren Eiseley, "or to tolerate, if not promote, the life of genius, then its unwieldy slumbers may be its last."

Archaeology is constantly digging up the remains of societies like that.

In fact, there appears to be enough known about the necessary social conditions for creativity that we can predict, with reasonable accuracy, the kind of innovations that are likely to be produced.

"Can we," asks Harold D. Lasswell in The Social Setting of Creativity, "improve our anticipation and understanding of innovation by analyzing all the significant contours to be found in a given social context as a whole, or in selected situations within it? If we locate the contours we may even predict that the corresponding innovations will be made by several individuals at the same time. . . .

"By considering in advance a range of environmental changes, can we predict innovations?. . . If we are successful, it should be possible to locate the centers, routes and zones where innovations of a given kind will occur."

It seems quite possible that, in the near future, properly programmed computers may well be able to construct models of creativity for the societies in which they function and that the prediction of creativity may become a creative act itself. One would assume that prediction would be accompanied or followed by search and reward systems.

If, and when, this happens, we may have something that was foreshadowed by nature long ago, when it set upon the organizing ability of organisms as the expression of life—a truly and deliberately creative society in which each individual is able to enjoy the fullest development of his abilities, whatever they may be.

It seemed to me that much boiled down to the relative absence of fear (in creative persons). . . . They seemed to be less afraid of what other people would say or demand or laugh at. . . . Perhaps more important, however, was their lack of fear of their own insides, of their own impulses, emotions, thoughts.

—Abraham Maslow
Creativity in Self-Actualizing People

To be creative, in short, is to be unpredictable; it is to be decidedly suspect in the world of affairs. The creative aspect of life is rightly viewed as action. Never simply contemplative, the creative act at its highest brings about notable differences in things, thoughts, works of art and social structures. What is to be changed fights back; perhaps with success.

—George D. Stoddard
Creativity in Education

What are the conditions of the creative attitude, of seeing and responding, of being aware and being sensitive to what one is aware of? First of all, it requires the capacity to be puzzled. Children still have the capacity to be puzzled. . . . But once they are through the process of education, most people lose the capacity of wondering, of being surprised. They feel they ought to know everything, and hence that it is a sign of ignorance to be surprised or puzzled by anything.

—Erich Fromm

Henry Eyring commented, "A keen observer once said of Einstein that part of his genius was his inability to understand the obvious" (in "Scientific Creativity").

Sidney Parnes once said, "Our discipline is the unknown; the mind has a window toward infinity."

With me, a picture is a sum of destructions. I make the picture, and proceed to destroy it. But in the end nothing is lost; the red I have removed from one part shows up in another.

—Pablo Picasso
Conversations avec Picasso

Eugene Speicher likened painting to playing with electricity. "Touch one part of the canvas," he said, "and something immediately happens to some other part."

Old Bureaucrat, my comrade, it is not you who are to blame. No one ever helped you to escape. You, like the termite, built your peace by blocking up with cement every chink and cranny through which the light might pierce. You rolled yourself up into a ball in your genteel security, in routine, in the stifling convention of provincial life, raising a modest rampart against the winds and the tides and the stars. You have chosen not to be perturbed by our great problems, have trouble enough to forget your faith as a man. You are not a dweller upon an errant planet and do not ask yourself questions to which there are no answers. . . . Nobody grasped you by the shoulder while there was still time. Now the clay of which you were shaped has dried and hardened, and not in you will ever awaken the sleeping musician, the poet, the astronomer that possibly inhabited you from the beginning.

—Antoine de Saint-Exupéry
Wind, Sand and Stars

The reciprocal relationship between culture and creativity is such that a creative product is not really an invention unless it is socially accepted. The creative product has to operate within the culture; it has to work. If it does not work, it is a failure as an invention.

—Morton I. Teicher
Culture and Creativity

Perhaps if we were franker on personal creativity, we might reach out and occasionally touch, with a passing radiance, some other star in the night.

—Loren Eiseley
The Mind as Nature

The Job Blahs

Newsweek

Few of us seem to mind hard work as long as it is a task that is meaningful to us. Teenagers (according to popular parent opinion, one of the laziest groups alive) will happily spend hours of their "leisure time" tearing apart and putting together an old car. A working man or woman who comes home "dog tired" from the job may in a short time be happily "at work" on a building, sewing, or gardening project. In short, work is what you make it, and many people enjoy the jobs they are paid to do.

But almost no one can really be said to enjoy a dull, monotonous assembly-line job, putting the same bolt in the same spot on the same machine for thirty years. Large corporations are beginning to recognize boredom as a primary cause of job dissatisfaction and low morale among workers. This Newsweek article discusses the effect of boredom on workers and productivity, and what some large companies are doing to alleviate the problem.

The sullen refrain, it sometimes seems nowadays, is heard everywhere—at a Kaiser Steel Corporation plant in Fontana, California, at a blue-collar saloon in Houston, Texas, at a production workers' conference called in Atlanta by the United Auto Workers' union. "The one thing I have is security," says Fidencio C. Moreno, a $5.60-an-hour Kaiser steelworker. "But it's a boring, repetitive job—nasty, hot, and dirty work. I go there 'cause I have to." "It's getting to be a bore to me," grumbles J.E. (Andy) Anderson, a $15,000-a-year machine-shop manager in Houston, who seeks companionship over a couple of lunch-hour beers in Jimmie's Bar. "Every day, for eight hours, we fight that black devil-chain [the assembly line]," said R.J. Soptic, a Kansas City, Missouri, autoworker at the recent UAW conference in Atlanta. And even James M. Roche, the retired $790,000-a-year board chairman of General Motors, wisecracked recently: "What is more boring than lugging home a big briefcase of papers to be read before going to bed every night?"

Roche, presumably, was just being sardonic. But the other complaints reflect the discontent of an angry new breed that some say is growing faster than the labor force itself. These men and women are the new problem children of the American economy: the "alienated" workers, afflicted with the blue-collar blues, the white-collar woes and the just plain on-the-job blahs. They are bored, rebellious, frustrated; sometimes they're drunk on the job or spaced out on drugs. And though they are the newest darlings of the sociologists and industrial psychologists, they're still largely a mystery to many of the people who should understand them best: their bosses and their union leaders.

Today some 83 million Americans are holding full-time or part-time jobs. Of the total—62 percent of them men—about 19 million are engaged in manufacturing and 1 million of these are tied to the dull, routine tedium of an assembly line like that satirized four decades ago by Charlie Chaplin in "Modern Times." But there are actually more white-collar workers (49 percent of the total) than blue (35 percent)—the rest are service workers and farm workers. There are more women at work in the nation today than ever before, and more young people.

The mood of this vast work force is obviously of tremendous importance to the country as a whole as well as to the individuals themselves. Worker attitudes affect productivity—how competitive the nation is versus nations such as Japan . . . and how high America's standard of living can go. On a more philosophic but no less significant level, a nation's attitude toward work is a reflection of its sense of itself. The work ethic President Nixon is so fond of celebrating involves not only a job but a way of life.

The "Enrichment" Boom

While people have been complaining about work since it was invented, there is a widespread feeling that there is something different about today's discontent. As a result, the managers of American business and industry are now coming up with plan after plan—some pure public relations, some quite innovative, but all designed to pacify unhappy workers. From giant General Motors Corporation to a tiny, 50-worker unit of Monsanto Chemical's textile division in Pensacola, Florida, literally hundreds of companies have instituted "enrichment" programs to give workers a sense of satisfaction on the job and send them home with a feeling of accomplishment.

And the movement is growing rapidly. Lyman Ketchum, a manager of organizational development for General Foods and the father of a pioneer enrichment program at GF's Topeka, Kansas, Gaines Pet Food plant, has been practically forced to get an unlisted telephone number. "I was getting ten to twelve calls a week from corporation executives who wanted to talk to me about it," Ketchum reports. "I have just had to say no. I have too much of my own work to do."

In the automobile industry, where about 25 percent of the work force assembles cars with robot-like monotony, General Motors is experimenting with a "team" approach to the assembly of its new $13,000 motor home. Rather than having the chassis roll down an assembly line, with each worker performing only one or two functions, teams ranging in size from three to six workers are now building selected coaches from hubcap to horn. Ford is trying a team assembly program at its Saline, Michigan, parts plant while Chrysler has given some Detroit-area plants virtual carte blanche to try any experiment they choose. So far these have ranged from employees operating without a foreman to assigning assembly-line workers the relatively pleasant chore of test-driving the new cars they have just built.

While experiments by the auto industry's Big Three are still inconclusive, others are not. Indiana Bell Telephone, for example, used to assemble its telephone books in 21 steps, each performed by a different clerk. It now gives each clerk individual responsibility for assembling an entire book. One result: employee turnover in recent years has been cut by as much as 50 percent.

At Kaiser Steel in Fontana, California, a group of 150 workers literally kept the continuous-weld pipe mill from closing—at least temporarily—when they were given full responsibility for making it competitive with Japanese pipe producers. Recalls Timon Covert, a grievance committeeman for the United Steelworkers union and a leader of the worker group: "I told management, 'Look, we don't believe anybody in the damned world can outproduce us.' I hear all this bunk about how good they do it in Japan and Germany and we told management to let us try some things." The workers overhauled some tools, rearranged the production flow to make it more efficient and worked out changes in the production schedule. The result: production jumped 32.1 percent during the final three months of 1972, while the spoilage rate dropped from 29 percent to 9.

The Search for Solutions

As another example, the 50 workers at the Monsanto plant in Pensacola set up task forces to restructure certain jobs through automation, and managed to eliminate certain "dirty" chores that nobody wanted or did well. The workers also became their own managers. In the first year of the new deal, waste loss dropped to zero and productivity improved by 50 percent.

With such programs proliferating, the search for the roots of the problem and for possible solutions goes on apace. In New York next week, a group of major firms and labor unions will gather to discuss "The Changing Work Ethic." In Washington, the Nixon Administration, for all its reluctance to accept job dissatisfaction as a matter on 0i concern, is at least reported willing to spend $2 million this year to study it. In the Senate, Senator Edward Kennedy has introduced a bill calling for a $20 million investigation to determine just how serious the problem is and what efforts might be taken by the United States to solve it.

But even as businessmen and government officials search for new solutions to worker alienation, a lively debate goes on in business, labor and academic circles over the basic question of whether the whole thing hasn't blown out of all proportion to begin with.

On one side are such social scientists as Harold L. Sheppard and Neil Q. Herrick, whose book *Where Have All the Robots Gone* (Free Press) is considered by some to be a definitive work on the subject. After an in-depth study of 400 male union workers, Sheppard and Herrick concluded that one-third of them—particularly the young ones—were alienated from their jobs and could not be assuaged with the typical rewards of more money, shorter hours or longer vacations. Sheppard and Herrick went on to assert: "Worker dissatisfaction metamorphosed from a hobby horse of the 'tender minded' to a firebreathing dragon because workers began to translate their feelings of dissatisfaction into alienated behavior. Turnover rates are climbing. Absenteeism has increased as much as 100 percent in the past ten years in the automobile industry. Workers talk back to their bosses. They no longer accept the authoritarian ways of doing things."

"Dull, Repetitive, Meaningless"

In large measure, Sheppard and Herrick are supported by a controversial Health, Education and Welfare Department report issued last December. While short on specific evidence, the HEW report indicated that nearly half of American workers are dissatisfied with their jobs and suggested that something had better be done to make work more attractive, interesting and meaningful. According to the 200-page HEW study, the work force in America is changing and more and more workers are growing restless because of "dull, repetitive, seemingly meaningless tasks, offering little challenge or autonomy."

These are foreboding words indeed, but they don't pass unchallenged—and the challenge often comes from the very workers who are supposed to be unhappy. "I like it all right," says 30-year-old Rico Veneas of his job as a paint sprayer for a lighting-fixture firm in Inglewood, California. "I mean, I know how to do it so it doesn't tire me out." This may seem like an unscientific sample of one when arrayed against the Sheppard-Herrick and HEW studies. But in actual fact, the thesis that most Americans are indeed contented with their jobs finds powerful support among public-opinion specialists and some thinkers.

For example, a Gallup poll reports that, contrary to what HEW and the others say, eight out of ten Americans are satisfied with the work they do. And the situation is getting better, not worse, says Gallup. Back in 1949, "three out of ten whites and nearly half the blacks said they were dissatisfied or had qualifications about the work they were doing," versus the two out of ten for today, according to Gallup.

More than that, the Sheppard-Herrick and HEW studies start out with preconceived notions and then find statistics and other evidence to "prove" their point, charges Irving Kristol, professor of urban values at New York University. George B. Morris Jr., General Motors' vice president in charge of industrial relations, compares the current debate with the furor over automation a decade or so ago. "The academics started talking about it and pretty soon they were quoting each other. They said people were on their way out, which simply wasn't true," he says. "Well, today the same thing is happening; there is a lot of writing being done on this subject of 'alienation' by people who don't know what they are talking about."

For their part, most union leaders seem to be gingerly skirting the subject, waiting for someone to offer some definitive answers. UAW president Leonard Woodcock concluded a meeting of his union's production workers not too long ago with a blast at "academics" whom he accused of writing "elitist nonsense" that degraded factory workers. "Sure," Woodcock said, "work is dull and monotonous. But if it's useful, the people who do it are entitled to be honored and not degraded, which is what's goind on in this day and time." But a few weeks later, UAW vice president Irving Bluestone said that the blue-collar blues were indeed a problem and called for an intensive search for answers. As one UAW source summed up: "I guess you could conclude everybody's confused about things."

Indeed, perhaps the best sense on the subject these days is being made by observers far removed from the industrial-relations firing line. One is Fred Foulkes, an assistant professor at the Harvard Graduate School of Business and author of the book "Creating More Meaningful Work." As Foulkes sees it: "Jobs haven't changed. People's expectations have, and this has been expressed in high absenteeism, low morale, high turnover, etc."

Greater educational achievement has helped raise expectations. The average worker in 1940 had an eighth-grade education, he notes, but now about 80 percent of the work force has gone beyond high school. Changing life-styles outside the job affect attitudes at work. Says Foulkes: "[Workers] want some sort of participation. There's more freedom around. So why should employees want regimented, autocratic jobs?"

So far, the White House hasn't taken a public position on the alienated-worker issue. But according to insiders, President Nixon has privately expressed displeasure with the HEW report, claiming that it is the work of soft-headed sociologists who don't know much about work and worker motivation. This may be so. But where it exists, it is important, and increasing numbers of companies are trying to do something about it. Among the best-known and most successful are on-going programs in Topeka, Hartford, Fort Lauderdale, and Medford, Massachusetts.

"I used to work as a construction laborer and every morning I hated to get up," 21-year-old Andy Dodge recalled as he relaxed in the comfortably furnished employee lounge at the Topeka Gaines Pet Food plant. "Now, it's different. I'm still just a laborer, but I have something to say about my job. If I get sore about something, I bring it up at the team meeting in the morning. If I want to go to the bathroom or make a phone call, I do it. I just ask someone else on the team to cover. I really feel more like a human being than a worker. After this, there is no way you could get me to go back to regular employment."

Andy Dodge is one of the lucky 72 production workers at the revolutionary, five-story Gaines plant, a brainchild of General Foods' Lyman Ketchum. Until two years ago, pet-food production was limited to the company's plant in Kankakee, Illinois, run along conventional lines and plagued by conventional factory problems: a lackadaisical work force, a 5 percent absentee rate and occasional acts of sabotage. (Someone once dumped a batch of green dye into a hopper and spoiled an entire day's production of dog food.) Thus, when the demand for pet food outstripped Kankakee's capacity, Ketchum persuaded his superiors to try something new: a plant designed around people, not jobs. The result is the Topeka facility.

While it is highly automated, the plant is still burdened with a number of menial jobs with a sizable potential for boredom. So, to insure that both the rewarding and unrewarding jobs are shared equally, Ketchum devised a model workers' democracy. The employees are split into semiautonomous teams, ranging in size from six to seventeen, depending on the operation. Each team selects its own foreman and, at the start of each shift, determines how to meet production quotas, divides up job assignments and airs grievances. Moreover, each worker is trained to do practically any job in the plant, from filling bags on an assembly line to monitoring the complicated controls of machines that cook and mix the pet food.

Even more unusual, the team leaders interview and hire replacements, and the teams discipline malingerers. "If someone is goofing off," says William Haug, 38, "the team members get on him. If this doesn't work, we have a team meeting. If there is a personal or family problem, team members often help. Sometimes it is just a matter of time off to straighten out problems, but we don't have many of them."

To further expand the individual worker's feeling of involvement and responsibility, Ketchum erased most of the lines dividing the white- and blue-collar workers at the Topeka plant. There are no time clocks, no special parking privileges for executives, and everybody eats in the same cafeteria. At lunchtime, it is not unusual to see plant manager Ed Dulworth, a 38-year-old graduate of General Motors Technical Institute, playing Ping Pong with a production worker.

Predictably enough, the result is an exceptionally high level of worker contentment. "Everything is left up to the individual to expand himself," sums up 26-year-old Joe Ybarra. "We are responsible for the product we turn out. A guy can come to work here without a feeling that management is on his neck." As one result, the absenteeism rate at Topeka is less than 1 percent, versus 5 percent at Kankakee.

Even more important to the executives back at General Foods' headquarters in White Plains, New York, the Topeka plant is a glowing financial success. "Even after [allowing for the new] technology, we get a productivity rate here that is 20 to 30 percent higher than at Kankakee," says Dulworth. "We need only about two-thirds of the Kankakee work force to get the same production."

Could the Topeka plant work in a larger, more complicated setting? To a degree, says Ed Dulworth. "I think it is transferable in terms of the basics, and the basics are that work can be organized for both business needs and people needs and it pays off both ways," he told *Newsweek*'s Tom Joyce. "The problem with this is that managers are looking for models. They want a package you can put in place and have it pay off. Well, the nature of job design is complex and each program must be developed to fit specific situations."

Diversity Boosts Morale

At the huge, 21,000-employee Travelers Insurance Co. headquarters in Hartford, Connecticut, the raw material is punch cards rather than dog food, but the problem was the same: high absenteeism and low morale and productivity. So three years ago, Travelers hired Roy W. Walters and Associates, a New Jersey management consultant firm, to undertake a job-enrichment program.

As a pilot project, the Travelers selected a key-punch operation involving 100 operators and ten supervisors. "What we attempted to do here is create a structural change for employees and supervisors which forces a behavior change and eventually an attitude change," said Jewell Westerman, second vice president in charge of management services.

Basically, the project involved transferring some supervisory functions to the operators and broadening their jobs so that instead of dealing day after day with only one phase of an operation they carried it through from start to finish. Ordinarily, a worker would handle receipts or collections or any of the separate punch-card functions. But work was rearranged so that one employee is now responsible for the entire punch-card operation for a particular corporate or individual customer and establishes a firm operator-customer relationship. "Typically, work is assigned on the basis of who has the least to do," explains Norm Edmonds, Travelers' director of management services. "So the operator has no commitment to the job. That's been reversed, and people are aligned with their own group of clients."

The first-year results of the pilot project were dramatic: a 26 percent increase in productivity and a 24 percent decline in absenteeism. The enrichment program has since been expanded to cover some 2,000 employees in four departments at Travelers' headquarters and eight branch offices. As Dale Menard, a 27-year-old supervisor in the premium-collection department, sums up his "new" job: "I'm much more involved in decision-making than my peers at other insurance firms. Before, we went down the syndrome of 'the more you specialize the more efficiency you have.' It got to the point where tasks were divided into smaller and smaller bits and pieces. Now, with combining certain jobs, the problem takes care of itself."

Studies in Boredom

At the Corning Glass plant in Medford, Massachusetts, the attitude is so gung-ho that work teams give themselves such nicknames as "The Dirty Half Dozen" and stick around after the 4:30 afternoon whistle to discuss the best way to meet their production schedule. At the Motorola Corp. plant in Fort Lauderdale, Florida, the work teams compete in production races and the winning team is treated to a dinner each month by the company.

The Medford plant turns out such products as hot plates, while the Fort Lauderdale facility produces a pocket-size electronic signaling device called the Pageboy, both of them prime candidates for the impersonal attention of an assembly line. However, in each plant, the hot plates and the Pageboys are assembled in their entirety by a member—usually a woman—of work teams that set their own production goals and, in the case of Corning, even decide when they will take some of their holidays.

The results have been highly encouraging. Last year, the Medford plant increased its hot-plate production by 20 percent and it is expecting an even larger increase this year. And while the plant increased its work force by 50 percent last year, efficiency improved by 100 percent. Even though the pay is relatively low ($2.95 an hour), the plant has many more job applicants than it can satisfy. Margie Bell, a 54-year-old mother of three, sums up: "I love this place. It's not like at Raytheon where I used to work. Here you start with nothing and you make something yourself."

At Fort Lauderdale, Motorola officials say that productivity is about 5 percent lower than it would be on a normal assembly line, but that the quality is better and the morale of employees vastly improved. "It's technology having advanced to a state that permits this kind of operation," one official notes. "We're now back to something simple enough for one girl to make a total contribution, and that is very significant, I think."

Admittedly, the experiments at Gaines, the Travelers, Corning and Motorola would be impossible to impose on many operations; it would be ridiculous, for example, to split the 30,000 employees of Ford Motor's River Rouge plant into work teams and allow them to decide production schedules and assembly-line speeds. However, there is no question but that job enrichment will continue to grow as a subject for both management soul-searching and collective bargaining between companies and their unions. The Ford Foundation has found the subject worthy of further study and plans to spend nearly $500,000 evaluating experiments industry has undertaken to stimulate worker satisfaction. And the conference on "The Changing Work Ethic" in New York . . . [enjoyed] the full-scale participation of labor for the first time; autoworkers, steelworkers and machinists were all represented.

But all of the conferences, all of the studies, all of the books may be too late to help some workers, such as steelworker Fidencio Moreno. "I should have quit long ago," he said sadly last week. "Now my dad, he ran a bar. When he'd come home, us kids would run up to him and say, 'How'd it go?' My dad always had pride in his work. He'd talk about all the things the customers would say and do. Me, I go home, they don't understand a damn thing. All I do is dump a little coal into an oven. Why would my wife or my kids be interested in that?"

Women M.B.A.'s, Harvard '73— How They're Doing

Wyndham Robertson
Research Associate: Philip Mattera

The women's movement is often misunderstood. This is particularly true in the area of work. Women are not only asking for access to all occupations but also for equal pay for equal work. Money is a source of power in our society. Even though a woman may be doing the same job, it is not unusual to find that she is paid less money. This article takes a look at the 1973 class of women M.B.A.'s at Harvard over the five-year period following their graduation.

Those red faces in the sea of blue ones represent the women who graduated from Harvard Business School in 1973—thirty-four in a class of 776. Although they entered the B-school only seven years ago, they were pioneers, leading the way for the surge of women who followed them into business schools, and later into the kinds of promising jobs that have traditionally propelled talented men to the top. The pace of women's progress has been so brisk of late that it is hard to remember how different things were in 1971.

But the women of the class of '73 remember very well. One memory in particular still rankles, and invariably comes up when they reminisce about their initial impressions of Harvard. Their male classmates had an unfortunate penchant for wondering aloud, "What are *you* doing here?" Recalls Linda Taylor, who now helps oversee the $500 million in the United Mine Workers pension fund, "I finally got to the point where I just laughed and said I was there to get a man."

That unsettling question is almost never asked at Harvard these days, which is just one testament to how much things have changed. Harvard didn't even admit women into its two-year business program until 1963, and in the Sixties only a few of them trickled through. The class of 1973 was the first to have as many as 5 percent women. (There were forty at the start; six dropped out, or flunked out, before graduation.) Female enrollment at other business schools took off at about the same time. Among the top-ranking business schools, only Columbia admitted as many as 8 percent women into the class of 1973. In this fall's entering classes, by contrast, Harvard, Stanford, Wharton, and the University of Chicago will all have more than 20 percent women, and at Columbia the proportion will be 35 percent.

Those ballooning statistics reflect the new opportunities for women in the workplace. Things changed dramatically, in fact, while the class of '73 was undergoing Harvard's rigorous "case method" training. In late 1971, the year they entered, the Labor Department decreed that companies holding federal contracts had to have written affirmative-action plans for women, to bring them into jobs where they were underrepresented. And in January, 1973, the year they graduated, A.T.&T. signed a consent agreement that required the company to fork over $15 million to 15,000 employees— mostly women—for past discrimination in hiring practices.

Against that backdrop, it can be argued that these thirty-four women entered the job market at what was, up to that point, the most propitious time in history for career-oriented women. And they had the quintessential business credential of the day, a Harvard M.B.A.

In "Men's Jobs" All Over the World

Today, five years later, all thirty-four are in the labor force—working or looking for work. On average they are thirty-two years old, and precisely half are married. Six are mothers. Of the unmarried half, fourteen have never married; one is divorced; two are separated. They are all over the world—working in "men's jobs" in banking, investment banking, consulting, sales and marketing, advertising, accounting, money management, corporate planning, college administration, and government. One, who also graduated from Harvard Law School, is an associate in a law firm.

Fortune recently interviewed all thirty-four women to find out how they have fared. Twenty-six of them are full-time salaried employees. One works part-time for a bank, two are currently unemployed—temporarily, it appears—and five are self-employed. One of the full-time salaried employees, Judith Gehrke, who has a planning job at International Paper, also has a company of her own, called Design Lines. To juggle both jobs, Gehrke works from 7:00 A.M. until 11:00 P.M., helped by the same energy, drive, and intellect that led her to finish in the top 5 percent of her class at Harvard and thus to win the designation Baker Scholar.

The only other woman in the class to attain that distinction was Tabb Taylor, who has just received her doctorate in business administration from Harvard. Her dissertation, which she hopes to have published as a book, is entitled "Management Succession Under Conditions of Crisis: the Role of the Board of Directors." It deals with real-life situations in which chief executives were dismissed for unsatisfactory earnings performance.

The median compensation of the twenty-six salaried women working full time is $32,250. That's a respectable figure, to say the least. The latest government figures show that in 1976 only 8.4 percent of U.S. *households* had incomes above $30,000. And only one-half of 1 percent of all women had incomes above $25,000.

The lowest salary among the twenty-six is $22,200—which, however generous in the national scheme, is well below the median starting salary of $25,555 that *this* year's Harvard M.B.A.'s commanded. At the top of the pay scale, five women have reached or passed the $40,000 mark, and a sixth could join the group if certain incentive-compensation goals are met. One is likely to earn as much as $50,000 this year, again depending on her performance.

More than half the class lives in New York, Boston, or their suburbs, where salaries reflect the higher cost of living. The median compensation for the ten salaried women working in New York City or its environs is $38,250.

A Feminist in Agribusiness

One of the unemployed women is unsure about women's prospects in her field, which is agribusiness. She is Christopher Mock, who has just passed the oral exams for a Ph.D. in agricultural economics and is looking for a job doing fieldwork on the agricultural problems of Third World countries. An ardent feminist, Mock believes the kind of work she wants to do is often dominated by men with a "macho" mentality. To prove she can handle the rigors of the job, she has crossed the Andes twice in a jeep, camped out in the Sahara, driven all over Tunisia on a management-consulting job (for which she developed an estimate of the size of the Tunisian black market for wheat), and traveled in Thailand and South Korea on other consulting jobs—some of them subcontracted by a Harvard agribusiness professor. Despite that, Mock is having trouble getting a job she wants. One problem, as she sees it: "Some men don't like to ride in jeeps with women." As evidence, she cites the comment of one man in the business whom she ran across at a conference. "Where would I pee?" he asked.

The other unemployed woman has also been across the globe since graduation. She is Susan Haberland, who has worked for three and a half years in Iran, most recently for an Iranian management-consulting company where she was the only American professional (and one of two women). She returned to the U.S. in May, with a working knowledge of Persian, and is taking her time to find what she calls a "suitable career opportunity." The opportunities should be there because, in addition to her M.B.A., Haberland holds an undergraduate degree in chemical engineering from Carnegie Tech. Not long ago she contacted an executive placement service in San Francisco and was told that "male chauvinism" would cut her chances of advancement by 50 percent, a remark that struck Haberland as "ridiculous."

Both of the unemployed are single, which means they can look for jobs wherever they like. The married couples, on the other hand, operate under geographical constraints. Several of the women have switched jobs because their husbands relocated. Among them is Cecilia Healy Herbert . . . who left her job with Morgan Guaranty in New York when her fiancé (now her husband) bought a business in Richmond. Healy got very high marks from her superiors at Morgan Guaranty, which has been recruiting and promoting lots of women in recent years. But her future may be no less bright at the Bank of Virginia, where she is an assistant v.p., and highly visible as the only female commercial-loan officer. Herbert's territory includes Texas, Louisiana, and several major cities in other states. One of these cities is New York, and since the bank's chairman also travels there on business, he and Herbert often team up for meetings with clients.

Another woman in the class, Linda Kent Boothby, left her position with Avon to accompany her husband when his job at Morgan Guaranty took him to Japan. She now works for McCann-Erickson in Tokyo, and believes the international experience can only help her career.

Resolving problems in dual-career households is apt to get trickier as both husbands and wives become more entrenched with their present employers. Husbands of thirteen of the seventeen women are also M.B.A.'s—eleven from Harvard and four of those from the class of '73. Career conflicts might be expected to cause marital conflicts, but so far that kind of problem hasn't surfaced.

A Powerful Tug

In fact, the job of being a wife, the women say, combines easily with the paying kind. But they stress that this is because their husbands are generally proud of what they are doing and are "supportive" (a word that gets much use). Husbands typically share in the housework—or don't care if it doesn't get done. And with two incomes, the couples can afford to, and do, eat out a lot.

Combining careers with having children, on the other hand, is perceived by the mothers—and most of those asked to speculate about motherhood—as a delicate juggling act. Most say it does, or would, drain energy from paying jobs and make the workday less stretchable. This is one of the reasons only six are mothers. And only two of these six are full-time employees. Three are self-employed and one is the part-time bank employee. None of the four is currently putting in a full workweek. Partly because they don't want to make such trade-offs, three of the married women have decided to forgo motherhood.

The mothers are feeling their way, because the tug between children and careers is powerful. Susan Ness was moving rapidly up the hierarchy at First Pennsylvania Bank when she quit early last year to have a child. She wanted to see "what it was like" staying home with the baby. Very quickly, she found out. "Being a mother was more tiring than I expected," she says. "It's a full-time job, either mine or someone else's." After six months, Ness went back to First Pennsylvania on a part-time basis. She now works two days a week as assistant to the head of the national department. Although eventually she wants a full-time job, and although her ambitions are still high, she says she no longer dreams of "making it to the top." As she sees it, "You have to give 110 percent to your job to make it to the top—which you just can't do with children."

Another mother, Ilene Lang, is surprised at her own reaction to motherhood. Lang, who will be thirty-five this fall, had always wanted to be her own boss, and so, after graduation, she opened a store in Cambridge called The Big Picture. There a piece of equipment she bought from Itek enables her to convert customers' snapshots into poster-sized blowups. Though Lang was married when she graduated, children weren't then a part of her own big picture. "I never *liked* babies until I had my own," she says. "I'd never even baby-sat." But at thirty-three (an age that more than half the class has yet to reach, incidentally) she told herself, "If I'm gonna do it, I better do it." In can-do fashion, she did it, and baby Sarah arrived a year ago. . . .

Now Lang, who had once thought of opening more stores, says she has less energy to devote to her business, and she works only five and a half hours a day. A joyful mother, hipped on "wonderful" Sarah, Lang marvels at her own transformation. "I am conflicted right now about my goals," she says, adding with B-school logic, "I think I should know where I'll be in five years." She doesn't now, she admits. Then, with a laugh, she throws up her hands, "I'll be forty, and have a couple more kids."

Neither Lang nor any other woman in the class expressed the slightest interest in quitting work permanently to raise a family. Overwhelmingly, however, the mothers—and those who were asked to speculate about motherhood—felt with Ness that the trade-off for having children would be lower career aspirations. (One who said she expected someday to earn $100,000—in 1978 dollars—lowered the figure to $70,000 when children were added to the equation.)

A Wild Outbreak of Pregnancies?

More may make the trade-off when the final decision time comes toward the end of their childbearing years. Margaret "Peg" Walker, a '73 graduate who is a Quaker Oats brand manager (Aunt Jemima frozen waffles, French toast, and pancake batter), is thirty-three and separated from her husband, but wants to have children "next time." Walker ticks off the number of women with M.B.A.'s in responsible positions in the Quaker foods division—six brand managers out of eleven, and three group brand managers out of five. A lot of women at Quaker, she says, including the married women, are considering not having children. But Walker, who is older than most brand managers, suspects that many will opt for motherhood before it's too late. "I just have a feeling that in about five years there's going to be a wild outbreak of pregnancies around here," she predicts.

A few of the women think they can manage it all—children and really big, demanding jobs. For the most part, they are not yet mothers, and don't intend to be until they are in positions lofty enough to enable them to call their own shots (and arrange their schedules flexibly) at the office. Some of those who talk this way are among the most impressive businesswomen in the group, and their chances of "having it all," as one puts it, appear reasonable.

One of them is twenty-nine-year-old Cecilia Herbert at the Bank of Virginia. "I think eventually we would like to have kids," she says. "But I don't have any intention of considering the subject until I'm thirty-four or thirty-five. I would very much like to be the equivalent of a senior vice president before I do that—to be sufficiently senior so that when I start wearing big dresses, people don't rush to tell the personnel department to warm up because I'm coming in to quit."

A Lack of Female Stars

In any discussion of women M.B.A.'s, the question inevitably arises, how are they doing as compared with the men? Harvard will be collecting salary data and other information on the class of 1973 later this year; in the meantime comparisons must rest on sketchy evidence. Alumnae who went to the class's fifth reunion in June tend to think the women are doing about as well as the men, except that some of the men (but no women) have emerged as "stars"—most often cited is the classmate who is president of Design Research, the Cambridge fabric and furnishings company.

Assistant Professor Anne Harlan of Harvard Business School has done some research comparing the progress of the school's men and women graduates. Based on information for the year 1976, she found that in her sample the median monthly salary range for those who graduated between 1970 and 1975 was $1,500 to $2,000 for women and $2,000 to $3,000 for men. She also found the men in this group twice as likely as women to hold upper-level managerial positions and be involved in setting organizational policy.

At *Fortune's* request, Harlan broke out her data on the class of 1973. The sample contained only fourteen of the thirty-four women and only thirty-two of the men, so Harlan has some reservations about what conclusions can be drawn from it. The data show that by 1976, a higher proportion of men than women were earning more than $24,000. (The median starting salary for the class was $17,000). Only one of the women in Harlan's sample, but four of the men, were earning more than $36,000. Harlan also found that men held all of the six top-executive titles reported (vice president or higher)—and that three times as many women as men were in professional or nonsupervisory staff jobs.

Today there are three vice presidents among the women of '73, all in the field of finance. Elizabeth Spector is one of about a dozen female vice presidents of Merrill Lynch, Pierce, Fenner & Smith. Joyce Anson is a vice president of Paine Webber's investment-banking subsidiary. And Frederica Challandes-Angelini is a vice president (in London) of American Express International Banking Corp. Two besides Herbert are assistant vice presidents of banks, and as it happens, these are the two Oriental women in the class: Constance Chan of Citibank and Carol Wong, also with the American Express banking subsidiary (in Hong Kong). All of these women—and others, like Bettina McKee, an audit manager with Arthur Young in Rio— have considerable responsibility in dealing with clients. But internally their management responsibility is still quite limited, as it is for most of the women in the class of 1973.

There is no simple and reliable way to measure degrees of managerial responsibility in different kinds of jobs and in different companies, but the number of people who report to an executive is sometimes taken as a rough indicator. Among the women of the class of '73, only four have as many as eight people regularly reporting to them. One is Patricia McGrath, the only controller in the group, who holds that position at Logical Machine Co., a privately held outfit that makes technologically advanced minicomputers in Sunnyvale, California. Eight men and women work under her and report to her.

Only One Chose Sales

Adrienne Houel, another financially oriented woman in the class, also supervises eight. One of five black women in the class, she married a French classmate after graduation and moved to Paris, where she works for a home-construction company. (It was founded a few years ago by Olivier Mitterrand, a Harvard M.B.A. who is a cousin of the French Socialist leader.) Her area of responsibility is finance and accounting; she also heads the computer operations, which have been expanded at her urging. She is, incidentally, pregnant with her second child, and is one of two mothers in the class who work full time.

Another woman with broad supervisory responsibility is Paula O'Hara, general manager of Canadian operations for Tri-Chem Inc. Tri-Chem uses 35,000 housewives, and the "party system," to sell some $40 million worth of hobby products. Four thousand operate in O'Hara's domain. An economics major at Mount Holyoke before she went to the B-school, O'Hara is the only woman in the group with a career in sales. She normally works sixty hours a week, and even more when she is traveling—which is much of the time. The Canadian sales manager reports to her, as do six district managers (two of whom are men) and two people who run a distribution center employing thirty people. O'Hara's husband (Harvard Business School '71) is working on a doctorate in business administration and intends to teach. He will be looking for a job in Toronto when O'Hara's job requires her to move there in the fall.

The only woman with nine other M.B.A.'s reporting directly to her is Lois Juliber, a product group manager at General Foods. She is responsible for the marketing of all General Foods children's cereals, a line of four brands with estimated sales of some $115 million. Juliber too works a long day; she leaves her New York apartment at 6:30 for the drive to her office in White Plains, arrives just after 7:00, and generally goes home twelve hours later. Two nights a week she does "heavy work" at her apartment, and she usually works on Sunday nights as well. A single woman, she enjoys an active social life—and relishes tennis on summer weekends in the Hamptons. She seemed genuinely surprised when an interviewer added up her workweek hours and found they total seventy.

A Hot Start at Kool-Aid

Juliber has been promoted faster at General Foods than is usual, even for M.B.A.'s. She was lucky enough to spend her apprenticeship on Kool-Aid, a business that grew rapidly after she joined the company in 1973. Her promotion—and the shift to cereals—came in February. As the senior product manager on Kool-Aid, she had only two people working for her, and though she is confident and self-possessed, she admits when she made the shift, it was "scary." "At first," she says of her new job, "it almost seemed like an empire. The people were new to me, and so was the business. I was also afraid of the 'woman' issue [the product managers under her are men]. But that turned out to be a non-issue."

Two men from the class of '73 are also at General Foods. Both product managers in other areas, they are junior to Juliber in the General Foods hierarchy. But lest anyone generalize from that example, just the reverse is true at Tri-Chem: two men of '73 have made vice president, ahead of Paula O'Hara.

With a few exceptions, the women say they haven't felt discrimination where promotions are concerned. Many do say they encountered initial skepticism, both inside their organizations and with clients, but they found it vanished when they had a chance to prove themselves. (They note that inexperienced men dealing with new clients have the same problem.) Some give examples to show that men they encounter on the job still feel awkwardness, as when women suddenly show up at confabs that were once all-male. (Men don't know whether to stand up when women enter, or to clean up their language—or just apologize for it. For that matter, the women seem unsure what amenities they like, except that they can live without the apologies.) But most don't know whether these little reminders that they are different add up to anything meaningful or not.

And they can cope with them. Judy Gehrke, the International Paper planner who set up her own company, says that when she and her designer, a man, meet with people in the factories where her products are produced, "the performers play to him, not to me, even though he's not the businessman and I am." She adds, "Sometimes that's good, because it gives me a chance to figure out what the next sentence should be."

Some women in the group find the subject of unique treatment barely worth discussing, and express sentiments only slightly milder than those of Sandra Smith, a senior associate at a Washington consulting company. When Smith was asked if being a woman made a difference on her job, she replied, "I don't think anyone gives a damn."

Whether anyone will give a damn in the tougher competition for higher-level jobs is still unknowable. Some women wonder whether their sex will be a hindrance as they reach for more visible jobs. Will prejudices too subtle to be perceived block their way? And will they be able to compete successfully against men as the scramble gets more political? Some admit they are not accomplished at the art.

Patricia Kosinar, a member of the class who is now director of Simmons College's two-year-old middle-management program for women, found out during her second year at Harvard how much she had to learn about gamesmanship. She was standing in a line of second-year students, all waiting to have their résumés duplicated. "I had a one-page résumé," she recalls, "because we had all been told that was the way it's done. A guy in front of me was holding a *sheaf* of papers. I thought, 'Oh, you poor dummy!' But what he had, it turned out, was twelve one-page résumés, each with a different career objective, tailored for different job interviews. I think I suffered a crisis of confidence that day!"

Linda Taylor, of the Mine Workers pension fund, has lots of confidence but feels a lack of aggressiveness. Says she: "I was never brought up to say, 'Me first,' and yet in the business world you have to be me-first. Also, it's very difficult for me to go storming in and say, 'Listen you ----, I want more money.' I was raised to think of that as boorish, a preoccupation of people who haven't made it."

Despite their experience in the Harvard classroom, which Kosinar describes as "the big leagues of verbal dominance," some of the women aren't as dominant in group sessions as their male counterparts. Says one of them: "I can be over-yelled—even though my performance may be three times better than the person's doing the yelling."

An Expectations Gap

Some are consciously trying to learn the political ropes. In this category is Theresa Wyszkowski, who has a job in inventory accounting at Digital Equipment Co. She is trying to develop what she calls a "sensitivity to the political environment," by talking to and watching her male colleagues. A thoughtful woman, Wyszkowski has no patience with some of the complaints she hears from her female friends in business. "I get fed up," she says, "with women who say, 'I can't put up with the politics' and give up. Politics, after all, is not unique to business." Wyszkowski says her "ultimate" goal is to be a D.E.C. plant manager, and since no woman has ever held such a job, she appears to regard it as a minor triumph that higher-ups at the company have encouraged her to believe the goal is realistic.

Would an ambitious *male* M.B.A. from Harvard give plant manager as an "ultimate goal"? It seems unlikely. For Wyszkowski, it would be a breakthrough; for a man equally motivated, just another job on the way to something bigger. Differences like these may help explain why women's aspirations—which after all have something to do with how far they go—are usually lower than men's.

Dramatic evidence of this shows up in a study conducted by Myra Strober, assistant professor at Stanford Business School, and Francine Gordon, formerly of the Stanford faculty. In May, 1974, Gordon sent questionnaires to the men and women who were about to graduate from Stanford Business School. The answers revealed that in the jobs they were about to take, the average salary of the men and women was almost the same ($17,000 for men, $16,938 for women). But women's expectations were lower. Asked the peak salary they expected to earn (in 1974 dollars), the men said, on average, $75,927. For women, the comparable figure was $44,222. Moreover, on the question of what the respondents would like to earn, the wide gap remained. Men averaged $135,083; women, $81,471.

Without a doubt, one explanation for the difference in expectations is the scarcity of women—or, to use the sociologists' term, role-models—in top management. As one woman in the class of '73 puts it, "I wish I could say, I want her job." Adds Linda Taylor, "There aren't enough Mary Wellses or Kay Grahams." And Lois Juliber says that although no woman in marketing at General Foods currently has a title higher than hers, it helps to know that at least one formerly did. (Sandra Meyer, now a vice president of American Express, was consumer-marketing manager of the giant Maxwell House division.)

A possible explanation of Gordon and Strober's finding about what women want to earn is even simpler—it could just be that they don't care as much about money as men do. Ask most women in the class of '73 why they work, and money is the last thing they mention. Some volunteered that they have no interest in making vast amounts of it. But they clearly enjoy what they're raking in, because—they will invariably tell you—it's a measure of how they're doing. Others, especially the married women, say they value being financially independent.

And whether this is true down deep or not, several of the women volunteered that their egos aren't as tied to their job status as they suspect men's are. Some work because it forces them into pursuits more worthwhile than any they can dream up on their own. "It's not easy to think up constructive things to do at home," says Linda Taylor, a mother who works full time. "I say if I had the time I would read more or do other good things. But, heck, if I had the time, I probably wouldn't. I really like to use my mind, and I have a great fear of its going to pot." Adds Smith, the Washington consultant: "I guess, you know, it's like a series of little tests—you like to see what you can do." Says Cecilia Herbert: "I just think working is a kick."

Be More Than Qualified

But Herbert also says, unabashedly, and speaking for her husband as well, "We both really want to be very rich." Her salary is one of the lowest in the group, reflecting the difference in pay scales between Richmond and the northeastern area where most of the other women work. But, at twenty-nine, she's got plenty of time.

Some researchers on women in business have found them to be so preoccupied with mastering each job that they neglect to focus, the way men do, on the higher jobs up the ladder. Not Assistant Vice President Herbert. "I'm a big believer in *process*," she says. "Promotions don't come in stair steps. You don't get increased responsibility because you're almost qualified, but because you're *more than* qualified. There's a period of looking like a vice president, sounding like a vice president, and then all of a sudden you are one." Herbert believes she's acting like one now, and hopes to be one before the year is out.

And looking much farther down the road? "This company," says Herbert, after mulling over the question, "has usually been headed by a Mr. Inside and a Mr. Outside. I don't think they'd make me Mr. Outside, but I think I have a fair shot at Mr. Inside." She laughs at the confusion of gender, and then reaffirms: "Maybe president and inside man."

7 The Self at Play

People work. Why? Because they are part of a pattern or tradition that says they must. Freud (and indeed we ourselves) often intimates that one of the truly meaningful ways of expressing and experiencing significant selfhood is through work. But people have enormous reserves of energy and, increasingly, of time. Work isn't the only avenue of expression. What of play? What of fun? What of love, humor, relaxation, laughter, enjoyment, creative meditation, and even not-particularly-creative-doing-of-nothing?

People are capable of and often surprisingly committed to an impressive amount of relaxation and play. This is as important a part of finding and expressing one's uniqueness, one's significance, as anything else we can do. Yet, our Puritan tradition, our Work-Sin Ethic, has made many of us afraid to have a good time. We feel work or school is only meaningful if it's laborious, tedious, and serious.

Unfortunately, this dichotomous way of thinking is so pervasive that we often think of "play" as the opposite of "work." To be truly holistic in our thinking and feeling, we should consider the division into either work or play as artificial as the division into good or bad, right or wrong, love or hate, beautiful or ugly, emotion or reason. Humans are total, integrated creatures. Yet, their ways of thinking have trapped them into compartmentalized ways of understanding.

In the chapter that follows, we present four articles for your perusal. In the first, journalist-educator George B. Leonard describes the necessity of recapturing the lost virtue of ecstasy in one of our most important endeavors, education.

In the second article, Sidney Jourard, humanistic
psychologist, tells us of our need for periods and
places of creative "time out."

The third article, by Ursula Vils, examines Dr.
Robert Shomer's ideas about why many of us don't
enjoy ourselves when we play. Shomer sees the subject
as so important that he has begun to teach college
courses in it, and he shares here some suggestions for
true enjoyment of your recreational time.

The fourth article, written by Linda Garrison,
Phyllis Leslie, and Deborah Blackmore, teaches you
how to relax and remain sane.

The Uses of Ecstasy

George B. Leonard

We are often such grim creatures. Certainly, life is often hard,
and so is much of our labor, including our schooling. But is this all
there is to our lives? Have we lost our sense of the ecstatic, the
humorous, the fun?

In this excerpt from his book, Education and Ecstasy, George B.
Leonard, a journalist and educational consultant, tells us what we
are missing by losing sight of our need for ecstasy.

Unlimited amounts of power are coming into human hands, perhaps
surpassing what even Huxley could have imagined a few short years ago.
For example, the "breeder" reactors now under development promise to
produce more nuclear fuel than they can use. Human control of the death
rate already has set in motion a possibly catastrophic population rise,
though the means for controlling the birth rate also are available. . . .

. . . It seems to demand a new kind of human being—one who is not
driven by narrow competition, eager acquisition, and aggression, but who
spends his life in the joyful pursuit of learning. Such a human being, I feel,
will result not so much through changed ideologies or economic systems as
through changes in the process I have called "education." . . .

As a chief ingredient in all this, as well as an alternative to the old reinforcers, I have named "ecstasy"—joy, *ananda*, the ultimate delight.

Our society knows little about this ingredient. In fact, every civilization in our direct lineage has tended to fear and shun it as a threat to reason and order. In a sense, they have been right. It is hard to imagine a more revolutionary statement for us than "The natural condition of the human organism is joy." For, if this is true, we are being daily cheated, and perhaps the social system that so ruthlessly steals our birthright *should* be overthrown. . . .

Perhaps it is time for scholars and pundits to engage in the serious study of delight. What are its dangers? What are its uses? I would suggest three primarily negative considerations as a beginning:

1. *Ecstasy is not necessarily opposed to reason.* On the other hand, it may help light the way toward relationships, societies, and educational systems in which reason and emotion are no longer at odds; in which, in fact, the two are so in tune that the terms themselves, as opposites, will atrophy.

2. *Ecstasy is not necessarily opposed to order.* On the other hand, it may help us redefine order. In the new definition, a balanced natural ecology in which all creatures grow and act freely represents order. . . . Life is an ordering force. Man is an ordering animal. Order will continue to evolve. Ecstasy is implicated in changing not the quantity, but the quality of order.

3. *Ecstasy is neither immoral nor moral in itself.* At times, forms of ecstasy have powered some of mankind's most destructive movements. The Third Reich, for example, exhibited a certain ecstatic mania. But Hitler's "joy" was used to bolster the old reinforcement system— competition, acquisition, and aggression—carried to the most destructive extremes. It was not brought into play as an *alternative* reinforcement system designed to replace the old.

In dealing with ecstasy, as with all powerful forces, context is crucial. The context I have suggested is neither the wantonly Dionysian nor the purely contemplative, but the educational. Ecstasy is education's most powerful ally. It is reinforcer for and substance of the moment of learning.

Knowing this, the master teacher pursues delight. Even those best known as great lecturers have turned their lecture halls into theaters, shameless in their use of spells and enchantments. Great men, as every schoolboy knows, have greeted their moments of learning with crazy joy. We learn how Archimedes leaped, crying, "Eureka!" from his bathtub; how Handel, on finishing the "Hallelujah Chorus," told his servant, "I did think I did see all Heaven before me, and the great God himself"; how Nietzsche wrote *Thus Spake Zarathustra:*

There is an ecstasy such that the immense strain of it is sometimes relaxed by a flood of tears, along with which one's steps
either rush or involuntarily lag, alternately. There is the feeling that
one is completely out of hand, with the very distinct consciousness
of an endless number of fine thrills and quiverings to the very toes.

What we fail to acknowledge is that every child starts out as an
Archimedes, a Handel, a Nietzsche. The eight-month-old who succeeds in
balancing one block on another has made a connection no less momentous
for him than Nietzsche's. He cannot verbalize it so eloquently and probably
would not bother to if he could; such moments are not so rare for him as for
Nietzsche. Much of his life at that age, in fact, is learning. The possibilities
of an endless series of ecstatic moments stretches before him. We quell the
ecstasy and the learning but this is hard work and rarely is it entirely
successful. Explaining why he was unable to think about scientific problems for a year after his final exams, Albert Einstein said:

> It is in fact nothing short of a miracle that the modern methods
> of instruction have not yet entirely strangled the holy curiosity of
> inquiry. . . . It is a very grave mistake to think that the enjoyment of
> seeing and searching can be promoted by means of coercion and a
> sense of duty.

And yet, life and joy cannot be subdued. The blade of grass shatters the
concrete. The spring flowers bloom in Hiroshima. An Einstein emerges
from the European academies. Those who would reduce, control, quell
must lose in the end. The ecstatic forces of life, growth, and change are too
numerous, too various, too tumultuous. . . .

Life has one ultimate message, "Yes!" repeated in infinite number and
variety. Human life, channeled for millennia by Civilization, is only just
beginning to express the diversity and range of which it is easily capable. To
affirm, to follow ecstasy in learning—in spite of injustice, suffering, confusion, and disappointment—is to move more easily toward an education, a
society that would free the enormous potential of man. . . .

William Golding's novel of some years back, *Lord of the Flies*,
generally has been interpreted as a bitter commentary on man's nature. In
it, a group of children, marooned on a deserted island, turn from Ralph, the
voice of Civilized reason, and Piggy, his myopic egghead sidekick, to join
Jack, who has been interpreted as the villain, the savage, the dark spirit in
man that invariably emerges when the Civilized restraints are removed.

But Golding stacked the deck in a way that comments more on Civilization than on "human nature." Ralph is "good," but dull, unimaginative, and indecisive. Piggy has "mind," but not much else. He is physically and sensorially inept. Jack, on the other hand, is physically and mentally alert, resourceful, imaginative, and creative. He encourages his followers in games and chants, colorful costumes and face paint, ceremonies and a sense of community. He organizes successful pig hunts and provides his meat-hungry children with torchlit feasts. Meanwhile, Ralph and his dispirited followers sicken on their unvarying diet of fruit. What child would not follow Jack? When Golding makes Jack's group evil, he reveals the usual inability in our time to equate the ecstatic with the good. When he makes Civilized Ralph dull and inept, he reveals what he really feels about Civilization as he knows it.

When men must serve as predictable, prefabricated components of a rigid social machine, the ecstatic is not particularly useful and may, in fact, erode the compartments so necessary for the machine's functioning. But when a society moves away from the mechanistic, when an individual may function as a free-roving seeker, when what we now term "leisure" occupies most of an individual's hours, ecstasy may usefully accompany almost every act. Technology is preparing a world in which we may be learners all life long. In this world, delight will not be a luxury but a necessity.

I can recall little of what happened in school the winter I was fifteen. Perhaps that was the year everyone in my English class had to do a chapter-by-chapter synopsis of *Treasure Island*. But the afternoons and nights of that period still are vivid. I was infected by the ham radio bug. My next-door neighbor, a boy two years older, had got me started, and I lived for months in a state of delicious excitement. I would rush home from school, knowing the day would not be long enough. I would work steadily, practicing code, devouring ham manuals and magazines, poring over catalogues of radio parts, building simple shortwave receivers. I loved everything about it. When later I read Gerard Manley Hopkins' "Pied Beauty," the phrase, "all trades, their gear and tackle and trim," immediately summoned up the coils and condensers, the softly glowing vacuum tubes, the sizzle and smell of hot solder, the shining curls of metal drilled out of a chassis.

One night, my radio experience came to a moment of climax. For weeks I had been working on my first major effort, a four-tube regenerative shortwave receiver. The design was "my own," derived from circuits in the manuals and approved by my knowledgeable friends. Every part was of highest quality, all housed in a professional-looking black metal cabinet.

Every knob and dial was carefully positioned for efficiency and esthetics, and there was an oversized, freewheeling band-spread tuning knob. That particular night I had been working ever since running most of the way home from school. I had skipped dinner, fiercely overriding my parents' protests. And now, at about eleven o'clock, I soldered the last connection.

With trembling hands, I connected the ground and the antenna, plugged in the socket, and switched on the set. There was a low, reassuring hum and, after a suspenseful wait, the four tubes lit up. I increased the volume. Dead silence. Nothing. I checked all the switches and dials. No problem there. Perhaps it was the speaker. I plugged in the earphones. Still nothing.

I couldn't imagine what was the matter. For the next hour or so, I went over every connection, traced the circuit until I was dizzy. Since I had splurged on all-new parts, I didn't even consider that one of them might be defective. The mystery, so powerful and unfathomable, could obviously have been cleared up in a few minutes by any well-equipped radio repairman. But, for me, its unraveling was momentous.

The radio's circuit consisted of two stages. The first stage converted radio frequency waves to electrical impulses of an audible frequency; the second stage served as an amplifier for the electrical impulses coming from the first stage. I hit upon the idea of tapping the earphones in at the end of the first stage. Success! Static, code, voices. This seemed to indicate to me that the trouble lay somewhere in the second stage. On an impulse, however, I tied in a microphone at the very beginning of the second stage. Success again. The second stage worked. I could hear my voice coming from the speaker.

At that very instant, the answer was clear: Both stages worked separately. The trouble had to lie in the coupling between them. My eyes went to a little green and silver coil (*the broken connection between subconscious and conscious, the hidden flaw between individual and community*). It *had* to be that impedance coil. With this certainty, I was quite overcome. I would gladly have broken into a radio store to get another one, but my friend, I found, had a spare. I tied it in, not bothering for the moment to solder it. And a universe poured into my room from the star-filled night. I spun the dial: a ham in Louisiana, in California; shortwave broadcasts from England, Germany, Mexico, Brazil. There was no end to it. I had put out new sensors. Where there had been nothing, there was *all of this*.

Ecstasy is one of the trickier conditions to write about. But if there is such a thing as being transported, I was transported that night. And I was, as with every learning experience, forever afterwards changed.

Society's Need for Respectable "Check-out Places"

Sidney M. Jourard

Schoolchildren aren't expected to spend the entire day at their desks, heads buried in their books. We have, in this enlightened age, seen fit to space their workday with recess periods, time when they can exercise their bodies as they also do their brains. In most businesses, lunch and coffee breaks are now a regular part of the workday. Most of us also have vacation periods, giving us a break in the routine.

Sidney Jourard proposes a further step: periods of "time out" with special places to go. Jourard is not just fantasizing; he is serious in his intent. People need opportunities for re-creation. In the following excerpt from Disclosing Man to Himself, *he spells out for us how his theory would work and with what benefits.*

A person needs a place to go when he finds his life unlivable. Society seems to conspire such that there is nowhere to go when you want to be offstage, free from your usual roles, free to discover and define your being-for-yourself. Judges, critics, and commissars are omnipresent. If a man steps out of line and departs from his usual roles, someone is there to remind him of who he is, to define him, and to punish him for daring to define himself. The upshot is many wives and mothers find they cannot face their families another moment without shrieking in protest against the sameness of their unappreciated daily grind. But they stifle the shriek and carry on. Fathers and husbands become bored with their wives, infuriated by their children, and worn out by work that lacks joy—continued only because there is no other work to do, and the bills fall due each month. The children, in turn, cannot get along with each other, or with their parents. Grandparents, aunts, and uncles live a thousand miles away and cannot take the youngsters in for a week or month of respite. And so the trapped ones persist on their joyless, desperate treadmills until physical illness grants them a ticket of admission to a hospital or sickroom. Or they "blow up," have a nervous breakdown, and are treated as "not in their right minds." They may enter a mental hospital, there to be placed in storage until the regime of shock, tranquilizers, and periodic consultations with an overworked psychiatrist brings them "to their senses." But even in the hospitals, there is no respite from roles; patients are cast into new ones and lack the freedom to choose their being. They return to the way of life they lived before, perhaps with the protest in them electroshocked or drugged out of existence.

Before this drama reaches its climax in the sickroom or the state hospital, it would be helpful if new alternatives could be provided. What would life in our society be like if we had acceptable "check-out places"? In moments of reverie, I have invented some. Let me describe one such, a healing-house that appeals to me. It is probably healing only for middle-class people.

It is a place where one can enter and find confirmation for *any* way one has chosen to be, or any way that circumstances have brought one to. If a man wishes solitude, he can find it there; and no one will speak to him if he wishes to remain silent. If he wishes congenial and enlivening body-contact, a masseur or masseuse (he can choose which) is available to provide service. If a housewife wants to paint, listen to music, or just sit and meditate, there is a room for her to do so. The place would be like the now outdated retreats and monasteries that once were available for the defeated and the sick in spirit.

Each person would be entitled to a cell with inviolate privacy. There he could go, and stay for a day, a week, a month, or years. No one could enter this little womb without his invitation; and once a person closed the door, no one else could enter.

Routine would be simple and minimal in such a haven. Meals would be spartan. A person could take them communally, in the dining hall, if he wished to socialize, and take part in the preparation and clean-up from the repast. Otherwise, the pantry would be always available, with abundant supplies of fruit, bread, milk, raw vegetables, and similar snacks. A resident could come and go, nibbling as he wished.

If he wished conversation, he could go to the common room, where he could sit; and his presence alone would signify that he would be willing to talk. Or he could invite someone to the privacy of his cell, if he wished to enter into uninterrupted dialogue.

The rule of the house would be freedom for the self, with respect for the freedom of the other.

People who entered would leave their roles at the doorstep. No status, no rank, would interpose itself between the guests—who would have a first name, or a surname, or no name, or a pseudonym, if that was what they chose.

This would be a place where people could quite freely go out of their minds and roles, as these were known outside.

The house would not be solely for those harried, middle-class people who needed a place to go before they broke down. It would also be a place where creative people—writers, painters, dancers, poets—could go to live awhile and present their more tender creations in an accepting, or better, honest milieu, where commercial criteria for judging art and ideas are irrelevant.

This would be a place where one could go to redefine himself, apart from the people "back home," who have a vested interest in keeping the person in the roles by which they knew him, but which were sickening him. The fat ones could slim down, the thin ones increase in girth. The tense and nervous could find surcease and relaxation; the aimless might meet people with aims that could inspire and redirect their lives.

These houses would be the place one went *before* he got sick, or mad. The directors would eschew drugs and medicines. They would heal by letting healing take place. The houses would be places where joy could be experienced, and peace.

These islands or oases could exist in every community. The Howard Johnson- or Holiday Inn-builders could design them cheaply and simply enough—but with more taste, I would hope, than is shown in those rooms designed for everyone and hence no one. The staff of permanent residents could include professional psychotherapists, resident artists, playwrights, dancers, masseurs, writers and teachers, and musicians. Some of these residents might come and go; but all would provide seekers with an atmosphere of spiritual freedom, and examples of the quest for new avenues of being and expression. A workman, professional man, wife or mother, or lonely person could come daily for an hour or so, or weekly, and find relaxation, edification, or companionship. Americanized versions of geisha girls, or geisha men, would be available, not for illicit and illegal prostitution, but for the purpose of inviting a person into the dialogue that leads a man beyond his usual consciousness, even to delight.

I have little doubt that such houses would pay for themselves if they were on a private, pay-as-you-go basis. And I suspect that if they were underwritten by some grant, or by public-health moneys—but with their operation strictly in the hands of the director of each house—they would more than pay for themselves, in the form of physical breakdown that did *not* happen and mental breakdown which would *not* materialize. I suspect that for the people who patronized such a house, intake of drugs and medicines would diminish radically, to the dismay of the pharmaceutical houses. The mass invasion of physicians' clinics and waiting-rooms would be reduced to manageable dimensions. And the waiting lists of practicing psychotherapists would doubtless be less packed with names.

Such houses of retreat and healing will, alas, not become part of every village, town, or city neighborhood. But sensible people will find ways to pool resources so that they can organize them by themselves. Or if they can afford it, they will buy or rent a "pad" on the other side of town, away from family and friends. Perhaps some organizational genius will find the necessary staff, and the capital to invest; and he will become a millionaire by providing what everyone needs, at a price all can afford to pay.

If such places came into being as a normal part of society, I suspect psychotherapists would lose some of their present *raison d'être*, and would have to apply their knowledge of how people sicken and become whole to teaching, and to living fulfilled lives themselves, so that by their being, they would represent viable ways. And I suspect that physicians would find their practices confined to delivering babies, setting broken bones, and stanching the flow of blood. Sales of drugs would diminish, and the directors of pharmaceutical firms would send lobbies to Washington to persuade legislators the houses were subversive and un-American.

A Serious Look at the Way We Play

Ursula Vils

Play is not just what we do when we have nothing "constructive" to accomplish. Some people do not play during their recreational hours; they make work out of such activities. Some enjoy their work so much, and approach it with such an attitude, that they consider it play. In any case, play and the spirit of play are essential aspects of full living.

Dr. Robert Shomer is trying to get people to think more about the essential nature of play. In contrast to work, he says, play should be a free-choice activity, and ideally the sense of engaging in such activity should permeate our lives. As you read the article, compare your own definition of play with Shomer's.

When it comes to play, Dr. Robert W. Shomer likes travel, billiards and pool, and teaching UCLA Extension courses—especially if they're about—what else?—play. "I want to get people thinking about play," he says, "about the essential nature of play."

He [has done] just that ... in an eight-session course designed to examine how and why we play, if we do so constructively or destructively and what may lie ahead for our leisure hours, especially in the light—or dim, as the case may be—of the energy crisis. "I think we're going to have a lot more games and family activities," said Dr. Shomer, associate professor of psychology at Pitzer College and Claremont Graduate School.

That may not be as homey-warm as it sounds. "That can lead to a tremendous amount of tumult and aggravation, even marriage dissolutions," he said. "Winning at Monopoly becomes important, and competition becomes a divisive force."

In fact, says Dr. Shomer, the difference between healthy play and unwholesome play is competition. "It's bad if play becomes dominated by the end involved," he said. "Play should not be dominated by specific narrow competencies with no translatable ability in another area. I admire football and football players, but I know that that's not play. And where we so live our lives as to vicariously identify with a team or hero, it becomes unwholesome."

Americans, often criticized as a nation of spectators rather than participants, are not unique, he said. "It is not specifically an American problem. I have seen the same thing in South America, Britain, most of western Europe," he said. "It comes about in a society that is socialized to a win-lose situation. Play becomes business. Certainly professional baseball, football, and basketball are big business. And what about Arnold Palmer, a millionaire? Does he play golf for relaxation, or does he do something else to relax from golf?"

Yet play is a common human need. "Someone once said that the only difference between men and boys is the price of their toys," Dr. Shomer said. "We have a need to engage in activities which are diversions from our relatively narrow work activities—a freedom from having to do it. Perhaps it's to be a conspicuous consumer—you know, the expensive skis, the finest tennis racquet, the 28-foot motor home."

Dr. Shomer said that "man is the only species that plays until dead. Look at Picasso—play and exploration into his nineties." But the psychologist acknowledges that play is difficult to define. "Some say it is self-validating behavior, a major provider of joy, an essential for human life, an instinctual way to drain off surplus energy," he said. "Piaget says play is a biological vehicle for assimilating information about the environment, a way to learn to accommodate oneself to the environment."

Permeating Activity

"The problem is that we know when we're playing and when somebody else is playing. We can be very accurate about somebody's playing, yet fuzzy about how we know. Perhaps play is an end in itself, a permeating activity. Some psychologists think that man even learned to use tools through play, that much of his progress originated with play. One once said, 'Necessity may be the mother of invention, but play is its father.'

"Play needs to be 'free, wide-ranging, unfettered,' to allow us to learn about our own capacities," he said, "and wholesome play must allow for the possibility of more than one winner, more than one loser. We have been socialized into the kinds of games with only one winner," he said. "Monopoly, chess, cards, football.

"We must develop a different mental set. We must find how to win without making everybody else a loser. There is not enough emphasis on play in the sense of exploring the possibilities of cooperation. In some societies, the game ends when a tie occurs. We need interdependent cooperativeness, and we haven't learned to play that way yet."

He thinks the energy crisis, with its limiting of mobility, may make a significant impact on family life. "If we can't go out and play," Dr. Shomer said, "we must stay home and play. We can listen to music, read aloud, play team games, build something. We must do things in which no one wins and no one loses—a jigsaw puzzle that everybody can work on would be great.

"Play is a way of coping. We will really be able to gauge the seriousness of the energy crisis by how fast we convert it into play, by how soon the energy games come. Look at how quickly we had Watergate jokes and games."

Some forms of play, Dr. Shomer said, manifest man's need to calibrate himself against another human being. "In tennis," he said, "we are filling a need to calibrate our own abilities against our opponent's. That can be important, but if that's the only kind of play I have, it's not good. There is something about the infantile nature of play that needs to be reestablished, a need to keep a childlike, free, open creativeness. We need to do things at which everybody can be a winner. Riding bicycles—everybody can be competent at their own level, everybody can be a winner. In our future games we need somehow to give individuals the notion not to calibrate against others but against oneself, to see how much one can improve oneself."

Dr. Shomer reiterated that "one of the real problems in marriage is man's and woman's different conceptions about what play is." He also thinks women's ways of playing may be changing. "The increased self-awareness of women may result in different kinds of play for them," he said. "They will not be bound as much by stereotypes. They'll get away from that 'Get out of that tree—you're a girl' attitude. Up to now, women's play has been with men—by playing at manipulating men. I don't say that in a negative or derogatory way. It has been the kind of play women have had to play—the only potentiality for influencing men.

"From now on, women will grow into play more directed at self-fulfillment. They won't have to compete about men or compete about what it means to be a good woman, masculinely defined, of course. They will be more interested in finding out 'What am I as a person?' "

The Sanity Exercise—Relaxation

Linda Garrison, Phyllis Leslie, and Deborah Blackmore

Stress is one of the major factors in the cause of illness and death. We live in a very stressful society. Sometimes we are not aware when we are under stress. The authors of this article state, "Exercising our powers of relaxation has become necessary to offset the fast pace of living and the pressures of time. . . ." They present a set of exercises to teach you how to relax and manage stress. This is a survival article.

We have mentioned the relationship of the mind and body throughout our book. In no other exercise do they work together as closely as in the conscious process of relaxation. Relaxation is time given to renew and refresh our strengths—physical, mental, and emotional. We call relaxation the sanity exercise because of the calming effect it has on our lives. No matter what life brings, we are able to face it with less fatigue, and evaluate the consequences of our actions with better judgment, when our minds are relaxed and decisions are not made in haste.

Exercising our powers of relaxation has become necessary to offset the fast pace of living and the pressures of time, which are constantly undermining our own mental organization. The psychological difficulty in keeping up today's changing values and patterns of living is taking its toll on our energies. The sharp rise in emotional illness in America today is clear evidence of this fact. Until we meet the need to direct and reinforce inner strengths, the flow of our energies may be misdirected or drained to a breaking point. When we feel physically and mentally tired, we operate less efficiently, and consequently live with insecurity, worry, tension, and anxiety. These circumstances, continued over a period of time, may manifest themselves in several ways—difficulty in falling asleep or getting restful sleep, moodiness, depression, and ultimately mental and emotional breakdown.

When we have control of our thoughts, we have mastered the technique of concentration, which allows us to focus our energy on one thing at a time and act decisively. Any drain on our energy reserves will disrupt our mental concentration. Perhaps one of the most damaging influences on our mental well-being is negative thinking. An imagined situation may evoke almost the same emotional response as a real one. When we dwell on imaginary problems or anticipate trouble of some sort, we create a threat to our well-being. Our bodies grow tense with anxiety and emotion. By turning from negative to positive thoughts, we ultimately control our emotional responses, saving energy for productive and pleasant situations.

Tension has been singled out by the American Medical Association as a major cause of heart attacks. Tension is the sensation and emotion you feel as a result of continuous mental and emotional stress, theoretically in response to a physical or psychological threat. The physiology of the body's response to tension and stress is as follows: "The body responds—or attempts to respond (barring disease or injury to vital organs)—to any type of stress in the same manner. Interpreting the stress as a call to action, it mobilizes itself through the interaction of the nervous and glandular systems which control the level of body activity. Adrenalins are secreted, stored energy is released, blood sugar level rises, and heart rate and blood pressure increase. When the stress is removed, calming hormones are released and the body returns to normal."[1] Using electromyography, we can measure the response of the muscles to various kinds of stress. *Muscular tension is always an accompanying symptom of general tension.* The next time you sense a feeling of pressure, indecisiveness, excitement, anger, or frustration, notice the tightness in your muscles.

Interestingly enough, you will also find that a release of muscular tension eases overall tension. By focusing the mind on the control and relaxation of muscular tension, we have a release mechanism for our entire system. Brief periods of relaxation bring us back mentally and emotionally refreshed. The cultivation and use of relaxation techniques and exercises are an effective method of obtaining relief from the build-up of tension. As with other types of exercise, you must practice relaxing in order to experience the benefits. The following exercises and techniques for relaxation are provided in the sincere hope that they will be practiced with real effort and concentration. Above all, you must reach your mind to master the art of relaxation and the process of easing tensions within the body.

1. Frank Vitale, *Individualized Fitness Program* (Englewood Cliffs, N.J.: Prentice-Hall, 1973), p. 200.

Exercises

The following are exercises to use when you have the advantage of solitude, and a quiet place for a retreat. Music will help promote relaxation if it is soothing and quiet. Do not let your emotions or thought processes interfere with physical relaxation. Particularly in the beginning, the most important point of concentration should be your body.

1. Choose a particular time of day and make an effort to sit quietly for a few minutes each day at that time.
2. Sitting in a cross-legged position, rest your hands in your lap or on your knees. Gently close your eyes and concentrate on a single thing. Choose something that is pleasing for you to think about. Each time your mind is distracted, bring it back to your object of concentration.
3. Sitting quietly with your eyes closed, tighten your fists and mentally explore the feeling of tension within your hands. Slowly release the hands, studying the feeling of relaxation. Practice this several times until you are able to identify relaxation as it happens. Try this with different parts of your body.
4. Find a comfortable position lying on the floor. Try lying on your back, your head turned to one side, your arms away from your body, your feet and ankles loose. Turn your palms up and tighten your hands into a fist. Slowly let your hands relax. Concentrate on the feeling of relaxing your hands. Send the release up through your arms and relax the entire body.
5. Lying on the floor, roll to one side and curl up, bringing your knees to your chest. This is a position familiar to us as children. Turn your thoughts back to the day when you were young and life was full of adventure and curiosity. As you return to the present, bring back with you that sense of wonder and open your eyes to the adventures that lie ahead.
6. Find a position of relaxation. As you slowly close your eyes to the visual world around you, open your mind to experiencing the depths of your internal environment.
7. Sitting quietly or lying down, empty your mind of unhappy thoughts—anger, irritation, resentment, disappointment—and change to a positive outlook. Concentrate on being positive!
8. Think of yourself as a rag doll and collapse your body. Practice completely loosening every muscle you have.
9. Relax your mouth, lips, tongue, and throat. This is one method of turning off the constant words we turn over in our minds.

10. Practice releasing the muscles in the different areas of your face—cheeks, temples, lips, chin. Your face should be blank of all expression.

Techniques for Handling Stress

Many stressful situations may confront us during our normal daily tasks. Here are a few techniques for handling such situations.

1. Learn mental priority. Become aware of how rapidly and continuously your mind operates throughout the day. Periodically examine your thoughts, learning to sort out that which is worthwhile and that which is a waste of mental energy. Eliminate thoughts which are unnecessary and don't dwell on situations you can't change.
2. Develop your own plans for handling hectic situations when they occur. Practice these and your reactions to such situations will be controlled and relaxed.
3. When a bad situation does occur, resolve to handle it without emotion. That will drain your energies. Take a deep breath, gather your thoughts, and make a businesslike effort at resolving it.
4. When you are the busiest, take a few moments to relax your thoughts and control preoccupation with your work. A brief retreat to a favorite spot or a quiet corner will keep tension under control and ultimately help you master your time.

In addition, we recommend recreational forms of physical and social activity as an enjoyable release. The list of possibilities is endless—learn to play tennis or golf, take a walk or a hike, try sailing or skin diving, enroll in a yoga class. Explore the possibilities and enjoy the pleasure—you've got a life to live!

8 Masking and Unmasking

In the process of living, we play games with ourselves and with others, and we fill a variety of roles. In this section, we want to look at how masks, both those we put on ourselves and those others impose on us, hinder the self-actualization process. Traditionally, certain groups in our society have been forced to wear the masks and play the roles assigned them by others. That was usually because the majority—or those in power—have been able to maintain their positions only by having others play specific roles. A person is more than any one mask. But we all know that some individuals show only those parts of their identities which they think are safe, which they know will be accepted.

Recently, we have seen new identities emerging in America. Many have thrown aside the masks they've been forced or expected to wear. They now stand before us demanding to be seen, known, and acknowledged. We don't always like such people—not because they are necessarily bad, wrong, unpleasant, or dangerous, but because they upset our expectations. We refer, of course, to women in the feminist movement, who are insisting that women are not things, but full, free persons. We refer, also, to those in various minority groups, who refuse to play the mask game any longer. Negroes, preferring the term "blacks," are saying that white America can have its "nigger masks" back; they aren't needed anymore. Young people are also discarding the masks given them by parents and teachers in particular, by society in general, and showing in many ways that they are full-fledged persons.

It's an interesting commentary that those who

refuse to wear the expected masks are labelled "militant," "radical," "revolutionary." Some are, of course. But, the majority impress us as simply people who are discovering some of the pleasures of significant Selfhood.

Many whites see sports as one of the few areas in which blacks have escaped the confines of racism, but that may not be true. Sociologist Jonathan Brower gives us a behind-the-scenes look at how blacks are treated in professional football, and the masks they are expected to wear.

What happens when people unmask and share something personal about themselves with others? Our second article describes a research study done by psychologists to determine what happens when a person discloses something about him- or herself to a stranger.

The choice of a life-style is in a way a voluntary commitment to adopt a given mask—one that is radically important. In the third excerpt, drawn from Future Shock, Alvin Toffler describes his feeling that one's commitment to a life-style is a "super-decision" in one's life.

In the next article, Janice Trecker, a former secondary school teacher, presents a very strong case that our secondary schools perpetuate sex stereotyping, and she suggests some remedies for that problem.

In the last article, Nora Ephron takes a very sensitive but humorous look at how women are dehumanized in our society.

Whitey's Sport

Jonathan J. Brower

Asked to name professions in which nonwhites have a better-than-average chance to succeed or even excel, many people would name professional sports. Outstanding nonwhite players, particularly blacks, are legion, and most whites believe that such players are subject to relatively little prejudice.

In this article, Dr. Jonathan Brower explores the white-controlled world of professional football. He summarizes the results of a study he conducted to determine the subtle and unsubtle forms of prejudice, the problems blacks encounter in sports, and the attitudes they are required to exhibit in order to be considered "good team players." His findings may startle you.

On a Sunday afternoon in autumn, the game is pure escape. The competition is tough, the rules are strict, and a man is judged solely by how well he plays and not by his personal attributes. Sport, we can let ourselves believe, is blissfully immune to the social problems that plague our society. In particular, it's easy to think of it as a showcase of interracial harmony and understanding.

From the distance of the television screen or even the fifty-yard line, it seems to be so. There has been an increasing number of blacks entering professional sports in the past two decades and many have become superstars. Some knowledgeable fans may even argue that the prime mythology of sport and an important part of American folklore is integration and democratization. Sport should serve as a mirror, as it were, of American ideals.

However, I recently completed a two-and-a-half-year study of institutional racism in the National Football League, and I found that such notions are a long way from objective reality. Sport is part of the large society; indeed, it is embedded in the society. And while it does reflect its ideals, or at least those of the dominant group, it also carries the stresses and strains of the society. What I discovered was a subtle but pervasive form of racism. It is called culture clash and involves the inappropriateness of the black subculture in the white world of professional football.

Fortunately for the sociologist, the world of professional football is relatively open to view. A wide range of publications is available for analysis. Over the period of the study, I read popular magazines, books, official football publications such as record books and programs and newspaper articles. Several months prior to the football season, each team publishes an annual media guide that gives information on the team's personnel—front office and players—and general team operations. I studied these media guides covering the twelve-year period of 1960–1971.

Interviews with participants in professional sports are usually easy since football people are used to and expect to be interviewed. This makes the sociological investigator a less obtrusive research instrument than he or she would be in many other types of social settings. In the course of the study, I talked to dozens of players, coaches, scouts, and owners.

Finally, I was granted permission to study an NFL team during two successive summer training camps in 1970 and 1971. The team, fictitiously called the Jaguars here, had no idea I was studying racism. I felt the topic was too emotionally loaded.

My experiences later bore this out. At dinner one evening a high NFL team management official offered his views of social problems: "All Communists in America should be thrown out of the country," he said. "Any teacher *accused* of Communist affiliations should not be allowed to teach in our schools.... America has gone downhill ever since World War II when we fought to save the Jews.... There are too many intellectuals around today.... People like Sirhan Sirhan and Angela Davis shouldn't have trials wasted on them; they're guilty and everybody knows it.... Communism and socialism are the same bullshit."

At several points our conversation turned toward blacks in general. Early in the talk he referred to them as "negroes"; as it progressed, and he became more relaxed, he used the term "nigger" several times. He appeared to feel no uneasiness using this derogatory term; apparently, it was a natural part of his vocabulary.

I was allowed free range at camp with few restrictions. Although I did not stay overnight, I was a constant fixture there for much of every day, observing camp life and interviewing—formally and informally—trainers, players, coaches, management, and sportswriters.

Racism is a term with many different meanings or focuses. But here I was concerned with certain patterns of behavior the consequences of which maintain and reinforce present inequalities among ethnic groups. It does not matter whether the consequences are intended or not. In fact, the disturbing aspect of institutional racism is that many racist consequences are entirely unintentional.

Football is dominated and controlled by whites. At the professional level, as well as in the high school and collegiate ranks, the game is infused with traditional white middle-class values. It is considered by many self-appointed guardians of the sport to be one of the few stable aspects of a society engulfed in turbulent change. I discovered, moreover, that the people who control professional football spend a great deal of effort seeing that football remains the last bastion of traditional American values.

But more than 30 percent of the professional players today are black and they, like other blacks in the United States, are questioning white ethnocentric assumptions that have racist overtones and implications. And assertive blacks who want equality don't always fit easily into a system of traditional values.

The clash starts early in the recruiting process. The scouting system in professional football is the principal vehicle by which potential players are spotted, evaluated, and brought into the league. Once scouts were only interested in the playing ability of the candidates, but in recent years they have also developed a critical eye for the psychological or "adjustment" characteristics of athletes.

Supposedly, a player with the wrong attitude can't be an asset to the team, but determining just what that attitude is can be difficult. *Attitude* is a very general catch-all term meaning just about anything that helps or hinders the performance of the player and his team. And judgment of attitude is not only subjective but is measured against the norms of football and in the light of how a scout or a coach sees his own responsibilities.

One scouting report I saw on a black collegiate running back described in glowing terms his physical prowess. But then it went on to caution that he was "an individualist but worth the risk."

Why should an individualist be evaluated as a risk? The answer seems to be that any player, regardless of race, must be a team player, and in most team sports, individualists and team players are incompatible.

Scouts actually believe in the *individualist* as they use it, although most of the people in the scouting system are white, with little or no knowledge of the black experience, and their prejudices can color their judgment. In their context, blacks can be either accommodating Negroes or individualists. Thus, the "black individualist" tends to be evaluated more harshly than whites. The black individualist is too uncertain a quantity—a package of unexpected problems, and because his standards are less likely to match those of the white middle class, he is more readily tagged as a "team dissenter."

The coaches, almost exclusively a white group, believe in the traditional social values of football as much if not more than the scouts. While they may not be necessarily antagonistic toward black players, they often work with outmoded definitions and expectations that apply to white players but that are considered racist today.

For example, coaches generally prefer "respectful" players who show the proper deference to their mentors. This rankles many black players who are loath to perform the subservient role and thus perpetuate behavior demanded of blacks throughout the history of the United States. This often causes misunderstandings between blacks, who do not defer in the expected manner, and the coaches.

The coaches' opposition to long-haired athletes is another rule that interferes with black pride. Sociologist Harry Edwards has argued that the long-haired white athlete is seen as a "hippie"—a role that embodies values opposed to the American sports creed of goal-oriented hard work—while the Afro or natural hairdo of blacks labels the wearer a "revolutionary." Whites can more easily slip out of the role of hippie, at least temporarily, than blacks can from the role of revolutionary, especially when a "revolutionary" is a black who is honestly expressing his identity and loyalty to his oppressed people.

The black ghetto subculture is generally misinterpreted, then found offensive to white football personnel. The everyday activities and most commonplace expressions of blacks, such as gait and speech patterns, are often read as both socially offensive and as rebellious behavior. One NFL scout told me that the coaches of the team for which he works interpret the characteristic walk of young men of the black ghetto, observable in many pro black players, as revealing "a chip on their shoulders." Black ghetto speech patterns, they also believe, are indicative of lazy people.

In the Jaguars' training camp, coaches would "overexplain" football techniques and assignments more often to blacks than to whites. In most cases, this was done without malice; the coaches just wanted to be sure all their players understood the assignments. Understandably, perhaps, it grew out of the coaches' own anxiety, since their tenure in the NFL is notoriously shaky.

But, at the same time, it was clear that they perceived the blacks to be intellectually hazy, and a vicious circle developed around the issue. The blacks who received this extra attention often would not respond to the explanations with the normal middle-class cures of head-nodding and "uh-huhs" to show that they understood. Instead, many of them would listen with expressionless faces and no outward signs of response. Then the coaches, not certain they had been understood, would reexplain things. The blacks, who may have been stony-faced for other reasons than lack of understanding—such as anger and defiance directed at an all-white coaching staff, grievances against the club for some perceived injustices or the habit of maintaining a "cool" demeanor—became even more unresponsive, since they saw the coaches' overexplanation as a condescending gesture.

I could see subtle reactions to the biracial issue in the Jaguars' training camp. The white players, coaches, and management feel liberal if not self-righteous. Coaches, maintaining that they only try to field the best team possible and run a well-disciplined unit, are sometimes quick to insist they are "color-blind."

Management likes to believe it is giving blacks a chance to "better themselves." One man from the front office said, "These guys are getting the chance of a lifetime. If it weren't for pro ball, they'd be poor." In addition to the direct benefits, management argues that the entire black community is gaining pride and a sense of commitment to the American system because blacks have made good in football and, moreover, that these blacks are living proof of the fact that opportunity and open competition flourish in America.

Black players, on the other hand, are becoming aware of the fallacy of this argument. They are conscious of the fact that the great majority of athletic hopefuls don't make the grade and so slip back into the oblivion of the ghetto. Many of the blacks who make it in the league are in a constant state of low-key anger. They feel that white players and management personnel are insensitive to their unique needs and problems. While many of the problems may at times be exaggerated, they are nonetheless real and immediate. And what is significant, of course, is that a group of blacks— well paid and well treated in relation to most blacks in the United States— *believes* these issues to be real.

Cultures clash off the field as well as on. A few sportswriters have noted the informal segregation that exists, but the issue has generally been ignored by the public and most social scientists who claim that sport is a vehicle for integration.

Social psychologists have maintained that when members of various racial groups are in prolonged contact in a variety of contexts and are working for a common goal, race relations will improve to the point where participants will see one another as unique individuals, not representatives of racial categories. I found little to confirm this in the training camp of the Jaguars.

I asked many players—black and white—if they felt that being in professional football had broadened their outlook in certain ways, helping them to get along with people from other regions and of other races and different political persuasions. A white Southerner, in the NFL for several years, expressed not untypical sentiments when he answered my question: "I don't believe that all people are created equal. It's just not possible. I may be wrong, but I don't think blacks are equal to whites. I've never been close with any blacks on the team, although I've been friendly with some. But I just don't think they're as good as whites. Maybe I'm wrong and maybe I'll change my mind some day, but I don't think so. It's the way I've been brought up and it's what I believe." This white player, while never rude to blacks at summer training camp, was always cool and reserved toward his black teammates, although quite the opposite toward his white ones.

The camp was conducted in a quiet college community. The college athletic facilities were used by the team while a privately owned dormitory, located about a mile from the football fields and locker room, housed all the team personnel (players, coaches, management, trainers, and doctor) except the one female secretary.

I asked one of the management officials how roommates were assigned. He explained that they were paired up alphabetically, both rookies and veterans. There was, in fact, a good deal of integration in the rookie rooms, but a rookie's presence there is likely to be temporary. Only about five of twenty-five or thirty rookies will make the team. If a rookie makes it then he ceases to be a rookie after one season of play.

But the veterans, in spite of management's claims, were not assigned alphabetically. If they had been, there would have been nine integrated veteran pairs. In the 1970 and 1971 summer camps I observed, there were only three such pairs.

One of the sportswriters then told me that frequently many veteran players are assigned on the basis of playing position, i.e., complementary positions such as quarterback and receiver. Only six pairs could have been assigned according to position. Obviously, veterans must be assigned roommates on the basis of nonofficial criteria, one of which is race. And since veterans, who have been in the league for a number of years, are accustomed to, and expect, segregated rooms, management finds it more comfortable to go along with the way things are usually done.

These compromises are not made as a result of major policy decisions; rather, given the way organizations work and the way people work and need to get through the day, a pattern develops as the result of seemingly inconsequential daily decisions. But it adds up to the same thing.

In 1970, the veteran room assignments consisted of twelve white, seven black, and three integrated pairs. Of the three integrated room assignments, one of the integrated pairs was cut from the team. The consensus around camp was that those two players were not expected to make the team anyway, so it was "safe" to room them together since they would be around for a short time and would help make the team look more integrated than it actually was. The other two pairs of integrated roommates were established stars, all of whom were likely to have publicized who their roommates were. No wonder several black players I talked to were convinced that integration was only a token gesture.

The players would have an hour or more to get ready for practice. Getting ready would not take any one player an hour, but it did take an hour to handle all the players. A team rule requires every player to have his ankles taped. Also, many players would have injuries that also needed taping or medication. Since there were only two trainers to administer to all the athletes, the arrival times at the locker room were staggered.

Most players don't like to wait around for an hour in the locker room. Therefore, those players with little or no seniority had to go first. The rookies were expected to be in the locker room an hour before practice. The veterans came later, reporting according to the length of time they had been playing professional football. Thus, reporting to the locker room fifteen minutes before practice was not only a luxury but also a badge of seniority.

But I saw that black and white veterans with equal seniority didn't report at the same time. Blacks came in earlier than required. I asked a black veteran why this was so. "We can't look too secure," he said. "It's just not expected of blacks to take all the privileges. If we appear too comfortable, the man will come down on us in one way or another."

Even on the field there was a kind of informal segregation. Between the players' arrival and the arrival of the coaches, visiting and talking among the players were, for the most part, on a segregated basis. Usually, players jogging or warming up before practice would do so either by themselves or with other players of the same race.

In the dining commons, there were two types of segregation. The rookies were separated from the veterans, a time-honored professional football tradition; then, within each group there was further segregation along racial lines.

The rookies sat farther from the food, which was served cafeteria style, than the veterans. But the black veterans, it turned out, sat farther from the food than the white veterans. Apart from the random integration of the rookies, there was also a small degree of mixing among the veterans when whites would sit in the black section.

The veterans most likely to be integrated were teammates of many years' standing. But veterans who had been recently acquired from other teams would not enter the few integrated circles. In any case, not too many whites were enthusiastic mixers. Of those who were, most belonged to the Fellowship of Christian Athletes. But even so, many blacks, including even a few who belonged to the FCA, felt that the white FCA members were intent only on demonstrating and proselytizing for their Christian ideology.

The blacks, on the other hand, seldom mixed voluntarily with the whites. For some this was a dilemma. In order to convince coaches and management that they could get along with all types of teammates, they felt obligated to eat with a wide variety of players, but they found it an uncomfortable experience.

One player told me, "After a hard day of practice, I'm tired. I don't feel like expending much energy at dinner. I want to have easy communication. I don't want to have to explain in detail to a white what I can say in a few words to a brother."

Others agreed with this justification, but still there were black players who had grown up in non-ghetto middle-class environments where the traditional black-ghetto manner of speaking was seldom if ever used. They appeared articulate and comfortable when talking to whites, but more often than not I found them at mealtime rapping with their black brothers. Said one, "Sure, I can talk like a white guy. But we don't have all that much in common. We can use the same words but still not communicate worth shit."

Once again, a time-honored arrangement that had grown into a structured hierarchy had become institutionalized for some kind of biracial interaction. But on white peoples' terms.

Even during the two free nights each week, blacks and whites went their separate ways to bars, parties, or other forms of entertainment. Time off from the training grind would find many more blacks than whites remaining at the dormitory because blacks often felt they had no place to go in a town with few entertainment spots that catered especially to them.

Much of the institutional racism in professional football starts and ends at the top with the owners. Most men who own football teams originally go into the venture to have fun. To mingle with the players and take an active part in dealing with the team's strategy help the owner to enjoy vicariously an identity as an athlete and thus fulfill a lifelong fantasy.

But fun and ego fulfillment, for many owners, cannot be realized by simply owning a team. They are also prudent financial investors, and football teams are expensive toys; the going price for an NFL franchise currently is $20 million, and clearly these toys are for the exceedingly wealthy. Most professional athletic team owners are hard workers who also want to see results in terms of financial profit. Given these two factors—fun-and-games and financial profit—it is not hard to understand the impatience of owners with troublemakers.

The owners comprise a small and fairly exclusive sort of club. Not only do their sports endeavors afford them common outlooks and policy standpoints on club ownership matters, but these men usually share many of the same social values. Since they are tuned in on the same wavelength, they can readily agree on collective action regarding the operation of the NFL.

In my interviews with professional athletic team owners, I always asked the same question: "What qualities do you like in your players besides actual playing ability?" The answer was always much like the one given by one team owner, who said, "I like good citizens, morally upstanding men." From the interviews, this could be translated to mean that these qualities insured cooperative players who readily accept the authority of the team as it is manifested through actions of the owner, front office, and coaches.

One candid owner told me that he and others prefer players "with blond hair and blue eyes." He is by no means a hooded klansman or Southern redneck; rather, he is a prudent businessman who views the white middle-class standards of America as the appropriate standards for human conduct.

When he admitted this, he paused a moment in the conversation and gave a nervous, quiet laugh, then went on to explain his reasons, implying that he was not personally negative towards black people. There were two points, he said. First, from an economic point of view, white players are desirable because white fans identify with them more readily than with blacks, and most paying customers are white.

Secondly, there are fewer problems with whites since blacks today have chips on their shoulders. He felt the mistreatment and discrimination by management that some blacks claim to exist were really imaginary. This incorrect perception, he maintained, disrupts the effective functioning of a team during athletic competition.

Owners, then, want cooperative players who conform to the accepted, dominant-group ideal standards of the white middle class. As a cohesive collective, they keep in touch about troublesome players. This is not to say that owners are seething with paranoia, obsessed with staying on top of the latest scuttlebutt concerning "coach baiters" or "locker-room menaces." They don't need to be. The front-office management, coaches, and scouts are well aware of the potential power of the owners.

Why can't blacks do something about it within the system? One of the answers is that these forms of racism are usually apparent only to the blacks. The discrimination and relative deprivation of black players in comparison to their white counterparts are often so subtle they cannot even be articulated. And white players feel they are accommodating themselves to the needs of the blacks and usually believe they are doing everything possible to create harmony within the team. When the occasional charge of racial discrimination is brought into the open, white owners, coaches, and players are usually genuinely dumbfounded.

Procedures for redressing grievances or hearing appeals are rigged, and blacks are particularly affected. Players see no point in taking their complaints to the NFL commissioner, since he is paid by the owners; hence, in the player's eyes, he cannot be impartial.

Furthermore, football players have an average career span of only 4.6 years, so they cannot afford to wait out the several years it takes for a grievance to go through the channels of the National Labor Relations Board. Under this board's current rules, a player filing a grievance must win his case at several different levels before going to court. "If you want to play ball," said one player representative resignedly, "you can't go through all the rigamarole."

The channels—such as they are—discourage reform. The white world of professional football is fairly new to blacks, who are aware of and encounter in it the problems that are uniquely theirs in any white institution. What they find is that avenues of due process lead nowhere. The dead ends occur because the methods for rectifying blacks' grievances are under the control of the team owners—and their employee, the commissioner. Thus, the players, required to work through the power structure of professional football, have little hope for redressing wrongs, and redressing racist practices is even more difficult.

Equally significant is the fact that for the most part black players will not speak out publicly about such grievances. White players may complain about injustice, but a black player who may complain about the same injustice runs the risk of being labeled a "troublemaker." And the black player who steps out of his accepted role too often or too blatantly will either be traded to another team or blackballed from football completely.

More than that, the black football player wants to succeed; hence, he is concerned about himself as a professional athlete as well as a black man. Most blacks are willing to tolerate a good deal of racial unpleasantness since salaries in professional football are considerably higher than most players, black or white, could earn in any other work they are qualified to do. And when their playing careers are over, other lucrative occupations may be opened to them as a result of the status as a former professional athlete.

Meanwhile, the tensions continue. Many of the whites sense the resentment but they cannot understand the smoldering, poorly concealed anger of these "privileged" blacks. Blacks, on the other hand, are impatient with and frustrated by the white football establishment. Meanwhile, the patterns of institutional racism persist. And so do the myths and folklore of sport.

Disclosing Oneself to Others

Zick Rubin

What is the purpose of wearing a mask? Is it easier for a woman to disclose something personal about herself than for a man to do so? What happens to a relationship when you share some intimate bit of information about yourself? Dr. Zick Rubin attempts to answer these and other questions in the following article. His unique research demonstrates what happens to strangers when one discloses something personal about one's self to the other. His conclusion, based on his research, shows the close relationship between personal disclosure and trust.

The most literal meaning of "intimate" is to get into another person—to really know another. Yet there often is considerable reluctance among people to be known. Self-disclosure invariably entails a risk, and the greater the disclosure, the greater the risk. When we reveal to another person something of our "true self," we must be prepared for the possibility that he will examine what we have revealed and find it wanting. Or he may use the information to take advantage of us. In courtship, for example, one partner's revelation of some blemish in his background may prompt the other to abandon him. Or one partner's disclosure of the depth of his affection for the other may enable the other to exploit him by making large and unreasonable demands. In light of these risks, it is no wonder that many of us learn early in life to be wary of revealing ourselves. "We conceal and camouflage our true being before others," psychologist Sidney Jourard writes, "to foster a sense of safety, to protect ourselves against unwanted but expected criticism, hurt, or rejection." But this protection, Jourard goes on to argue, is purchased at a steep price: "When we are not truly known by other people in our lives, we are misunderstood. . . . Worse, when we succeed too well in hiding our being from others, we tend to lose touch with our real selves, and this loss of self contributes to illness in its myriad forms." Thus, disclosing ourselves to others may be necessary not only for the establishment of close relationships, but also to permit us to keep in touch with ourselves. "A friend is a person with whom I may be sincere," Emerson wrote. "Before him, I may think aloud."

Although self-disclosure is often difficult for men and women alike, it seems to be especially difficult for men in our society. Women surveyed by Jourard typically report that they have revealed more information about their feelings and experiences to family members, friends, and lovers than men do. As Jourard suggests, "The male role, as personally and socially defined, requires men to appear tough, objective, striving, achieving, unsentimental, and emotionally unexpressive. . . . If a man is tender, . . . if he weeps, if he shows weakness, he will likely be viewed as unmanly by others, and he will probably regard himself as inferior to other men." During the first of the 1972 Democratic Presidential primaries, Senator Edmund Muskie, at that time the leading candidate for the nomination, expressed his displeasure with a New Hampshire newspaper publisher in an outburst that was simultaneously indignant and tearful. The incident was widely reported to have seriously weakened his drive for the nomination. It was not his indignation that hurt the senator, for this is an expression that men are generally permitted, but rather his tears. Muskie's genuine expression of feelings was considered a sign of unmanliness and weakness.

The rise of women's consciousness-raising groups has served to emphasize the relative inability of men to reveal themselves—especially to other men. Marc Festeau writes:

> Can you imagine men talking to each other saying: "Are you sure you're not angry at me?" . . . "I'm not as assertive as I would like to be." . . . "I feel so competitive that I can't get close to anyone." . . . "I just learned something important about myself that I've got to tell you." . . . "I don't have the self-confidence to do what I really want to do." . . . "I feel nervous talking to you like this."
>
> It just doesn't happen. . . .
>
> As a man, my conditioning and problems are not only different, but virtually the inverse of those of most women. We've been taught that "real men" are never passive or dependent, always dominant in relationships with women or other men, and don't talk about or directly express feelings; especially feelings that don't contribute to dominance.

In Jourard's view, men's inability to disclose themselves to others is a literally lethal aspect of the male role, contributing to the shorter life expectancy of males. "Men keep their selves to themselves and impose an added burden of stress beyond that imposed by the exigencies of everyday life. . . . The time is not far off when it will be possible to demonstrate with adequately controlled experiments the nature and degree of correlation between level and amounts of self-disclosure, proneness to illness and/or death at an early stage." I frankly cannot imagine what sort of "controlled experiments" Jourard has in mind—all of the possibilities that occur to me are rather macabre. Nevertheless, the point that openness is likely to be related to psychological and perhaps even physical health is well taken. People of either sex who are totally unable to reveal their feelings to others are likely to be labeled as poorly functioning or, in extreme cases, as autistic or schizophrenic. One recent study of Peace Corps trainees documented the link between self-disclosure and psychological adjustment by showing that those trainees who were most willing to reveal personal information about themselves to others also tended to be the most cognitively complex, adaptable, flexible, and popular.

It would be highly misleading to equate the ability to disclose oneself with positive mental health, however. People who disclose *too much* are apt to be considered as sick or sicker than those who disclose too little. To be a hallmark of psychological health or interpersonal competence, a person's disclosure must be appropriate to the particular situation and relationship in which it occurs. The appropriateness of disclosures is important in fleeting encounters between strangers as well as in the development of intimate relationships over longer periods of time. In the next section I will describe one of my own studies of encounters among strangers. The study will hopefully be of interest in its own right. But my main reason for introducing it at this point is my belief that these fleeting encounters illustrate certain mechanisms that are central to the development of intimate relationships.

Notes from the Departure Lounge

Several recent laboratory experiments have been concerned with the exchange of self-disclosure among unacquainted pairs of subjects. Their general finding is that, as one would expect, self-disclosure tends to be reciprocal. The more Person A reveals about himself to Person B, the more Person B is likely to reveal to Person A in return. My own experiment also concerned the exchange of self-disclosure among pairs of strangers, but it was conducted in a real-life setting—departure lounges at Boston's Logan Airport—rather than in the laboratory. Its central goal was to go beyond another demonstration of the "reciprocity effect" toward a better understanding of the mechanisms that underlie it.

The reciprocity effect may in fact be ascribed to at least two different mechanisms. One mechanism is that of *modeling*. Especially when norms of appropriate behavior are not completely clear, people look to one another for cues as to what sort of response is called for. If a person sitting next to you on a train talks about the weather, you are likely to respond in kind. If he proceeds to discuss his recent illness—and at the same time seems to be in command of the situation—then you may well infer that disclosing personal matters is the proper thing to do under the circumstances. Such modeling phenomena can also be observed in the initiation of new recruits to sensitivity training or encounter groups. At first unsure about how they should behave, the new members observe their fellows disclosing themselves intimately and as a result conclude that they too are expected to reveal personal information.

A second mechanism that may underlie the reciprocity effect goes beyond modeling, however, and may be called *trust*. When another person reveals himself to you, you are likely to conclude that he likes and trusts you. He has, after all, made himself vulnerable to you, entrusting you with personal information that he would not ordinarily reveal to others. A common motivation in such a situation is to demonstrate to the other person that his affection and trust are well placed. One effective way to do this is to disclose yourself to him in return. It is by means of such reciprocal displays of trust and affection that people are most likely to move from acquaintanceship to friendship.

In many instances the two mechanisms operate simultaneously and lead to essentially the same end-state. In the encounter group, for example, members not only model one another's levels of disclosure, but also demonstrate their increasing trust for one another by means of reciprocal disclosure. There are instances, however, in which the two mechanisms should lead to rather different results. These are the cases in which the first person reveals *too* much, going beyond the level of intimacy with which the second person feels comfortable. To the extent that reciprocal disclosure is dictated by modeling, even extremely intimate revelations may lead to intimate disclosures in return.[1] But excessively intimate disclosures will often breed suspicion rather than trust. If, for example, a person reveals the details of his sex life to a co-worker on their first day at the job, the second person may have reason to suspect the first's motives or discretion. Instead of being motivated to reveal the details of his own sex life in return, he will be likely to clam up.

In the experiment that I conducted at the airport, the experimenter, either a male or a female college student, began by approaching a prospective subject, an adult man or woman sitting alone in the departure lounge, and asking him if he would write a sentence or two about himself to be used as part of a class project on "handwriting analysis." There is, to be sure, a deception involved here that I wish we could avoid. In a previous experiment my students and I found, however, that when we asked people to write something about themselves as part of a study of "the way people describe themselves"—which is of course the true purpose—several problems emerge. Foremost among these was that over half of the male subjects approached by male experimenters refused to take part. As we have already noted, men find it particularly difficult to express themselves to other men. In the all-male context, "self-description" seemed to be a threatening word. When we represented the study as concerned with handwriting analysis, on the other hand, we were able to reduce male refusal rates substantially. In addition, by obtaining "handwriting samples" rather than "self-descriptions" I hoped to minimize the subjects' self-consciousness about the content of their messages. As far as the subjects knew, only their handwriting, and not their personal disclosures, would later be evaluated for research purposes.

1. This modeling effect may explain in large measure why laboratory experiments have failed to find withdrawal as a common response to excessively intimate disclosures. In the laboratory context, the subject typically experiences considerable pressure to determine and accede to the "demand characteristics" of the experiment, those subtle cues that define the experimental situation for the subject and suggest to him how a "good subject" should behave. Thus, he utilizes his partner's disclosure as a cue to what sort of behavior is appropriate to the situation and responds in kind. As a result, laboratory studies of disclosure tend to overemphasize those aspects of encounters that evoke modeling and to underemphasize those that are relevant to trust.

After the subject had agreed to participate, the experimenter explained that the class would be comparing the class members' own handwriting with the handwriting of other people. Therefore, the experimenter would write a few sentences about himself or herself in the top box of the response form, labeled "Class Member's Sample." The subject was invited to look at the experimenter's sample and then to write a sentence or two about himself or herself in the bottom box. The "Class Member's Sample" was the device by which I was able to vary the intimacy of the experimenter's self-disclosure to the subject. The "sample" provided by the experimenter was either a non-intimate, moderately intimate, or extremely intimate statement about himself. In all cases the experimenter began by writing his or her name and the fact that he was a junior or senior in college. In the "low intimacy" condition, he proceeded to write: ·

> ... right now I'm in the process of collecting handwriting samples for a school project. I think I will stay here for a while longer, and then call it a day.

In the "medium intimacy" condition he wrote:

> ... Lately I've been thinking about my relationships with other people. I've made several good friends during the past couple of years, but I still feel lonely a lot of the time.

And in the "high intimacy"—or, if you will, "excessively high intimacy"—condition the experimenter wrote:

> ... Lately I've been thinking about how I really feel about myself. I think that I'm pretty well adjusted, but I occasionally have some questions about my sexual adequacy.

The experiment included a further variation. In half the cases within each of the intimacy conditions, the experimenter simply *copied* the message from a card in front of him. It was obvious to the subject that the experimenter was not directing the message to him personally, but rather was working from a prepared script. In the other half of the cases the experimenter pretended to *create* the message especially for the subject. He did not have a cue card in front of him, and he occasionally glanced up at the subject thoughtfully as he wrote. My purpose in setting up this variation was to establish conditions in which the two mechanisms of modeling and of trust would be differentially salient.

When the experimenter copied his message, it presumably furnished the subject with a cue as to what sort of statement would be appropriate to the situation. Since the experimenter was not singling the subject out for his revelation, however, there was little reason for the subject to interpret the experimenter's disclosure as a demonstration of any particular affection or trust. Under these circumstances the subject was relatively unlikely to react suspiciously or defensively to the "extremely high" message. The experimenter was not being excessively forward or indiscreet; he was merely doing his job. Following this reasoning, I predicted that as the intimacy of the experimenter's message varied from "low" to "medium" to "high," the intimacy and length of the subject's own message would correspondingly increase.

When the experimenter seemed to create a unique message for the subject, on the other hand, considerations of trust inevitably entered the picture, supplementing the modeling mechanism. Up to a point the subject might be expected to respond positively to the experimenter's apparent demonstration of affection and trust and, as a result, to disclose himself in return. Thus the reciprocity effect, considering only the low-intimacy and medium-intimacy messages, was expected to be stronger in the "create" than in the "copy" condition. But the high-intimacy message, when delivered in a personal way, might indeed be going too far and consequently should arouse sentiments of mistrust and defensiveness. "After all," a typical subject might think, "it's nice to have a young person confide in you, but this bit on 'sexual adequacy' is really going too far. I wonder what his *real* problem is. I had better write something short and be done with it."

Before revealing the results of the study, let me present a few of the "handwriting samples" provided by subjects, to give you a sense of the ways in which airport passengers responded to the request to write a sentence or two about themselves. Some of the responses were not intimate at all. They were personally uninformative or even evasive:

005[2]   Today is the 29th of October and this is Logan Airport. It is very warm for this time of year especially when waiting for a late airplane.

031   This is the start of a trip to Atlanta and other states in the adjacent area.

047   I've got to go.

Other subjects provided factual information about themselves but did not get into highly intimate revelations:

028   My name is Frank Peterson and I'm a retired police officer. I served for 30 years on the Boston Police department.

---

2. Numbers are the subjects' identification numbers. Names and other potentially identifying information provided by the subjects have been altered.

133   My name is Bertha Schwartz. I am a housewife and very happy.

236   My name is Ronnie, live in Boston—like art, studied at B.U., think handwriting analysis is a great hobby.

Still other subjects did reveal what seemed to be much more personal and private thoughts and feelings:

144   My name is Gloria Baker. I'm a grandmother but I too have been thinking of myself—where I've been—what to do—I too question my identity.

089   I've just been attending Alumna Council at Cooper College—looking ahead to my 40th Reunion. I still feel sexually adequate—never felt otherwise.

197   My name is Thomas O'Day. I'm a 3rd year medical student. Recently I haven't been getting much sleep and have been under extreme pressure; thus, my handwriting is terrible. Generally I am well-adjusted, but 3rd year students have many adjustments to make, and I often question my ability to function under pressure.

It is possible to have raters code the intimacy of these samples with quite good reliability. In some cases, however, interesting patterns emerge quite as clearly, or even more so, simply by using the number of words in the subject's sample as a measure of his or her self-disclosure. This is the measure employed in Figure 1 (page 182). As the graph indicates, the predictions outlined above were very neatly confirmed. In the impersonal, "copy" condition, the length of the subject's statement increased steadily as the intimacy level of the experimenter's statement increased from low to medium to high. The modeling mechanism apparently operated across the entire range of the experimenter's disclosures. In the personal, "create" condition, on the other hand, the length of the subject's statement increased sharply as intimacy of the experimenter's message increased from low to medium, but it dropped off just as sharply as the intimacy of the experimenter's message increased from medium to high.

Lovers and Other Strangers

Although the airport study involved encounters between strangers, I believe that the results contain several lessons about the development of intimate relationships. In every sort of interpersonal relationship, from business partnerships to love affairs, the exchange of self-disclosure plays

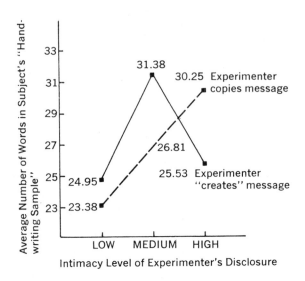

Figure 1   Length of subjects' messages in departure lounge experiment. Each point
represents about 40 subjects. The statistical interaction between the two
experimental factors is significant at the .014 level.

an important role. In some respects this exchange closely resembles other
transactions on the interpersonal marketplace. . . . Just as people may exchange such commodities as approval, assistance, and status, they also
exchange information about their experiences and feelings. But the exchange of self-disclosure is governed by several additional motives and
mechanisms. In some cases, it is not really an exchange at all, even though
the two people are sequentially emitting similar behaviors to one another.
In fact they are not exchanging anything, but instead are imitating or
modeling one another's behavior. Such modeling is an important aspect of
the development of relationships, especially in their early stages. At such
times, when people are tentatively exploring each other's potential as a
friend or lover, they are especially concerned about responding in ways
that are appropriate to the situation, and they frequently do so by picking
up and modeling one another's cues.

At a deeper level, the exchange of personal disclosures is in fact an
exchange of trust. The discloser shows that he likes and trusts the person to
whom he discloses, thereby implying that he might value the establishment of a relationship with him. The person disclosed to must decide how
to respond to this "move" on the part of the discloser. If he is disposed to
keep relations cool, and at the same time to retain a position of relative

power, he may disclose little in return. Knowing more about another person than he knows about you is a way to remain "one-up" in interpersonal relationships.

The Power of Style

Alvin Toffler

Counterculture, alternative life-style, in-group, subculture, identity crisis, liberation group—all these words are indicative of an increasing number of choices as to how one will live. You can probably go to a party and find a hippy who is a former housewife, a couple who were formerly a priest and nun, a radical who is a former reactionary, a businessman who used to be a dropout, and a dropout who used to be a businessman. Each of us has an overwhelming choice of life-styles, and each of those choices carries with it a certain mode of dress, manner of speech, set of values, and so on. Alvin Toffler discusses here the process we go through to make such a choice, and the effect of the pressure of maintaining or changing a life-style.

Of course, not just any life style will do. We live in a Cairo bazaar of competing models. In this psychological phantasmagoria we search for a style, a way of ordering our existence, that will fit our particular temperament and circumstances. We look for heroes or mini-heroes to emulate. The style-seeker is like the lady who flips through the pages of a fashion magazine to find a suitable dress pattern. She studies one after another, settles on one that appeals to her, and decides to create a dress based on it. Next she begins to collect the necessary materials—cloth, thread, piping, buttons, etc. In precisely the same way, the life style creator acquires the necessary props. He lets his hair grow. He buys art nouveau posters and a paperback of Guevara's writings. He learns to discuss Marcuse and Frantz Fanon. He picks up a particular jargon, using words like "relevance" and "establishment."

None of this means that his political actions are insignificant, or that his opinions are unjust or foolish. He may (or may not) be accurate in his views of society. Yet the particular way in which he chooses to express them is ine capably part of his search for personal style.

The lady, in constructing her dress, alters it here and there, deviating from the pattern in minor ways to make it fit her more perfectly. The end product is truly custom-made; yet it bears a striking resemblance to others sewn from the same design. In quite the same way we individualize our style of living, yet it usually winds up bearing a distinct resemblance to some life style model previously packaged and marketed by a subcult.

Often we are unaware of the moment when we commit ourselves to one life style model over all others. The decision to "be" an Executive or a Black Militant or a West Side Intellectual is seldom the result of purely logical analysis. Nor is the decision always made cleanly, all at once. The research scientist who switches from cigarettes to a pipe may do so for health reasons without recognizing that the pipe is part of a whole life style toward which he finds himself drawn. The couple who choose the Tiffany lamp think they are furnishing an apartment; they do not necessarily see their actions as an attempt to flesh out an overall style of life.

Most of us, in fact, do not think of our own lives in terms of life style, and we often have difficulty in talking about it objectively. We have even more trouble when we try to articulate the structure of values implicit in our style. The task is doubly hard because many of us do not adopt a single integrated style, but a composite of elements drawn from several different models. We may choose a cross between West Side Intellectual and Executive—a fusion that is, in fact, chosen by many publishing officials in New York. When one's personal style is a hybrid, it is frequently difficult to disentangle the multiple models on which it is based.

Once we commit ourselves to a particular model, however, we fight energetically to build it, and perhaps even more so to preserve it against challenge. For the style becomes extremely important to us. This is doubly true to the people of the future, among whom concern for style is downright passionate. This intense concern for style is not, however, what literary critics mean by formalism. It is not simply an interest in outward appearances. For style of life involves not merely the external forms of behavior, but the values implicit in that behavior, and one cannot change one's life style without working some change in one's self-image. The people of the future are not "style conscious" but "life style conscious."

This is why little things often assume great significance for them. A single small detail of one's life may be charged with emotional power if it challenges a hard-won life style, if it threatens to break up the integrity of the style. Aunt Ethel gives us a wedding present. We are embarrassed by it, for it is in a style alien to our own. It irritates and upsets us, even though we know that "Aunt Ethel doesn't know any better." We banish it hastily to the top shelf of the closet.

Aunt Ethel's toaster or tableware is not important, in and of itself. But it is a message from a different subcultural world, and unless we are weak in commitment to our own style, unless we happen to be in transition between styles, it represents a potent threat. The psychologist Leon Festinger coined the term "cognitive dissonance" to mean the tendency of a person to reject or deny information that challenges his preconceptions. We don't want to hear things that may upset our carefully worked out structure of beliefs. Similarly, Aunt Ethel's gift represents an element of "stylistic dissonance." It threatens to undermine our carefully worked out style of life.

Why does the life style have this power to preserve itself? What is the source of our commitment to it? A life style is a vehicle through which we express ourselves. It is a way of telling the world which particular subcult or subcults we belong to. Yet this hardly accounts for its enormous importance to us. The real reason why life styles are so significant—and increasingly so as the society diversifies—is that, above all else, the choice of a life style model to emulate is a crucial strategy in our private war against the crowding pressures of overchoice.

Deciding, whether consciously or not, to be "like" William Buckley or Joan Baez, Lionel Trilling or his surfer equivalent, J.J. Moon, rescues us from the need to make millions of minute life-decisions. Once a commitment to a style is made, we are able to rule out many forms of dress and behavior, many ideas and attitudes, as inappropriate to our adopted style. The college boy who chooses the Student Protester Model wastes little energy agonizing over whether to vote for Wallace, carry an attaché case, or invest in mutual funds.

By zeroing in on a particular life style we exclude a vast number of alternatives from further consideration. The fellow who opts for the Motorcyclist Model need no longer concern himself with the hundreds of types of gloves available to him on the open market, but which violate the spirit of his style. He need only choose among the far smaller repertoire of glove types that fit within the limits set by his model. And what is said of gloves is equally applicable to his ideas and social relationships as well.

The commitment to one style of life over another is thus a super-decision. It is a decision of a higher order than the general run of everyday life-decisions. It is a decision to narrow the range of alternatives that will concern us in the future. So long as we operate within the confines of the style we have chosen, our choices are relatively simple. The guidelines are clear. The subcult to which we belong helps us answer any questions; it keeps the guidelines in place.

But when our style is suddenly challenged, when something forces us to reconsider it, we are driven to make another super-decision. We face the painful need to transform not only ourselves, but our self-image as well.

It is painful because, freed of our commitment to any given style, cut adrift from the subcult that gave rise to it, we no longer "belong." Worse yet, our basic principles are called into question and we must face each new life-decision afresh, alone, without the security of a definite, fixed policy. We are, in short, confronted with the full, crushing burden of overchoice again.

A Superabundance of Selves

To be "between styles" or "between subcults" is a life-crisis, and the people of the future spend more time in this condition, searching for styles, than do the people of the past or present. Altering his identity as he goes, super-industrial man traces a private trajectory through a world of colliding subcults. This is the social mobility of the future: not simply movement from one economic class to another, but from one tribal grouping to another. Restless movement from subcult to ephemeral subcult describes the arc of his life.

There are plenty of reasons for this restlessness. It is not merely that the individual's psychological needs change more often than in the past; the subcults also change. For these and other reasons, as subcult membership becomes ever more unstable, the search for a personal style will become increasingly intense, even frenetic in the decades to come. Again and again, we shall find ourselves bitter or bored, vaguely dissatisfied with "the way things are"—upset, in other words, with our present style. At that moment, we begin once more to search for a new principle around which to organize our choices. We arrive again at the moment of super-decision.

At this moment, if anyone studied our behavior closely, he would find a sharp increase in what might be called the Transience Index. The rate of turnover of things, places, people, organizational and informational relationships spurts upward. We get rid of that silk dress or tie, the old Tiffany lamp, that horror of a claw-footed Victorian end table—all those symbols of our links with the subcult of the past. We begin, bit by bit, to replace them with new items emblematic of our new identification. The same process occurs in our social lives—the through-put of people speeds up. We begin to reject ideas we have held (or to explain them or rationalize them in new ways). We are suddenly free of all the constraints that our subcult or style imposed on us. A Transience Index would prove a sensitive indicator of those moments in our lives when we are most free—but, at the same time, most lost.

It is in this interval that we exhibit the wild oscillation engineers call "searching behavior." We are most vulnerable now to the messages of new subcults, to the claims and counterclaims that rend the air. We lean this way and that. A powerful new friend, a new fad or idea, a new political movement, some new hero rising from the depths of the mass media—all these strike us with particular force at such a moment. We are more "open," more uncertain, more ready for someone or some group to tell us what to do, how to behave.

Decisions—even little ones—come harder. This is not accidental. To cope with the pressure of daily life we need more information about far more trivial matters than when we were locked into a firm life style. And so we feel anxious, pressured, alone, and we move on. We choose or allow ourselves to be sucked into a new subcult. We put on a new style.

As we rush toward super-industrialism, therefore, we find people adopting and discarding life styles at a rate that would have staggered the members of any previous generation. For the life style itself has become a throw-away item.

This is no small or easy matter. It accounts for the much lamented "loss of commitment" that is so characteristic of our time. As people shift from subcult to subcult, from style to style, they are conditioned to guard themselves against the inevitable pain of disaffiliation. They learn to armor themselves against the sweet sorrow of parting. The extremely devout Catholic who throws over his religion and plunges into the life of a New Left activist, then throws himself into some other cause or movement or subcult, cannot go on doing so forever. He becomes, to adapt Graham Greene's term, a "burnt out case." He learns from past disappointment never to lay too much of his old self on the line.

And so, even when he seemingly adopts a subcult or style, he withholds some part of himself. He conforms to the group's demands and revels in the belongingness that it gives him. But his belongingness is never the same as it once was, and secretly he remains ready to defect at a moment's notice. What this means is that even when he seems most firmly plugged in to his group or tribe, he listens, in the dark of night, to the short-wave signals of competing tribes.

In this sense, his membership in the group is shallow. He remains constantly in a posture of non-commitment, and without strong commitment to the values and styles of some group he lacks the explicit set of criteria that he needs to pick his way through the burgeoning jungle of overchoice.

The super-industrial revolution, consequently, forces the whole problem of overchoice to a qualitatively new level. It forces us now to make choices not merely among lamps and lampshades, but among lives, not among life style *components*, but among whole life *styles*.

This intensification of the problem of overchoice presses us toward orgies of self-examination, soul-searching, and introversion. It confronts us with that most popular of contemporary illnesses, the "identity crisis." Never before have masses of men faced a more complex set of choices. The hunt for identity arises not out of the supposed choicelessness of "mass society," but precisely from the plenitude and complexity of our choices.

Each time we make a style choice, a super-decision, each time we link up with some particular subcultural group or groups, we make some change in our self-image. We become, in some sense, a different person, and we perceive ourselves as different. Our old friends, those who knew us in some previous incarnation, raise their eyebrows. They have a harder and harder time recognizing us, and, in fact, we experience increasing difficulty in identifying with, or even sympathizing with, our own past selves.

The hippie becomes the straight-arrow executive, the executive becomes the skydiver without noting the exact steps of transition. In the process, he discards not only the externals of his style, but many of his underlying attitudes as well. And one day the question hits him like a splash of cold water in a sleepsodden face: "What remains?" What is there of "self" or "personality" in the sense of a continuous, durable internal structure? For some, the answer is very little. For they are no longer dealing in "self" but in what might be called "serial selves."

Sex Stereotyping in the Secondary School Curriculum

Janice Law Trecker

Traditionally, society has relied on its schools to convey to children society's definition of what reality is all about. Janice Trecker feels that our secondary school curriculum continues the sexual myths and attitudes that encourage young girls to pursue the roles traditionally assigned to them. Strikingly few positive female images and role models are presented in the textbooks used in the secondary schools. Female students are discouraged from taking vocational courses, even though an estimated forty percent of them are currently in the labor force. And there is gross discrimination in the administration and funding of athletic programs for the two sexes. The author seeks profound changes in the schools, shifts that will require the cooperation of teachers, administrators, counselors, educational publishers, and students.

Reprinted by permission of the author and the *Phi Delta Kappan*, October, 1973, pp. 110–112.

One difficulty of dealing with sex bias in the public schools is that the integration of male and female students in most curriculum areas has led to a belief in educational equality. While such blatantly separate and unequal departments as physical education and vocational preparation are rationalized on the grounds of physical and attitudinal differences, other forms of bias are sufficiently subtle to be ignored altogether. At least until quite recently, stereotyped and biased curriculum offerings and materials were complacently accepted as either factually correct or not important enough to make changes worthwhile. The hidden assumption has been that girls, who were after all fortunate enough to have been admitted to secondary facilities over 100 years ago, could be adequately served by materials designed for boys.

Thus the standard in our secondary schools, after decades of coeducation, is still male. Texts and programs are designed to enhance the male self-image, promote identification with male spokesmen and heroes, explore the developmental and intellectual growth of young males, and reveal masculine contributions to our culture. So far as the typical secondary school curriculum is concerned, humanity is masculine. This is evident whether one examines the literary style or graphic design of textbooks, the topics and individuals chosen for consideration and emphasis, the administration of the curriculum, the manner in which students are tracked, or the underlying assumptions of the course offerings. Current curricula and textbooks present perhaps the clearest demonstration of sex prejudice in our schools.

A look at current United States history textbooks, for example, raises the question of how our country has maintained itself with a 99% male population. These books consistently refer only to men, i.e., "our revolutionary forefathers," "the men who conquered the West," or "the men who built our nation." The pictures, photographs, and paintings chosen for inclusion are almost exclusively about male subjects. Women are rarely chosen as spokesmen, and even books with ample sections of documentary material allot women writers and thinkers no more than the most meager space—if any at all. A recent linguistic study of social studies texts, "Equal Treatment of the Sexes in Social Studies Textbooks," by Elizabeth Burr, Susan Dunn, and Norma Farquhar, details the more subtle manifestations of sex bias, including demeaning terms for women, exclusive use of male pronouns and generic terms, and a perpetuation of images of women as fragile and timid.

Nor are history and social studies texts the only offenders. Recently, the New York City Chapter of the National Organization for Women (NOW) prepared a *Report on Sex Bias in the Public Schools*. Josephine Milnar, a contributor to the report, examined a number of junior high school mathematics and science texts. She found that female mathematicians and scientists of note were ignored, and that illustrative and problem-solving materials were consistently characterized by sexual stereotypes. For example, while boys in mathematical problems show a variety of activities—gardening, building, sports, and painting—girls and women were virtually confined to sewing, cooking, and child care. In science books nonbiased texts were frequently accompanied by illustrations showing only males using scientific equipment or solving problems. Considering the large numbers of female students with scientific and mathematical potential who do not pursue careers in these areas, it seems unfortunate that texts and materials do not present young girls with positive female images and role models.

The exclusion of women from pictorial material, the stereotyped descriptions of those who do appear, and the linguistic conventions of the texts show how supposedly objective school texts subtly encourage female students to pursue their traditional roles—the home, silence, and subjection. Any doubt about this message is soon removed by a closer consideration of the topics emphasized in the various curriculum areas. Reviewing virtually any catalogue of supplementary texts and novels for secondary school students reveals how few novels and biographies feature female protagonists. While one can find a plentiful supply of novels built around the experiences of young men and boys from Alabama to Ankor Wat, one is fortunate to find even one-fourth as many dealing with young women. Supplemental texts typically include few biographies of ourstanding women, and in volumes of collected lives, women receive only token representation. Both teachers and publishers seem to assume that males are involved in more interesting and important activities than females and that while girls are willing to read about boys, boys would be unconcerned about female protagonists.

Similar attitudes are evident in the social studies. Topics of particular interest to women are frequently omitted altogether, and the effects of sex bias and sex stereotypes on other problems and topics are ignored. How else can one account for the fact that, even today, young women are largely ignorant of their legal disabilities and of the prejudices they face in education, employment, and public policy, and that the general public remains uninformed about the role of sex bias in social problems? One reason is that very few social studies courses or text materials consider sex-role conditioning, women's current and historic legal status, social and philosophical attitudes toward women, or the connections between these attitudes and women's rights. It would be difficult to argue that citizenship courses are doing an adequate job when they fail to inform all students about the civic and legal disabilities affecting more than half of the student population.

Similarly, it seems difficult to justify the continuing neglect of the part that attitudes toward women play in other contemporary problems. Two-thirds of the adult poor are female, and the vast majority of the welfare population is comprised of women and children. For these reasons, it is impossible to discuss the problems of poverty without consideration of the status of women and of attitudes toward women and children. Similarly, now that 40% of the labor force is female, labor problems and unemployment cannot be explored realistically without consideration of the prospects of working women and of attitudes toward female employment. When women are trained virtually from birth to regard homemaking and child bearing as the primary and, in some cases, the exclusive "feminine" occupations, consideration of social attitudes and female roles would seem mandatory in any discussion of population control or ecology.

The same patterns of omission and neglect are evident in American history texts and courses, and it would be surprising if similar criticisms do not apply to European, Latin-American, and Afro-Asian history courses as well. Such topics as the evolution of the social and legal status of women, the importance of female and child labor in the industrial revolution, women's work in the wars and in social reforms, the women's movement, and the contributions of outstanding women are conspicuous by their absence. The typical U.S. history book generously devotes one out of its 500 to 800 pages to women, their problems, and their contributions. Looking at the typical history texts, the social studies programs, and the secondary school English and humanities reading lists, one must regretfully agree with the Pennsylvania report, "Sexism in Education." The authors, from the Pennsylvania Department of Education, the Human Relations Commission, and a state women's group, concluded that the Pennsylvania public school texts and library materials showed the following weaknesses:

> underrepresentation of women; representation in limited stereotyped roles—wives, mothers, teachers, nurses, secretaries, and other service-oriented jobs; reinforcement of culturally conditioned sexist characteristics showing as *female* such traits as dependency, passivity, noncompetitive spirit, and emotionality; and a very meager appreciation of women's contributions to history, literature, science, and other areas of American life. . . .

In light of current scholarly research on women's history and on the contributions of women to the arts, sciences, and ideas, it is simply no longer adequate to tolerate such weaknesses in American history texts.

Unfortunately, sex bias is not confined to the curriculum per se but extends to its administration and to the rationale of certain courses and procedures, especially with regard to athletics and vocational preparation courses. It would be difficult, for example, to defend most current athletic and physical education programs. In comparison with programs designed for male students, girls' athletic programs receive less money and equipment and show a narrower range in offerings. While some school systems offer no competitive programs for girls at all, many more show vast inequities in funding. *Let Them Aspire*, a report on the Ann Arbor (Michigan) schools, revealed that the budget for boys' interscholastic sports was 10 times as high as the corresponding female budget, a discrepancy by no means unique in this field. The view that boys' sports just happen to be more expensive is a frequent but inadequate justification. While school districts do not hesitate to introduce such costly boys' sports as football and ice hockey, the introduction of comparably expensive girls' activities as show jumping, horseback riding, or figure skating is almost beyond civic contemplation. It is not unusual for girls to be denied the opportunity for swimming, because pool time is limited, or for towns to reject funding for a girls' coaching staff, requiring talented young women either to abandon athletic excellence or to pay for private coaching.

In a number of cases, the neglect of female competitive athletics is paralleled by a neglect of physical education opportunities as well. Testimony from a 1971 New York City court suit against the administration of Junior High School 217 for sex bias included statements that girls were only rarely allowed to use outdoor recreation areas, and they were denied the opportunity to use the school's soccer fields, and that their indoor sports program was inferior in variety and quality to the corresponding boys' program.

Although there are glaring inequities in girls' physical education and athletic programs, they are of minor importance compared to the sexual inequities in vocational and technical education. It is still common practice to track students by sex for vocational training. Such tracking usually begins in the junior high school, where girls are steered into homemaking and boys into industrial arts. Even where sex prerequisites for these courses are absent, vocational training programs reflect rigid notions of appropriate masculine and feminine occupations. Thus females are an overwhelming majority in homemaking, health occupations, and business, while males predominate to an equally striking degree in agriculture, the skilled trades, and the industrial and technical fields. While as many girls as boys (indeed, more, if homemaking is included) receive vocational training on the secondary level, their training prepares them for a very narrow range of occupations, mainly in low-paying women's fields. Nonvocational homemaking courses received the lion's share of federal funds for home economics until very recently, but young women are not prepared in these courses for paid employment but for unpaid labor as housewives.

Whether or not female students are deliberately excluded from vocational schools and courses, these sex divisions are justified on the ground that young girls are not interested in the traditionally masculine fields. Considering the economic disadvantages of their vocational choices—the low wages and worsening economic position of the American woman worker—materials and programs which might enlarge the carer possibilities and raise the aspirations of young women should be a high priority item in any responsible school program. In addition to the legal and administrative changes needed to end tracking by sex, young women and men need information about the status of women in the labor force and about the new career opportunities available to women. Both ERIC and the Women's Bureau distribute informative material on women in the labor force, and the new interest in career education and vocational training will certainly make such material especially pertinent and useful. In perhaps no other area of the curriculum is there more need for non-stereotyped information and for positive role models for young women than in vocational training and career education. There is little doubt that traditional stereotypes about the proper work for women have combined with overt economic discrimination to greatly restrict the aspirations and opportunities of the female secondary school student.

Removal of bias in vocational training goes beyond a simple revision of textbooks and materials. It requires new ways of thinking about the needs of girls and women and revisions in thinking about their capacities. This is true of the curriculum as a whole, as well as of its constituent parts. School programs need to be evaluated from the point of view of female as well as male needs, and the supposition should not automatically be made that these are the same. For example, should the educational program include some form of women's studies, self-defense classes, the inclusion of material on contraception in sex education courses, and non-stereotyped courses about the family and marriage?

The removal of stereotypes and the development of a curriculum which is appropriate for both female and male students is a complex procedure requiring the cooperation of teachers, administrators, counselors, and educational publishers. The role of teachers is especially important. While a few subjects, such as history or science, lend themselves to a relatively small number of standardized texts, othere areas, such as the humanities, literature, family life, and sex education, use such diverse materials as to require the cooperation of several departments and teachers in researching material and evaluating textbooks. In research and evaluation, in creating alternative non-sexist books and materials, and in their dealings with the major textbook houses, policy-making bodies, and the public, teachers and teacher organizations can make major contributions to the elimination of sexual bias in the secondary schools. Hopefully, educators will begin to initiate and support efforts to evaluate school policies, curriculum, and educational materials with regard to sex bias and to work to eradicate stereotyping and bigotry in courses and programs.

A Few Words About Breasts

Nora Ephron

Having an appropriate-looking body is an important concern for most people. Look at how much time and energy is spent on diets and exercise for appearance rather than fitness. Yet one has no control over the development of certain parts of one's body. What you get is what nature gives you. Nora Ephron writes about her personal concerns as she grew into maturity.

I have to begin with a few words about androgyny. In grammar school, in the fifth and sixth grades, we were all tyrannized by a rigid set of rules that supposedly determined whether we were boys or girls. The episode in *Huckleberry Finn* where Huck is disguised as a girl and gives himself away by the way he threads a needle and catches a ball—that kind of thing. We learned that the way you sat, crossed your legs, held a cigarette, and looked at your nails—the way you did these things instinctively was absolute proof of your sex. Now obviously most children did not take this literally, but I did. I thought that just one slip, just one incorrect cross of my legs or flick of an imaginary cigarette ash would turn me from whatever I was into the other thing; that would be all it took, really. Even though I was outwardly a girl and had many of the trappings generally associated with girldom—a girl's name, for example, and dresses, my own telephone, an autograph book—I spent the early years of my adolescence absolutely certain that I might at any point gum it up. I did not feel at all like a girl. I was boyish. I was athletic, ambitious, outspoken, competitive, noisy, rambunctious. I had scabs on my knees and my socks slid into my loafers and I could throw a football. I wanted desperately not to be that way, not to be a mixture of both things, but instead just one, a girl, a definite indisputable girl. As soft and as pink as a nursery. And nothing would do that for me, I felt, but breasts.

I was about six months younger than everyone else in my class, and so for about six months after it began, for six months after my friends had begun to develop (that was the word we used, develop), I was not particularly worried. I would sit in the bathtub and look down at my breasts and know that any day now, any second now, they would start growing like everyone else's. They didn't. "I want to buy a bra," I said to my mother one night. "What for?" she said. My mother was really hateful about bras, and by the time my third sister had gotten to the point where she was ready to want one, my mother had worked the whole business into a comedy routine. "Why not use a Band-Aid instead?" she would say. It was a source of great pride to my mother that she had never even had to wear a brassiere until she had her fourth child, and then only because her gynecologist made her. It was incomprehensible to me that anyone could ever be proud of something like that. It was the 1950s, for God's sake. Jane Russell. Cashmere sweaters. Couldn't my mother see that? "*I am too old to wear an undershirt.*" Screaming. Weeping. Shouting. "Then don't wear an undershirt," said my mother. "But I want to buy a bra." "What for?"

I suppose that for most girls, breasts, brassieres, that entire thing, has more trauma, more to do with the coming of adolescence, with becoming a woman, than anything else. Certainly more than getting your period, although that, too, was traumatic, symbolic. But you could see breasts; they were there; they were visible. Whereas a girl could claim to have her period for months before she actually got it and nobody would ever know the difference. Which is exactly what I did. All you had to do was make a great fuss over having enough nickels for the Kotex machine and walk around clutching your stomach and moaning for three to five days a month about The Curse and you could convince anybody. There is a school of thought somewhere in the women's lib/women's mag/gynecology establishment that claims that menstrual cramps are purely psychological, and I lean toward it. Not that I didn't have them finally. Agonizing cramps, heating-pad cramps, go-down-to-the-school-nurse-and-lie-on-the-cot cramps. But, unlike any pain I had ever suffered, I adored the pain of cramps, welcomed it, wallowed in it, bragged about it. "I can't go. I have cramps." "I can't do that. I have cramps." And most of all, gigglingly, blushingly: "I can't swim. I have cramps." Nobody ever used the hard-core word. Menstruation. God, what an awful word. Never that. "I have cramps."

The morning I first got my period, I went into my mother's bedroom to tell her. And my mother, my utterly-hateful-about-bras mother, burst into tears. It was really a lovely moment, and I remember it so clearly not just because it was one of the two times I ever saw my mother cry on my account (the other was when I was caught being a six-year-old kleptomaniac), but also because the incident did not mean to me what it meant to her. Her little girl, her firstborn, had finally become a woman. That was what she was crying about. My reaction to the event, however, was that I might well be a woman in some scientific, textbook sense (and could at least stop faking every month and stop wasting all those nickels). But in another sense—in a visible sense—I was as androgynous and as liable to tip over into boyhood as ever.

I started with a 28AA bra. I don't think they made them any smaller in those days, although I gather that now you can buy bras for five-year-olds that don't have any cups whatsoever in them; trainer bras they are called. My first brassiere came from Robinson's Department Store in Beverly Hills. I went there alone, shaking, positive they would look me over and smile and tell me to come back next year. An actual fitter took me into the dressing room and stood over me while I took off my blouse and tried the first one on. The little puffs stood out on my chest. "Lean over," said the fitter. (To this day, I am not sure what fitters in bra departments do except to tell you to lean over.) I leaned over, with the fleeting hope that my breasts would miraculously fall out of my body and into the puffs. Nothing.

"Don't worry about it," said my friend Libby some months later, when things had not improved. "You'll get them after you're married."

"What are you talking about?" I said.

"When you get married," Libby explained, "Your husband will touch your breasts and rub them and kiss them and they'll grow."

That was the killer. Necking I could deal with. Intercourse I could deal with. But it had never crossed my mind that a man was going to touch my breasts, that breasts had something to do with all that, petting, my God, they never mentioned petting in my little sex manual about the fertilization of the ovum. I became dizzy. For I knew instantly—as naive as I had been only a moment before—that only part of what she was saying was true: the touching, rubbing, kissing part, not the growing part. And I knew that no one would ever want to marry me. I had no breasts. I would never have breasts.

My best friend in school was Diana Raskob. She lived a block from me in a house full of wonders. English muffins, for instance. The Raskobs were the first people in Beverly Hills to have English muffins for breakfast. They also had an apricot tree in the back, and a badminton court, and a subscription to *Seventeen* magazine, and hundreds of games, like Sorry and Parcheesi and Treasure Hunt and Anagrams. Diana and I spent three or four afternoons a week in their den reading and playing and eating. Diana's mother's kitchen was full of the most colossal assortment of junk food I have ever been exposed to. My house was full of apples and peaches and milk and homemade chocolate-chip cookies—which were nice, and good for you, but-not-right-before-dinner-or-you'll-spoil-your-appetite. Diana's house had nothing in it that was good for you, and what's more, you could stuff it in right up until dinner and nobody cared. Bar-B-Q potato chips (they were the first in them, too), giant bottles of ginger ale, fresh popcorn with melted butter, hot fudge sauce on Baskin-Robbins jamoca ice cream, powdered-sugar doughnuts from Van de Kamp's. Diana and I had been best friends since we were seven; we were about equally popular in school (which is to say, not particularly), we had about the same success with boys (extremely intermittent), and we looked much the same. Dark. Tall. Gangly.

It is September, just before school begins. I am eleven years old, about to enter the seventh grade, and Diana and I have not seen each other all summer. I have been to camp and she has been somewhere like Banff with her parents. We are meeting, as we often do, on the street midway between our two houses, and we will walk back to Diana's and eat junk and talk about what has happened to each of us that summer. I am walking down Walden Drive in my jeans and my father's shirt hanging out and my old red loafers with the socks falling into them and coming toward me is . . . I take a deep breath . . . a young woman. Diana. Her hair is curled and she has a waist and hips and a bust and she is wearing a straight skirt, an article of clothing I have been repeatedly told I will be unable to wear until I have the hips to hold it up. My jaw drops, and suddenly I am crying, crying hysterically, can't catch my breath sobbing. My best friend has betrayed me. She has gone ahead without me and done it. She has shaped up.

Here are some things I did to help:
Bought a Mark Eden Bust Developer.
Slept on my back for four years.
Splashed cold water on them every night because some French actress said in *Life* magazine that that was what *she* did for her perfect bustline.
Ultimately, I resigned myself to a bad toss and began to wear padded bras. I think about them now, think about all those years in high school I went around in them, my three padded bras, every single one of them with different-sized breasts. Each time I changed bras I changed sizes: one week nice perky but not too obtrusive breasts, the next medium-sized slightly pointy ones, the next week knockers, true knockers; all the time, whatever size I was, carrying around this rubberized appendage on my chest that occasionally crashed into a wall and was poked inward and had to be poked outward—I think about all that and wonder how anyone kept a straight face through it. My parents, who normally had no restraints about needling

me—why did they say nothing as they watched my chest go up and down? My friends, who would periodically inspect my breasts for signs of growth and reassure me—why didn't they at least counsel consistency?

And the bathing suits. I die when I think about the bathing suits. That was the era when you could lay an uninhabited bathing suit on the beach and someone would make a pass at it. I would put one on, an absurd swimsuit with its enormous bust built into it, the bones from the suit stabbing me in the rib cage and leaving little red welts on my body, and there I would be, my chest plunging straight downward absolutely vertically from my collarbone to the top of my suit and then suddenly, wham, out came all that padding and material and wiring absolutely horizontally.

Buster Klepper was the first boy who ever touched them. He was my boyfriend my senior year of high school. There is a picture of him in my high-school yearbook that makes him look quite attractive in a Jewish, horn-rimmed-glasses sort of way, but the picture does not show the pimples, which were air-brushed out, or the dumbness. Well, that isn't really fair. He wasn't dumb. He just wasn't terribly bright. His mother refused to accept it, refused to accept the relentlessly average report cards, refused to deal with her son's inevitable destiny in some junior college or other. "He was tested," she would say to me, apropos of nothing, "and it came out a hundred and forty-five. That's near-genius." Had the word "underachiever" been coined, she probably would have lobbed that one at me, too. Anyway, Buster was really very sweet—which is, I know, damning with faint praise, but there it is. I was the editor of the front page of the high-school newspaper and he was editor of the back page; we had to work together, side by side, in the print shop, and that was how it started. On our first date, we went to see *April Love*, starring Pat Boone. Then we started going together. Buster had a green coupe, a 1950 Ford with an engine he had hand-chromed until it shone, dazzled, reflected the image of anyone who looked into it, anyone usually being Buster polishing it or the gas-station attendants he constantly asked to check the oil in order for them to be overwhelmed by the sparkle on the valves. The car also had a boot stretched over the back seat for reasons I never understood; hanging from the rear-view mirror, as was the custom, was a pair of angora dice. A previous girl friend named Solange, who was famous throughout Beverly Hills High School for having no pigment in her right eyebrow, had knitted them for him. Buster and I would ride around town, the two of us seated to the left of the steering wheel. I would shift gears. It was nice.

There was necking. Terrific necking. First in the car, overlooking Los Angeles from what is now the Trousdale Estates. Then on the bed of his parents' cabana at Ocean House. Incredibly wonderful, frustrating necking,

I loved it, really, but no further than necking, please don't, please, because there I was absolutely terrified of the general implications of going-a-step-further with a near-dummy and also terrified of his finding out there was next to nothing there (which he knew, of course; he wasn't that dumb).

I broke up with him at one point. I think we were apart for about two weeks. At the end of that time, I drove down to see a friend at a boarding school in Palos Verdes Estates and a disc jockey played "April Love" on the radio four times during the trip. I took it as a sign. I drove straight back to Griffith Park to a golf tournament Buster was playing in (he was the sixth-seeded teen-age golf player in southern California) and presented myself back to him on the green of the 18th hole. It was all very dramatic. That night we went to a drive-in and I let him get his hand under my protuberances and onto my breasts. He really didn't seem to mind at all.

"Do you want to marry my son?" the woman asked me.

"Yes," I said.

I was nineteen years old, a virgin, going with this woman's son, this big strange woman who was married to a Lutheran minister in New Hampshire and pretended she was gentile and had this son, by her first husband, this total fool of a son who ran the hero-sandwich concession at Harvard Business School and whom for one moment one December in New Hampshire I said—as much out of politeness as anything else—that I wanted to marry.

"Fine," she said. "Now, here's what you do. Always make sure you're on top of him so you won't seem so small. My bust is very large, you see, so I always lie on my back to make it look smaller, but you'll have to be on top most of the time."

I nodded. "Thank you," I said.

"I have a book for you to read," she went on. "Take it with you when you leave. Keep it." She went to the bookshelf, found it, and gave it to me. It was a book on frigidity.

"Thank you," I said.

That is a true story. Everything in this article is a true story, but I feel I have to point out that that story in particular is true. It happened on December 30, 1960. I think about it often. When it first happened, I naturally assumed that the woman's son, my boyfriend, was responsible. I invented a scenario where he had had a little heart-to-heart with his mother and had confessed that his only objection to me was that my breasts were small; his mother then took it upon herself to help out. Now I think I was wrong about the incident. The mother was acting on her own, I think: that was her way of being cruel and competitive under the guise of being helpful and maternal.

You have small breasts, she was saying; therefore you will never make him as happy as I have. Or you have small breasts; therefore you are less woman than I am. She was, as it happens, only the first of what seems to me to be a never-ending string of women who have made competitive remarks to me about breast size. "I would love to wear a dress like that," my friend Emily says to me, "but my bust is too big." Like that. Why do women say these things to me? Do I attract these remarks the way other women attract married men or alcoholics or homosexuals? This summer, for example. I am at a party in East Hampton and I am introduced to a woman from Washington. She is a minor celebrity, very pretty and Southern and blond and outspoken, and I am flattered because she has read something I have written. We are talking animatedly, we have been talking no more than five minutes, when a man comes up to join us. "Look at the two of us," the woman says to the man, indicating me and her. "The two of us together couldn't fill an A cup." Why does she say that? It isn't even true, dammit, so why? Is she even more addled than I am on this subject? Does she honestly believe there is something wrong with her size breasts, which, it seems to me, now that I look hard at them, are just right? Do I unconsciously bring out competitiveness in women? In that form? What did I do to deserve it?

As for men.

There were men who minded and let me know that they minded. There were men who did not mind. In any case, *I* always minded.

And even now, now that I have been countlessly reassured that my figure is a good one, now that I am grown-up enough to understand that most of my feelings have very little to do with the reality of my shape, I am nonetheless obsessed by breasts. I cannot help it. I grew up in the terrible fifties—with rigid stereotypical sex roles, the insistence that men be men and dress like men and women be women and dress like women, the intolerance of androgyny—and I cannot shake it, cannot shake my feelings of inadequacy. Well, that time is gone, right? All those exaggerated examples of breast worship are gone, right? Those women were freaks, right? I know all that. And yet here I am, stuck with the psychological remains of it all, stuck with my own peculiar version of breast worship. You probably think I am crazy to go on like this: here I have set out to write a confession that is meant to hit you with the shock of recognition, and instead you are sitting there thinking I am thoroughly warped. Well, what can I tell you? If I had had them, I would have been a completely different person. I honestly believe that.

After I went into therapy, a process that made it possible for me to tell total strangers at cocktail parties that breasts were the hang-up of my life, I was often told that I was insane to have been bothered by my condition. I was also frequently told, by close friends, that I was extremely boring on the subject. And my girl friends, the ones with nice big breasts, would go on endlessly about how their lives had been far more miserable than mine. Their bra straps were snapped in class. They couldn't sleep on their stomachs. They were stared at whenever the word "mountain" cropped up in geography. And *Evangeline*, good God what they went through every time someone had to stand up and recite the Prologue to Longfellow's *Evangeline*: ". . . stand like druids of eld . . . / With beards that rest on their bosoms." It was much worse for them, they tell me. They had a terrible time of it, they assure me. I don't know how lucky I was, they say.

I have thought about their remarks, tried to put myself in their place, considered their point of view. I think they are full of shit.

9 The Self in Conflict

Not all of our enemies are outside forces. In addition to masks we choose or have forced on us, each of us is continually struggling with a whole host of internal forces: negative attitudes, doubts, fears, unfulfilled dreams, self-hatred, and contradictory expressions of Selfhood.

Some of these enemies within produce only minor impasses in the Struggle for Significant Selfhood. Others produce more serious consequences, some of which hurt us very badly. Sometimes the conflict eats into the very being of an individual and he or she lives a crippled, partially fulfilled existence. The latter situation is sometimes called "mental or emotional illness."

It's important to remember that some of these internalized conflicts are self-chosen and self-imposed. Many of us find it easier to carry a load of doubt or guilt or unresolved hostility than to let it out for resolution. Often it's a matter of childhood training or religious teaching. Whatever the causes or the reasons, these dammed-up conflicts often limit our self-fulfillment and the actualization of our potential for Significant Selfhood.

In the first selection, psychologist Rollo May tells us the tale of a man who was imprisoned in a cage as an experiment to determine how a human would react in such a situation. The story, a parable of sorts, should hold real meaning for those of us who live in "cages" of various kinds in exchange for a given amount of security.

In the second selection, "Coping," Wendell Johnson and Dorothy Moeller give some sound advice on how to define and conceptualize a personal conflict in order to successfully cope with it.

*The last reading is the vivid story of a
sixteen-year-old schizophrenic girl named Deborah,
from Hannah Green's novel,* I Never Promised You a
Rose Garden. *In this excerpt, Deborah is struggling to
escape the pull of the fantasy world she has created in
order to blot out a too-painful reality.*

The Man Who Was Put in a Cage

Rollo May

*Rather than try to explain anything about this article, we will
simply let the author introduce it himself.*

> What a piece of work is a man! how noble in reason! how
> infinite in faculty! in form and moving how express and admira-
> ble! . . . The paragon of animals!
>
> —Shakespeare, *Hamlet*

We have quite a few discrete pieces of information these days about
what happens to a person when he is deprived of this or that element of
freedom. We have our studies of sensory deprivation and of how a person reacts when put in different kinds of authoritarian atmosphere, and
so on. But recently I have been wondering what pattern would emerge if
we put these various pieces of knowledge together. In short, what would
happen to a living, whole person if his total freedom—or as nearly total
as we can imagine—were taken away? In the course of these reflections a
parable took form in my mind.

The story begins with a king who, while standing in reverie at the
window of his palace one evening, happened to notice a man in the
town square below. He was apparently an average man, walking home at
night, who had taken the same route five nights a week for many years.
The king followed this man in his imagination—pictured him arriving
home, perfunctorily kissing his wife, eating his late meal, inquiring
whether everything was all right with the children, reading the paper,
going to bed, perhaps engaging in the sex relation with his wife or
perhaps not, sleeping, and getting up and going off to work again the
next day.

From *Psychiatry* 15 (1952): 469-472. Copyright © 1952 by The William Alanson White
Psychiatric Foundation, Inc. Reprinted by special permission of The William Alanson
White Psychiatric Foundation, Inc.

And a sudden curiosity seized the king, which for a moment banished his fatigue: "I wonder what would happen if a man were kept in a cage, like the animals at the zoo?" His curiosity was perhaps in some ways not unlike that of the first surgeons who wondered what it would be like to perform a lobotomy on the human brain.

So the next day the king called in a psychologist, told him of his idea, and invited him to observe the experiment. When the psychologist demurred saying, "It's an unthinkable thing to keep a man in a cage," the monarch replied that many rulers had in effect, if not literally, done so, from the time of the Romans through Genghis Khan down to Hitler and the totalitarian leaders; so why not find out scientifically what would happen? Furthermore, added the king, he had made up his mind to do it whether the psychologist took part or not; he had already gotten the Greater Social Research Foundation to give a large sum of money for the experiment, and why let that money go to waste? By this time the psychologist also was feeling within himself a great curiosity about what would happen if a man were kept in a cage.

And so the next day the king caused a cage to be brought from the zoo—a large cage that had been occupied by a lion when it was new, then later by a tiger; just recently it had been the home of a hyena who died the previous week. The cage was put in an inner private court in the palace grounds, and the average man whom the king had seen from the window was brought and placed therein. The psychologist, with his Rorschach and Wechsler-Bellevue tests in his brief case to administer at some appropriate moment, sat down outside the cage.

At first the man was simply bewildered, and he kept saying to the psychologist, "I have to catch the tram, I have to get to work, look what time it is, I'll be late for work!" But later on in the afternoon the man began soberly to realize what was up, and then he protested vehemently, "The king can't do this to me! It is unjust! It's against the law." His voice was strong, and his eyes full of anger. The psychologist liked the man for his anger, and he became vaguely aware that this was a mood he had encountered often in people he worked with in his clinic. "Yes," he realized, "this anger is the attitude of people who—like the healthy adolescents of any era—want to fight what's wrong, who protest directly against it. When people come to the clinic in this mood, it is good—they can be helped."

During the rest of the week the man continued his vehement protests. When the king walked by the cage, as he did every day, the man made his protests directly to the monarch.

But the king answered, "Look here, you are getting plenty of food, you have a good bed, and you don't have to work. We take good care of you; so why are you objecting?"

After some days had passed, the man's protests lessened and then ceased. He was silent in his cage, generally refusing to talk. But the psychologist could see hatred glowing in his eyes. When he did exchange a few words, they were short, definite words uttered in the strong, vibrant, but calm voice of the person who hates and knows whom he hates.

Whenever the king walked into the courtyard, there was a deep fire in the man's eyes. The psychologist thought, "This must be the way people act when they are first conquered." He remembered that he had also seen that expression of the eyes and heard that tone of voice in many patients at his clinic: the adolescent who had been unjustly accused at home or in school and could do nothing about it; the college student who was required by public and campus opinion to be a star on the gridiron, but was required by his professors to pass courses he could not prepare for if he were to be successful in football—and who was then expelled from college for the cheating that resulted. And the psychologist, looking at the active hatred in the man's eyes, thought, "It is still good; a person who has this fight in him can be helped."

Every day the king, as he walked through the courtyard, kept reminding the man in the cage that he was given food and shelter and taken good care of, so why did he not like it? And the psychologist noticed that, whereas at first the man had been entirely impervious to the king's statements, it now seemed more and more that he was pausing for a moment after the king's speech—for a second the hatred was postponed from returning to his eyes—as though he were asking himself if what the king said were possibly true.

After a few weeks more, the man began to discuss with the psychologist how it was a useful thing that a man is given food and shelter; and how a man had to live by his fate in any case, and the part of wisdom was to accept fate. He soon was developing an extensive theory about security and the acceptance of fate, which sounded to the psychologist very much like the philosophical theories that Rosenberg and others worked out for the fascists in Germany. He was very voluble during this period, talking at length, although the talk was mostly a monologue. The psychologist noticed that his voice was flat and hollow as he talked, like the voice of people in TV previews who make an effort to look you in the eye and try hard to sound sincere as they tell you that you should see the program they are advertising, or the announcers on the radio who are paid to persuade you that you should like highbrow music.

And the psychologist also noticed that now the corners of the man's mouth always turned down, as though he were in some gigantic pout.

Then the psychologist suddenly remembered: this was like the middle-aged, middle-class people who came to his clinic, the respectable bourgeois people who went to church and lived morally but who were always full of resentment, as though everything they did was conceived, born, and nursed in resentment. It reminded the psychologist of Nietzsche's saying that the middle class was consumed with resentment. He then for the first time began to be seriously worried about the man in the cage, for he knew that once resentment gets a firm start and becomes well rationalized and structuralized, it may become like cancer. When the person no longer knows whom he hates, he is much harder to help.

During this period the Greater Social Research Foundation had a board of trustees meeting, and they decided that since they were expending a fund to keep a man supported in a cage, it would look better if representatives of the Foundation at least visited the experiment. So a group of people, consisting of two professors and a few graduate students, came in one day to look at the man in the cage. One of the professors then proceeded to lecture to the group about the relation of the autonomic nervous system and the secretions of the ductless glands to human existence in a cage. But it occurred to the other professor that the verbal communications of the victim himself might just possibly be interesting, so he asked the man how he felt about living in a cage. The man was friendly toward the professors and students and explained to them that he had chosen this way of life, and there were great values in security and in being taken care of, that they would of course see how sensible his course was, and so on.

"How strange!" thought the psychologist, "and how pathetic; why is it he struggles so hard to get them to approve his way of life?"

In the succeeding days when the king walked through the courtyard, the man fawned upon him from behind the bars in his cage and thanked him for the food and shelter. But when the king was not in the yard and the man was not aware that the psychologist was present, his expression was quite different—sullen and morose. When his food was handed to him through the bars by the keeper, the man would often drop the dishes or dump over the water and then would be embarrassed because of his stupidity and clumsiness. His conversation became increasingly one-tracked; and instead of the involved philosophical theories about the value of being taken care of, he had gotten down to simple sentences such as "It is fate," which he would say over and over again, or he would just mumble to himself, "It is." The psychologist was surprised to find that the man should now be so clumsy as to drop his food, or so stupid as to talk in those barren sentences, for he knew from his tests that the man had originally been of good average intelligence. Then it dawned upon the psychologist that this was the kind of behavior he had observed in some anthropological studies among the Negroes in the South—people who had been forced to kiss the hand that fed and enslaved them, who could no longer either hate or rebel. The man in the cage took more and more to simply sitting all day long in the sun as it came through the bars, his only movement being to shift his position from time to time from morning through the afternoon.

It was hard to say just when the last phase set in. But the psychologist became aware that the man's face now seemed to have no particular expression; his smile was no longer fawning, but simply empty and meaningless, like the grimace a baby makes when there is gas in its stomach. The man ate his food and exchanged a few sentences with the psychologist from time to time; but his eyes were distant and vague, and though he looked at the psychologist, it seemed that he never really *saw* him.

And now the man, in his desultory conversations, never used the word "I" any more. He had accepted the cage. He had no anger, no hate, no rationalizations. But he was now insane.

The night the psychologist realized this, he sat in his apartment trying to write a concluding report. But it was very difficult for him to summon up words, for he felt within himself a great emptiness. He kept trying to reassure himself with the words, "They say that nothing is ever lost, that matter is merely changed to energy and back again." But he could not help feeling that something *had* been lost, that something had gone out of the universe in this experiment.

He finally went to bed with his report unfinished. But he could not sleep; there was a gnawing within him which, in less rational and scientific ages, would have been called a conscience. Why didn't I tell the king that this is the one experiment that no man can do—or at least why didn't I shout that I would have nothing to do with the whole bloody business? Of course, the king would have dismissed me, the foundations would never have granted me any more money, and at the clinic they would have said that I was not a real scientist. But maybe one could farm in the mountains and make a living, and maybe one could paint or write something that would make future men happier and more free. . . .

But he realized that these musings were, at least at the moment, unrealistic, and he tried to pull himself back to reality. All he could get, however, was this feeling of emptiness within himself, and the words, "Something has been taken out of the universe, and there is left only a void."

Finally he dropped off to sleep. Some time later, in the small hours of the morning, he was awakened by a startling dream. A crowd of people had gathered, in the dream, in front of the cage in the courtyard, and the man in the cage—no longer inert and vacuous—was shouting through the bars of the cage in impassioned oratory. "It is not only I whose freedom is taken away!" he was crying. "When the king put me or any man in a cage, the freedom of each one of you is taken away also. The king must go!" The people began to chant, "The king must go!" and they seized and broke out the iron bars of the cage, and wielded them for weapons as they charged the palace.

The psychologist awoke, filled by the dream with a great feeling of hope and joy—an experience of hope and joy probably not unlike that experienced by the free men of England when they forced King John to sign the Magna Charta. But not for nothing had the psychologist had an orthodox analysis in the course of his training, and as he lay surrounded by this aura of happiness, a voice spoke within him: "Aha, you had this dream to make yourself feel better; it's just a wish fulfillment."

"The hell it is!" said the psychologist as he climbed out of bed. "Maybe some dreams are to be acted on."

Coping

Wendell Johnson and Dorothy Moeller

Recent years have seen a number of performances of a musical with the intriguing title "Don't Bother Me; I Can't Cope." Coping in that setting meant getting along in the midst of all the problems of today's world. Many psychologists go beyond that in their definition, to include dealing productively and in a healthy, growing way with the problems of everyday life and one's own hangups.

In this excerpt, Johnson and Moeller propose that the first and most essential step in beginning to "cope" with any problem—whether internal or external—is to recognize and describe it. Only then, they say, can you begin to deal with it successfully.

We find, I think, that we cannot explain most problems by talking about one person. We can't explain much of anything this way, even though that still is the language we commonly use. Listen and you will hear it. It just makes for no end of confusion and misunderstanding, talking about each person as though he were alone with his problem, as though he were helpless in the face of outside forces, or as though within his skin he had everything that would account for his difficulties. No. The family is part of the problem. The neighborhood is part of it, and, in a rather meaningful sense of the word, very often civilization itself is part of it. The individual is doing something that he or someone else regards as a problem, but the patient is always the family or some other grouping of people. There are no delinquent children. There are delinquent societies. There are no stuttering children. There are stuttering interactions among persons and a child can get caught in them. Nobody comes to the clinic alone even though he is the only person sitting across the desk from his counselor. Everybody brings people and values of his culture with him.

There is this folk mind. We all share it. Parents share it. Teachers share it. Doctors share it. You can't find anybody who doesn't share it. Occasionally you will find someone who has discovered this, someone who knows what almost nobody else knows—that he is giving voice to what almost all men say. Most of us are not aware of this. But in the clinic we try to be.

So the question becomes not "Problem, problem, who's got the problem?" but "Who are the members of this problem?" Very often the individual who comes to the clinic, or who is sent, is the least powerful of all the members of the problem, the least able to do anything about the problem, and the last one who should be engaged in therapy. It could be, and often is, a form of very bad cruelty to treat him—especially if he is a child—because we then are asking him to take on his shoulders his whole problem, which has many other members, all bigger and older and more powerful than he. I think the same thing holds very often in the schools, in our other institutions, and in society generally. We are spanking the wrong bottom much of the time.

I think we need to examine very carefully our whole idea of punishment, and particularly our idea of the necessity of punishment, which has been handed down to us through the centuries, a complex orientation made up of many strands. Just who is to be punished and why and by whom? The members of the problem are behaving as they do under the influence of a culture and environment—social environment, semantic environment, an environment of values and meaning, attitudes, accepted statements that we call *morality*, statements having to do with what we call *right* and *wrong*, and so on. Everyone is caught up in this. And this we try to understand, and work from, in the clinic.

Those are the kinds of things I try to help my counselee consider. The questions I furnish I try to direct in this way. And my experience in doing this with many people these many years has convinced me that people want very much to think for themselves. I believe that every normal young person—well, any person of any age but here I think especially of today's restless and questing young people—wants very much to answer his own questions for himself. He doesn't want to be given answers. But he does want companionship and encouragement in searching for answers on his own. And by answers I mean formulations that lead to other and better questions.

The second thing I can do as a counselor is to share with my counselee such information and insights as I may have come by regarding procedures and techniques of coping. I offer him these. I make these available to him. But he must choose. Each counselee, every person with a problem, must choose what part, if any, he wishes to accept. After all, I can't move his muscles. I can't turn on his motivation. He must do this. What he does will be meaningful to him only if he feels he is doing it for his own purposes. It would be by mere accident that my purposes would coincide with his.

I think most people do what they do because they don't know what else to do. We keep on doing the things we are used to doing. I think this is the way most people are about most things that they might try to change about themselves to their advantage. They never get around it it because they are already doing other things and on top of that they wouldn't know how to make the decision they would have to make in order to do something else. They wouldn't know how to decide what to do. They lack information and techniques and procedures. As I see it, we do what is the most satisfying to us within the limits of our knowledge about what we might do. We take those known alternatives which are most satisfying to us. This is something to be investigated and evaluated on the basis of experience, it seems to me.

So I find it useful to explore with my counselees the matters we have been discussing here—basically, the concept of abstracting as a process, the ways we can borrow from science to make the process work, and the pathologies [illnesses] that are associated with dysfunctions of the process. I talk about the relation of talking to living, the map-and-territory idea, the answerability of questions, the scientific method, the neutrality of facts, et cetera. My counselee and I consider the words that are sort of misguided missiles, misguided verbal missiles that are not descriptive at all. They are, instead, projective of those rationalizations that seem necessary to us, necessary at least as long as we are not clear as to what we are talking about.

Then the third of the three things that as a counselor I can do for my counselee is this. When he has done his best, I can do one thing more. I can accept him. I can be a representative of all the millions of people who would accept him. And so, I tell him, I hope that he can accept himself.

I am convinced that this idea holds through the whole range of relatively subtle handicaps that most of us have, this great mass of us out here in the middle. However, it is more easily explored, I suppose, in terms of a problem that involves some grave and observable impairment. I think of a blind boy, for example. He came to me in the clinic not long ago. He has various problems. We are working on them. And some of them I think we will be able to manage pretty well. We can cope quite creatively with them. He can learn to use the scientific method, he can get his language in order, he can learn to get about using a cane or a dog or some other aid, he can go to school and prepare himself for a job, et cetera. Yet when everything has been done that can be done, there remains the blindness. He will still be blind. We shall have need for something to do when there is nothing to do. We shall have need for techniques of forbearance, techniques of compassion, techniques of self-acceptance: You do the best you can do and then when there is nothing more that you can do, you do this—you accept the rest. You learn to live with grace with your limitations. This is an art. This is a method too. And there is nothing bland about it. This is not an excuse mechanism. . . . It means facing reality. And it is based on the premise that you do the best you can do. That comes first.

Well, the question is: What *is* the best you can do? I suppose part of the answer depends on whether you see the glass as half-full or half-empty, as the old saying goes. But it seems to me that the heart of the answer is to be found in using a functional definition of normal. From the clinical point of view, a functional definition is basic. And that is why in the clinic we take great pains to define normal for each individual. An individual's par is normal for him. It is his unique and reasonable expectation.

A functional definition is the kind a good mechanic uses when he sizes up your ailing car. He doesn't say every car must run like a Cadillac, or a Porsche, or whatever, and therefore yours must too if it is operating normally. He checks the make and the model and he asks about gas mileage, engine performance, and things like that. He figures out what you can expect from such a car and if it is performing up to that expectation then it is operating normally. Normal for that wreck may be something pretty peculiar but it is normal for that wreck. A functional definition, here as with people, does something about expectations and evaluations and all the rest.

A common form of cruelty in our society, I think, is in defining normal to mean "like me." You know, you're normal if you're like me and you are not normal if you are not like me—either-or. This attitude filters down even to the way we fuss at little girls not to be chubby and not to get dirty, and we fix their hair as if to say, "You look terrible but I like you so I'll take time and I'll try to make you look like me if you'll just hold still." This is obviously not very constructive, any more than it is to act as if the crippled child were really not much good until he could run. But we do this all the time. The need is not for the crippled to run and the blind to see, or for you and me to sing like Marian Anderson. The need is to do the best we can with what we have, and to accept the rest.

The best we can do is probably very good indeed. I think it is usually a great deal more than we are doing. Whatever it is, I can see no sense in going around judging ourselves inferior to others. I see no harm in being even a little bit cocky at times. If there is some basis for feeling inferior, well, fine, accept it. But remember that nobody is inferior in everything. I can't sing like Marian Anderson but I can do a fine job of listening to her. That is much better than moping around because I can't sing. There are a lot of things all of us can't do. This doesn't mean we have to feel inferior. This just means we are not the people who do that. Everybody is different. How can we be inferior to ourselves? This is silly. Well, let's be ourselves to the hilt. The main thing is to be realistic. Don't exaggerate either way. Be the thing that you are but be a good one. If you are a plump woman, don't moon about it or pretend to be slender. Be plump. Face the fact that you are plump. Be a good, authentic, plump woman.

If you are deaf, and if that is a very important thing about you, well, tell people. Don't hide it. If ever a hearing aid was developed that you really couldn't detect at all, I think I would be against it. To make the hearing aid invisible is to destroy a large part of the value of having it. You probably have heard about the fellow who wore a shoebutton in his ear. It worked fine. People talked louder and that was all he needed.

People's degree of self-acceptance and their acceptance in general seem to me to be related. Those who reject books, plays, people, television, and new ideas tend to reject themselves too, whereas those who accept these things tend to accept themselves as well. In that strange and fascinating and somehow peculiarly human profession we call *politics*, I observe that some of the most successful people appear to be not exceptional but seem to have an awfully sure sense of what is acceptable about themselves. And they seem to have an awfully sure sense that the most acceptable thing about any individual is his own self-acceptance. And so Harry Truman could come out of a clothing store and run the country. He didn't pretend to be anybody but just old Harry. And that has an appeal to people. Somebody has said that people love us more for our little faults than for our virtues. Anybody who thinks probably knows this—as basic wisdom—but the more I work with people the more I am convinced that few people think. They read the ads and they try to look and act like the men of distinction, or whatever the current wording for that idea happens to be. But think? No. Be themselves? Well, not as much as they might, I fear, and I find that sad. If only they could accept themselves.

So I try to do these three things for my counselee: I try to serve as an empathic eavesdropper who furnishes clarifying questions; I try to give him information about matters related to his problem and try to make available to him such procedures and techniques as I may know; and, finally, after he has done the best he can do, I accept him.

I am convinced there is a way to cope with any problem. It is first recognizing what the problem is in terms of nonverbal reality, then stating it so clearly and so concisely that you have directed yourself toward changing what can be changed. And when you have changed what can be changed, you learn to accept the rest. That is, you accept what you must accept until you can state more clearly and more concisely the problem as you now see it. Then you go on to make another change. And you accept the rest until you can state it more clearly, et cetera, et cetera. You are behaving scientifically. You are engaged in productive behavior.

I have observed that as people really get interested in this approach to their problems, that is, interested in abstracting in the context of counseling, they discover in a way they had hardly noticed before that language, indeed, is the basis on which many important relationships are made. As they come to understand their blockages and their glibnesses they begin to develop hypotheses that they didn't know were possible. This can be almost unnerving because language behavior is subject to very great modification which, if carried through into their other behaviors, can change their life greatly. And this is something to adjust to.

It seems to me that the way man clarifies or beclouds his outlook on the world by his symbolic representation of that world, the way he thus stimulates and encourages or depresses and discourages himself and those around him, is for our major purposes the most important thing about him.

We may hear ourselves referring to the problems of our day as economic, or perhaps political, or maybe we say they are cultural, ecological, demographic, scientific, or spiritual. Or we say they are problems of maladjustment, anxiety, delinquency, violence, criminal behavior, disease, dis-ease, or whatever. Perhaps we speak of them too in some such terms as the social pathologies associated with urbanization, automation, the technologies of transportation, communication, weaponry, and all that. Since not one of these problems, except perhaps in extremely simple form, plagues any form of life but man, and since man is unique in the richness of his ability to symbolize, it seems to me difficult to escape the conclusion that symbolizing has something vital to do with both our triumphs and our difficulties. As I see it, then, nearly all the ways in which we can work on our problems, that is, make ourselves different from the way we are now, have to do directly or indirectly with our patterns of thinking and feeling, our attitudes and beliefs, our evaluations. And for me these reduce essentially to the symbols we make and the ways we use them.

from *I Never Promised You a Rose Garden*

Hannah Green

Deborah Blau is sixteen. She is a girl who lives in two worlds; she has been diagnosed schizophrenic. In her need to escape from reality's tortures, she fantasizes a kingdom in which she is at first a princess. In the Kingdom of Yr, there are gods and demons and people like the Collect. In the process of treatment, she gradually allows her therapist, Dr. Fried, to know about the Kingdom of Yr. The doctor's name in Yri is Furii, meaning "Fire-Touch." As Dr. Fried becomes closer to Deborah, the girl finds the creatures of Yr gradually turning on her, punishing her for her "betrayal."

Dr. Fried hasn't promised that life in the "real world" would be an easy thing, certainly not "a rose garden," but she has promised to be with her, to help her learn how to face the rough parts.

In this excerpt we find Deborah experiencing the early conflicts of giving up life in Yr and taking a fuller part in the world of reality.

For Deborah, the backfires became the only way of easing the pressure of the stifled volcano inside her. She continued to burn the same places over and over, setting layers of burns on top of one another. Cigarette butts and matches were easy to obtain, although they were supposedly guarded with great care; even D ward's precautions were no match for the intensity of her need. Because the effects of the burnings lasted only an hour or so and because she could only bear the building up of pressure for three or four hours, she had to have a large supply of used cigarettes and the matches to relight them.

For a few days the wounds remained secret, even though she had to change the site of the burning when they began to infect and drain. She was amused but not surprised at how oblivious the nurses and attendants were. The wounds drained and stank and no one noticed. She thought: It's because they don't really want to look at us.

At the end of the week, the new doctor came up to the ward again. "You look a lot better," he said, stopping by Deborah in the dayroom.

"I ought to," she said a little acidly, "I had to work like hell to keep it up."

"Well, with such an improvement, you should be ready to go back to B ward very soon."

When she heard this, she realized that B ward, with its unprotected time and free matches, was a perfect chance for the death she thought she wanted. Then she noticed that she was terrified, and wondered why. If he was letting her die as she wished, why was she angry?

"I have some more burns," she said simply.

He looked shocked, recovered quickly, and said, "I'm glad you told me."

She began to pull on her sweater, twisting it like wet laundry in her hands. *If I want to die, what am I saving myself for?* she demanded, still angry at the mental image of him permitting her to burn herself to death on B ward.

You told him because you are a coward! the Collect said. They began the old jibes again.

"How is the old sore?" the doctor said, loosening the bandaged place. She did not answer him because he was seeing for himself. The burn was stubbornly refusing to heal. "You haven't done any more to this?" he asked, a little bit accusingly and afraid to make it stronger.

"No," she said.

"We'll try another kind of bandage. Let me see the new burn." He looked at the other arm. "How many times did you burn this?"

"About eight."

He bandaged both places and left, no doubt to scold the nurses about the carelessness of leaving dangerous, fire-making materials on the ward. The burning cigarette he left behind him in the dayroom was long enough for two series of burnings.

When the lawgivers of D ward discovered that its patients were not so safe as they had thought, they swept the ward up and down with reforms to widen still further the distance between themselves and the patients. The fork that had been introduced on "D" a year before was now rescinded. The Age of Metal gave way to the Age of Wood and fire prevailed only within the precincts of the nursing station, the modern era. In the pleistocene beyond, *Pithecanthropus erectus* shambled and muttered gibberish, ate with its fingers, and wet on the floor.

"Thanks a lot, kid," Lee Miller said sarcastically as she walked past Deborah into the lighted place where Modern Man supplied the patients with his status symbols—cigarette and match.

"Go to Hell," Deborah answered, but her tone lacked conviction. Later, the Wife of the Abdicated accused her of being a spy and in league with the Secretary of the Interior, and as Deborah already knew, the Secretary of the Interior was one of the worst Enemies.

Getting matches and butts now became difficult, but by no means impossible. Modern Man was careless with the fire-tipped cylinders he burned and breathed, and waiting beside him was a fire-hungry primitive whose gray and flat world magically included the cigarette in sharp focus, color, small, and three dimensions of form.

But firing back at the volcano did not change its surface, its granite garment, as Anterrabae called it. And gods and Collect and Censor were wildly and inexplicably free with the Punishment. Even the logic of Yr seemed to have been erased and the laws overturned. Deborah began to believe that the volcano would erupt and explode. She remembered that the Last Deception had not yet come.

The days had long since become an Earth-form that was only a grammatical nicety. She woke up in one of them and found herself in pack, as so often before. A key turned in the lock of the door and a nurse entered. Behind the nurse, looking unbelievably different because she had not changed at all, stood Furii.

"All right," she said, and came in. The nurse brought a chair for her, and Deborah began to wish that she might escape the woman's face and the disgust she saw in it. Furii looked all around, sat beside the bed, and nodded with a kind of awe.

"My goodness!"

"You're back," Deborah said. The self-hate, terror, shame, pity, vanity, and despair never crossed the stone surface. "Did you have a good time?"

"My goodness," Furii repeated. "What happened? You were doing very well when I left, and now, back here. . . . " She looked around again.

Deborah was afraid of the joy she felt in seeing Furii alive. She said, "You've seen this . . . awfulness before; why are you so shocked?"

"Yes, I have seen it. I am only sorry to see you in it, and suffering so much."

Deborah closed her eyes. She was stricken with shame and she wanted to escape to the Pit, to be dark and blank, but Furii was back and there was no hiding place. Her mind held. "I didn't know you were coming."

"It is the day I said I would be back," Furii said.

"It is?"

"It is, and I think maybe you got in this bad shape to tell me how angry you are that I went off and left you."

"That's not true—" Deborah said. "I tried with Royson—I really did, but you were dead—at least I thought you were—and he wanted only to prove how right he was and how smart. I forgot that you would come back. . . ."

She began to thrash again, even though she was exhausted. "I'm all stopped and closed . . . like it was before I came here . . . only the volcano is burning hotter and hotter while the surface doesn't even know if it is alive or not!"

The doctor moved closer. "It is one of these times," she said quietly, "when what you say is most important."

Deborah pushed her head hard into the bed. "I can't even sort them out—the words."

"Well then, just let it come to us."

"Are you that strong?"

"We are both that strong."

Deborah took a breath. "I am poisonous and I hate it. I am going to be destroyed in shame and degradation and I hate it. I hate myself and the deceivers. I hate my life and my death. For my truth the world gives only lies; I tried with Royson time after time, but I saw that all he wanted was to be right. He might as well have said, 'Come to your senses and stop the silliness'—what they said for the years and years when I was disappointing them on the surface and lying to them with the inmost part of Yr and me and the enemy soldier. God curse me! God curse me!"

A soft scraping sound, a breathed rasp, came after, as she tried to cry, but the sound of it was so ridiculous and ugly that she soon stopped.

"Maybe when I leave," Furii said, "you can learn to cry. For now, let me say this: measure the hate you feel now, and the shame. That quantity is your capacity also to love and to feel joy and to have compassion. Also, I will see you tomorrow."

She left.

That evening Miss Coral came to Deborah holding a book. "Look," she said timidly, "my doctor has left this with me. It is a book of plays and I wondered if perhaps you might not wish to read them with me."

Deborah looked over at Helene, who was sitting against the wall. Had Helene been offering the book, she would have kicked it across the floor to Deborah, perhaps with a taunt. Did any two people, even in the World, speak the same language?

As she answered, Deborah could hear herself mirroring some of Miss Coral's elaborate form of speech and also her shyness. "Which one would you prefer?" Miss Coral asked. They began to read *The Importance of Being Earnest,* with Deborah doing most of the men and Miss Coral doing most of the women. Soon Lee and Helene and Fiorentini's Mary were reading, too. With the actors parodying themselves, the play was uproarious. Mary, laugh and all, was Ernest as a well-born bedlamite, while Miss Coral as Sybil reeked with magnolias and spiderwebs. Oscar Wilde's urbane and elegant comedy was being presented on the nightmare canvas of Hieronymus Bosch. They read the whole play through, and then another, aware that the attendants were laughing with them as well as at them, and thinking, for all the fear it caused, that it was a good night; one which, magically, was not included in their damnation.

Esther Blau faced Doctor Fried unable to speak. Then she cleared her throat.

"Did I understand you correctly?"

"I think so, but first——"

"Why! Why?"

"We are attempting to find out why."

"Can't you find out *before* she's burnt up!"

Esther had read the carefully general report, but something in its tone had alerted her and she had come down again, full of foreboding, to see Deborah. She had been told that it would be unwise; she had demanded to see Dr. Halle, and once in his office, she had heard the facts no word could modify or ease. Now she sat before Dr. Fried, angry and frightened and despairing.

"And what can I tell her father—what lie can I tell him now so that we can keep her here where she gets sicker and more violent all the time!"

Through her fear the doctor's words sounded long and slow. "I think perhaps that we are all letting ourselves go overboard with this burning business. It is, after all, a symptom of the sickness which we all know is there, and which is *still* responding to treatment."

"But it's so . . . *so ugly!*"

"You mean the wounds?"

"I haven't seen the wounds—I mean the idea, the thought. How could anyone do that to themselves! A person would be in—— " Esther gasped and put her hand before her mouth, and tears spilled over the rims of her eyes and rolled down her face.

"No, no," the doctor said, "it's the *word* that is making you so frightened. It is the old evil word 'insane,' which once meant 'hopeless and forever,' that is making you suffer so."

"I never let myself think that word for Debby!"

The facade is broken and what is behind the facade is not so bad, Dr. Fried thought. She wondered if she could let the mother know it in some way. It might be a small comfort. The telephone rang and Dr. Fried answered it in her affable voice, and when she turned again to face Esther, she found her composed.

"You do think, then, that there is still a chance for her to be . . . normal?"

"I think that there is certainly a chance for her to be mentally healthy and strong. I will say something to you now, Mrs. Blau, but it is not for your daughter and I will appreciate it if you never mention it to her. I am approached at least four times every week to do therapy with a patient. I have doctors' analyses also to supervise for the university School of Psychiatry, and at every session I must turn many away. I would be worse than wasteful to give a moment's time to a hopeless case. I do not keep her one moment longer than I think I can help her. Tell them this at home. You need not keep telling lies—the truth is not unbearable at all."

The doctor saw Deborah's mother out of her office, hoping that she had helped. Easy comfort might do for some other branch of medicine (placebo was a prescription more common than doctors themselves liked to admit), but the whole weight of her life and training was against it. And after her experiences, anything that sounded even faintly like placating would frighten Esther Blau; if she had been strengthened by this talk, the whole family would be strengthened in turn.

Dr. Fried understood that Esther had outgrown her subjection to her father. She was now a strong, dominant, even dominating person. The same force in her that had tried to conquer all of Deborah's enemies, to her detriment, might be the saving force as well. If she believed in this therapy for her daughter, she would stand against the whole family to see that it was carried out. Deborah's illness had done more than shake the portraits in the family album. Some of the family had had to question why, and had grown a little themselves because of asking. If this were true, it was a source of hope seldom mentioned in the psychiatric journals, maybe because it was beyond "science" and beyond planning for. Outside the doors of study, Dr. Fried's father had once told her, an angel waits.

Coming out of the doctor's house into the brisk autumn day, Esther looked toward the high, heavily screened porch behind which she knew was D ward. What was it like there? What was it like inside the minds of people who had to stay there? She looked away from it quickly, finding that it was blurred by a sudden overwhelming of tears.

Deborah sat on the floor of the ward having her burns dressed. She had begun to be of medical interest; the wounds refused to heal. The student nurses, delighted by so tangible a condition, worked faithfully and busily with their unguents, potions, bandages, and tape. The smokers were still angry at Deborah, holding her responsible for the new rules, and even Lee, who needed to talk, was sending scornful looks at her. While the nurses worked, Deborah watched what she had come to call the Breathing Frieze of other patients, sitting and standing, expressionless except for a look of great awe that their blood could move its ways so steadily, their hearts could beat beyond will or passion. When the nurses finished dressing the recalcitrant burns, they left the hall for a moment. Out of the corner of her eye, Deborah became aware that Helene was looking hard at Sylvia, who was standing next to her, immobile as ever. The next moment, Helene came close and struck Sylvia heavily once, and once again. Sylvia stood beneath the blows and gave no sign of being conscious of them. Challenged, Helene exploded into a whirlwind of rage. A wild creature seemed to be hurling itself against rock. Helene beat and screamed and scratched and flapped, spitting and redfaced, her hair flying. Sylvia reacted only by closing her eyes slowly. Her hands were still limp at her sides; her body, it seemed, was totally commended to the forces of gravity and inertia; she appeared to take no interest in the beating. The sudden, swift happening was interrupted by the standard six attendants required to get Helene away. Soon she was borne off drowning in a wave of khaki and white.

Deborah remained standing ten feet from Sylvia. Both of them seemed alone on the planet. Deborah remembered the time two years earlier when Helene had rushed at her to destroy the face that had witnessed, and be safe from its knowledge. Everything had been Helene—doctors, nurses, attendants, the ward's quickened rhythm, the wet sheets, and seclusion—all, all Helene, and Deborah had stood alone and shamed, because she had been too degraded to defend herself. She had stood as Sylvia was standing now, like a statue. Only her breathing betrayed her, wrenching in and out, almost as if she were snorting. Deborah was the only one who could know why Sylvia, who had failed to defend herself, needed as much attention as Helene was now getting.

I should go to her and touch her on the shoulder and say something, Deborah thought. But she stood still. I should go because it happened to me and no one knows as I do, how it is. . . . But her feet were in her shoes and her shoes were not moving toward Sylvia, and her hands stayed at her sides and were not moving. In the name of the dark night together when she broke her silence for me, I should go. . . . And she tried to wrench free of her granite garments and stone shoes. She looked at Sylvia, the ugliest of all of the patients, with her drooling and her pale, waxy face in its frozen grimace, and she knew that if she went to give what she of all people knew was needed, Sylvia might destroy her with silence alone. A fear came up to consume the wish to act. In another moment the subduers of Helene began to come back from the battle and the chance was lost. From the subsiding fear, shame rose. It grew up over her face so that she stood for a long time stone blind and wishing for death.

Later, she stood before Furii in the office and told her what she had seen and had not done.

"I never told you a lie!" Deborah said. "I never told you that I was human. Now you can throw me out because I have a guilt with no apology."

"I am not here to excuse you," Furii said, looking up at Deborah from the chair, and lighting a cigarette. "You will find no shortage of moral issues and hard decisions in the real world, and, as I have said before, it's no rose

garden. Let us bless the strength that let you see, and work toward the time
when you will be able also to *do* what you see to do. We have now to work
hard on the roots of this burning which you do in your anger at me and at
the hospital."

Almost at once Deborah knew that Furii was wrong about the reason
for the burning and the need for it, and most wrong about its seriousness.
While it had the semblance of terrible aberration, Deborah felt that this was
as deceptive as the quiet slopes of her volcano.

"Do you think the burning is very serious?" she asked Furii.

"Most serious, indeed," Furii answered.

"You are wrong," Deborah said simply, hoping that the doctor really
believed what she had so often said about the patient trusting her own deep
beliefs. There were over forty burns, inflicted over and over again on flesh
scraped raw to receive them, and yet they didn't seem worth the fuss that
was being made about them.

"I don't know why, but you are wrong."

Deborah looked around the cluttered office. For members of the world,
sunlight was streaming through the windows, but its goldenness and
warmth were only there for her to perceive from a distance. The air around
her was still cold and dark. It was this eternal estrangement, not fire against
her flesh, that was the agony.

"Restricted or not," she murmured, "I will do penance."

"Louder, please, I cannot hear you."

"Selective inattention," Deborah said, laughing at the words of
psychiatry, whose private language and secret jargon had not the beauty or
poetry of Yri. Furii saw, too, and laughed.

"Sometimes I think that our professional vocabulary goes too far, but
we speak to one another after all, and not only to ourselves and the falling
gods. Was it to them that you spoke just now?"

"No," Deborah said, "to you. I have decided not to be immoral, because
of what happened to Sylvia. If I couldn't do what I should have done after
Helene attacked her, at least I won't implicate her in my burnings, since you
say that they are serious."

"How do you mean this?"

"She smokes sometimes, but she is forgetful. She has put cigarettes
down when I was there to pick them up quickly and be gone. Both Marys
smoke like wild women and all I have to do is make sure that no one spots
me. They are contributing to my delinquency, aren't they?"

"I suppose, in a way they are. Actually you are taking advantage of
their symptoms."

"That must not be allowed to happen," Deborah said quietly. She
wondered why Furii had left matches in her waiting room, and cigarettes,

too. The nurse who had accompanied her was easily distracted; Deborah wondered if Furii knew how trying those minutes of waiting had been.

When the time was over, Deborah got up to leave, saying, "I am cutting my throat now myself. I won't steal burning butts from the patients unless they're left in the ash trays or are forgotten, and I won't let you contribute either because you wouldn't want to."

Then she reached into her sleeve and drew out the two packs of matches she had taken from Furii's table and threw them angrily on the paper-littered desk.

10 The Authentic Self

Throughout, our attempt has been to show ways in which we all search for means to experience personal significance, our authenticity, our real Selfhood. Those who live partial or conflicting lives, who never know they are really significant human beings, often require the intervention of another person.

Often this intervention is done by an act or word of love from a friend. Even total strangers have "worked wonders" in freeing a person's hidden potentials. Traditionally, people with incomplete or troubled lives have sought professional help, from their clergy or from professionally trained psychotherapists. Psychiatrists, psychologists, psychoanalysts, clinical social workers all function in this capacity, though their methods may be very different.

Psychotherapy is not a technique that promises a cure for a disease or conflict. It is a process-relationship—an involvement that is flexible, dynamic, changing, growing—that tries to reduce conflicts and bring out elements of full functioning and actualization that have been blocked or lost in the person needing help.

The first selection in this chapter, written by clinical psychologist Morris B. Parloff, tells you how to shop around for the right therapy if you feel you want it.

The second article introduces us to one of the newer ideas on how to recognize and deal with one's tensions—bio-feedback. Through bio-feedback techniques, one can learn to control one's heart rate, body temperature, brain wave patterns, and other functions related to stress and the feeling of well-being. Barnard Law Collier summarizes a number of recent studies on the subject.

225

Anthony Barton explores the therapeutic process as seen by followers of Carl Jung, Carl Rogers, and Sigmund Freud in the third selection. He discusses a variety of similarities and differences among these viewpoints.

The last article is an intriguing and unusual look at how behavioral modification techniques can be used to help children control their own environments. The authors have had excellent results in teaching students how to shape the behavior of their teachers, parents, and fellow students to make their contacts with those people more rewarding.

Shopping for the Right Therapy

Morris B. Parloff

If you ever need psychotherapy, there are more than 130 different "therapeutic techniques" from which you can choose. Don't be alarmed. Remember that there are 220 million people in the United States. The various approaches appeal to different individuals with different needs in our pluralistic society. The author examines the four major schools of therapy and what they have to offer the individual.

There is nothing absolute about the aims of psychotherapy. They are, rather, tied closely to current standards of well-being and social effectiveness. In the past, these social standards have seemed relatively fixed and stable. Today, however, our society changes its standards with ever-increasing speed, while the sciences keep fashioning new mirrors to reflect the new images of man. As a result, innumerable images are now simultaneously extant; which image we see depends on where we look.

At the same time, we make increasing demands on psychotherapy. In the past, religion and science were the main ways of achieving our aspirations. More recently, to the consternation of some and the satisfaction of others, the license for ensuring our well-being has apparently been transferred to psychotherapy!

The boundaries of the treatment, never firm, have become increasingly ambiguous and provisional; in fact, they now seem to be infinitely expansible. Within the past decade the role of the psychotherapist has been greatly extended. Not only is he expected to help the patient achieve relief from psychologically induced discomfort and social ineffectuality—that is, to treat "mental disorders"; he is also expected to help the client achieve positive mental health, a state presumably defined by the extent to which the patient experiences "self-actualization," growth, even spiritual oneness with the universe. Thus, some therapists have moved away from the earlier aim of "head-shrinking" to the loftier goal of "mind-expanding."

The range of problems brought to the psychotherapist has broadened to include not only the major mental disorders—the psychoses and neuroses—but also the celebrated problems of alienation and the meaninglessness of life. The conception of "pathology"—that is, what needs changing—has been modified. Where formerly the internal and unconscious conflicts of the *individual* were treated, the targets of change now encompass the interpersonal relationship, the family system, and, more recently, even society and its institutions.

Credentials for practicing psychotherapy have been broadened and, by some standards, lowered. What was initially almost the exclusive domain of the medical profession—of the psychoanalyst and psychiatrist—has slowly been opened up to include the related professions of clinical psychology, psychiatric social work, and psychiatric nursing. Among those more recently invited to provide some psychiatric services are the "paraprofessional," the nonprofessional, and even the former patient. The belief that "it takes [a former] one to treat one" has gained popularity, particularly in the treatment of drug abusers, alcoholics, criminals, and delinquents.

The number of "therapeutic techniques" also continues to grow. More than 130 different approaches are now being purveyed in the marketplace of psychosocial therapies.

New schools emerge constantly, heralded by claims that they provide better treatment, amelioration, or management of the problems and neuroses of the day. No school has ever withdrawn from the field for failure to live up to its claims, and as a consequence all continue to co-exist. This remarkable state of affairs is explained in part by the fact that each school seems to be striving for different goals—goals reflecting different views of the "nature of man" and his potential. All approaches to treatment are sustained by their appeals to different constituencies in our pluralistic society.

By way of general introduction, I shall briefly review the four self-proclaimed major schools of psychotherapy. Then I'll describe several other forms of treatment that are difficult to categorize but that currently also enjoy special popularity.

The four major schools of therapy are (1) analytically oriented therapy, (2) behavior therapy, (3) humanistic therapy, and (4) transpersonal therapy.

Analytically Oriented Therapy

The analytic (or psychodynamic, or depth) forms of therapy have evolved in a more or less direct line from classical psychoanalysis. While still flourishing, and perhaps the most frequently encountered form of treatment, this school appears—like unemployment and inflation—to be growing at a declining rate.

These psychodynamic therapies assume that people have innate and acquired drives which conflict with both the "external" requirements of society and the "internal" needs and "internalized" standards of the individual. Unacceptable drives are forced out of the conscious awareness—that is, repressed—but they continue, unconsciously or subconsciously, to press for expression.

A person's normal development may be interrupted by early-life experiences that either do not satisfy innate drives sufficiently or gratify them excessively. In either event, the child's development may be blocked. The emotions and fantasies derived from these unacceptable drives may be allowed partial expression in a disguised and compromised form. In some instances these emotions are "sublimated" into creative, socially beneficial channels. In other cases they "surface" as undesirable physical symptoms, or as socially unacceptable character traits and behavior patterns. The psychodynamic approach postulates that socialization is required in order for the person to become human.

Psychoanalytic treatment tries to unravel internal problems by bringing the unconscious neurotic conflicts into the patient's consciousness. The direct target of treatment is not the patient's *symptoms*, but rather the forces that are believed to generate these symptoms.

The formula for bringing this repressed material squarely into the patient's awareness is: clarify, confront, interpret. Understanding and insight of this kind are presumed to be in themselves "curative," provided that they evoke emotional experiences of a compelling nature.

Typically, psychoanalytic approaches involve analysis of the relationship that the patient attempts to establish with the therapist. This relationship is presumed to mirror the patient's unresolved pathological childhood conflicts.

More recently, the analytically oriented therapist has begun taking into account the social and cultural context in which the patient lives. The classical patient-therapist pairing has been widened to permit treatment in groups as well. Some psychodynamic therapies have moved from long-term to brief, time-limited courses of treatment. Though many of the classic procedures have been revised and relaxed, the basic assumption that dynamic forces underlie symptomatic behavior remains unchanged.

Behavior Therapy

Most behavior therapy derives from laboratory studies of learning processes. The therapist does not postulate the existence of any disease, aberrant personality development, or internal underlying conflict. The problem is defined in terms of specific behavior that the patient or society considers to be maladaptive. The aim of treatment is to change behavior—to change, specifically, its frequency, intensity, and appropriateness.

The behavior therapist does not consider maladaptive forms of behavior as evidence of "pathology" but rather as ways in which people have learned to interact with their environment. He believes that behavior disorders develop according to the same principles of learning evident in so-called normal learning.

"Behavioral" treatment begins with detailed study of the events that precede and follow occurrences of a particular behavior problem—phobic avoidances, compulsions, temper tantrums, sexual dysfunctions, and so on.

One major form of behavior therapy consists in changing environmental conditions that stimulate or maintain the unwanted behavior; this therapeutic technique is known as "operant conditioning." Behavior therapy now includes a broad spectrum of techniques, known by such names as systematic desensitization, assertiveness training, aversive conditioning, token economy, and modeling. These procedures are offered by psychologists, psychiatrists, educators, social workers, speech therapists, and others concerned with modifying behavior.

The procedure popularly labeled as *biofeedback* is used as a potential treatment for a variety of psychosomatic disorders, such as headaches, insomnia, high blood pressure, asthma, circulatory problems, and backache. The primary principle in biofeedback[1] is that if someone is provided with information about certain changes occurring in his body, that person can "learn" to (1) increase awareness of his or her bodily processes, and (2) bring these processes under conscious control. This control should then permit the patient to change the autonomic processes in a more benign or healthful direction. Awareness of events within the body is achieved by means of monitoring instruments, which detect the relevant internal physiological change, amplify it, and translate it into a visual or auditory display.

1. See "Biofeedback: An Exercise in 'Self-Control'" by Barbara Brown, *Saturday Review*, Feb. 22, 1975.

Humanistic Therapy

This umbrella term shelters a wide range of therapies and techniques. Perhaps the most important factor uniting them is their strong reaction against what they view as limited conceptions of human nature offered by the analytic and behavioristic therapies.

Humanists postulate that man is driven by an overarching need for self-actualization. Man's needs are, they assert, "higher" than simply mindless pleasure-seeking or avoidance of pain. Goodness, truth, beauty, justice, and order are not to be explained away as byproducts of man's efforts to sublimate, divert, or block the direct expression of the baser drives that lurk within—an explanation sometimes attributed to analytically oriented therapy. Humanists believe that the failure to express and to realize the potential of higher human needs, motives, and capacities is the cause of emotional distress.

The goals of humanistic therapy are self-actualization and the enrichment and fuller enjoyment of life, not the cure of "disease" or "disorders." To realize your potential, you must develop increasing sensitivity to your own—and others'—feelings. Such heightened awareness will help establish warm relationships and improve your ability to perceive, intuit, sense, create, fantasize, and imagine.

The humanists stress that the only reality that merits concern is one's own emotional experience—in contrast to what they view as the unwarranted faith that other therapists have placed in thought, insight, and understanding.

The analytic view holds that man's impulses must be frustrated and redirected in order that he be more fully human. But humanists argue that direct gratification of needs is ennobling and good.

Humanists such as the late Abraham Maslow hold that each individual has a biological essence, or self, that he must discover and develop, but that external influences are more powerful than biologically given characteristics and may distort or block our personal awareness and development.

The panoply of self-actualizing techniques ranges from nondirective counseling and gestalt therapy to the multiple and ever-evolving variants of "growth" groups: the encounter group, the T-group, sensory-awareness training, and so on.

Transpersonal Therapy

Unlike the humanists, the transpersonalists are not content with the aim of integrating one's energies and expanding the awareness of oneself as an entity separate from the rest of the universe. Instead, the transpersonalists' goal is to help the individual transcend the limits of ordinary waking consciousness and to become at one with the universe. The various levels and dimensions of awareness are as follows: "intuitive" states, in which vague, fleeting experiences of trans-sensory perception begin to enter waking awareness; the "psychical," in which the individual transcends sensory awareness and experiences integration with humanity; and the "mystical," representing a union of enlightenment in which the self transcends duality and merges with "all there is." Finally, there may be yet a further level of potential development—personal/transpersonal integrative—in which all dimensions are experienced simultaneously.

Transpersonalists do not share an organized theory or a clearly defined set of concepts, but, like all the humanists, they assume that we all have large pools of untapped abilities, along with a drive toward spiritual growth.

One may achieve these levels by means of various techniques, including Arica training, the Gurdjieff method, Zen, psychosynthesis, yoga, Sufism, Buddhism, and transcendental meditation.

Three transpersonal approaches have achieved considerable popularity: psychosynthesis, Arica training, and transcendental meditation.

Psychosynthesis was developed by a Florentine psychiatrist, Roberto Assagioli. As a form of therapy, it tries to help people develop "the will" as a constructive force guiding all psychological functions—emotion-feeling, imagination, impulse-desire, thought, and intuition. Treatment aims at enabling the patient to achieve harmony within himself and with the world as a path to attaining the higher self. It consists of techniques for training the will in order that one can master life and merge with "the universal will."

Psychosynthesis, the name Assagioli gives his model of personality *and* of psychotherapy, refers to the process of constructing a new personality. In psychosynthesis, three forces interact to give a new organization to the personality: (1) using our available energies, (2) developing new aspects of personality, and (3) coordinating and subordinating one's psychic energies and functions.

Arica training is an eclectic system, devised by Oscar Ichazo in Chile. It has incorporated many of the teachings of the Middle East and the Orient, including yoga, Zen, Sufism, Kabbala, and the martial arts. The branches of the Arica Institute now established in some major American cities stress these features: special diet, sensory awareness, energy-generating exercises, techniques for analysis in personality, interpersonal and group exercises, and various forms of meditation.

Transcendental meditation (TM), a variant of Raja yoga, has become extraordinarily popular in the United States and Europe. This form of meditation has been adapted to the habits of Westerners and does not require special postures, forced concentration, lengthy or arduous training, or religious belief. Each person is assigned a mantra—a special incantatory catch-phrase—which he is to keep secret and meditate on twice a day for about 20 minutes. This meditation helps people attain deep states of relaxation that are said to release creative energies. The advocates of TM hold that if 1 percent of the population in a given area meditate properly, the energies generated will benefit the rest of the population.

Special Treatment Forms

Most techniques of psychotherapy can be included under one or another of these four rubrics—analytic, behavioral, humanistic, and transpersonal—but there remain a number of approaches that do not claim allegiance to any school and are not claimed by any. Some of these special approaches may be termed "pan-theoretical"; others have evolved self-consciously "novel" techniques and procedures. The broad class of group psychotherapies and the many community-oriented therapies illustrate "pan-theoretical" approaches; the "novel" therapies will be illustrated here by perhaps the best known—primal therapy.

"Group psychotherapy" does not represent any particular set of techniques or common philosophy of treatment. It refers to the *setting* in which the particular views and techniques of the analytic, behavioral, humanistic, and transpersonal schools have been implemented. In addition to having a knowledge of his own school, the practitioner of group psychotherapy must understand the dynamics and processes of small groups.

One of the many forms of group therapy, one of the best known is *transactional analysis* (TA), of *I'm OK, You're OK* fame. TA was developed by Eric Berne and represents an adaptation and extension of the psychodynamic orientation. The treatment attempts to identify covert gratifications—the "payoffs" of the "games" that people play with one another. The tasks of both the therapists and the group patients include identifying the moment-to-moment ego states (parent, child, adult) that characterize each participant's interactions. A further step is to name the "game" that the individual is playing and, finally, to identify the "unconscious" life plan that the patient appears to have selected for himself during early childhood. The life plan involves the relatively enduring position of whether the self and others are "okay" or "not okay." The dynamics of change are believed to consist in the patient's learning to shift his "real self" from one ego state to another by an act of will.

Family therapy involves the collective treatment of members of the same family in a group by one or more psychotherapists. This appraoch treats not merely the individual but the family unit. The individual "patient" is viewed as but a symptom of a dysfunctional family system—a system that has produced and now maintains the problems manifested in a given family member.

The pan-theoretical approaches include those therapies which extend the therapeutic focus to the community and society. The premise that environmental influences may interfere with a person's development has been taken up by a variety of therapists loosely associated with humanistic psychology. Perhaps the most extreme position is that taken by the group espousing *radical therapy*, which holds that society is responsible for most mental and emotional ills, and that, therefore, society rather than the patient is sick. People in psychological distress are considered oppressed rather than ill, and traditional psychotherapy is "part of the problem rather than part of the solution to human misery." The therapist attempts to help the patient recognize not merely his own problems but also the realities of his life situation and the role played by society in generating and perpetuating emotional problems.

Like radical therapy, *feminist therapy* believes that the root of emotional problems may be found in society rather than in the individual. Feminist therapy emphasizes that all psychotherapy must be freed of its traditional sex-role biases. Sexism is viewed as a major force impeding the "growth" of both men and women. This approach is not characterized by any particular techniques, but rather by a shared ideology. Consciousness-raising groups, too, which were initially politically motivated, have recently become oriented toward providing women with help for their personal problems.

Primal therapy is viewed by its inventor, Arthur Janov, as unique in both its effects and its techniques, and as the "only cure of the neuroses." According to Janov, a neurosis occurs when the unexpressed physical and psychological pains experienced in childhood accumulate to the point where they are unbearable and can no longer be simply suppressed. The awareness of these feelings and needs is then "split off" when the child interprets the parents' behavior as meaning that they hate him. This formulation may occur at about the age of five or six and represents to Janov the "primal scene" that precipitates the neurosis.

In Janov's theory the pain of unmet needs is stored away somewhere in the brain and produces tension, which the patient may deal with by developing a variety of tension-relieving symptoms. Treatment requires the release and full expression of the underlying pain, by restoring physical access to the stored memories. Cure occurs only when each painful feeling is linked to its origins. The living and reliving of the primal scene is accompanied by a "tower of terror" usually associated with screaming, violent thrashing about, pounding, and even convulsions. The screaming may go on for hours and may be repeated periodically over a period of many months as one event after another is recalled.

According to Janov, the cured individual should ideally have no psychological defenses, nor need any, since all pain and its associated tensions have been dispelled. The recovered patient thus becomes a "natural man," who is "non-industrial, non-compulsive, and non-driving," and finds much less need for sex; women experience sexual interest no more than twice a month.

Even this truncated review of the major schools and techniques indicates the enormous complexity of any serious research effort that undertakes to compare the relative effectiveness of available therapies. Clearly, the basic conceptions differ as to who and what needs treating. It is not easy to prove that changes observed in patients and clients are due to the specific techniques and interventions. The therapist may wittingly or unwittingly provide the patient with experiences other than those assumed to be critical. It cannot be assumed that the same therapist will behave similarly with each of his patients—much less that different therapists espousing the same theory will behave similarly with all patients. The problems of research on the outcome of psychotherapy are further compounded by the concurrent impact of other events in the patient's life.

In terms of consumer guidance, then, I shall report only the most consistent trends that emerge from a review of a large number of studies:

- Most forms of psychotherapy are effective with about two-thirds of their non-psychotic patients.
- Treated patients show significantly more improvement in thought, mood, personality, and behavior than do comparable samples of untreated patients.
- Behavior modification appears to be particularly useful in some specific classes of phobias, some forms of compulsive or ritual behavior, and some sexual dysfunctions. Although behavior-therapy techniques appear to produce rapid improvement in the addictive disorders, such as alcoholism, drug abuse, obesity, and smoking, these changes are usually not maintained and relapse occurs in most cases.

- Biofeedback has been applied to tension headaches, migraine, hypertension, epilepsy, some irregularities of heartbeat. The evidence, while encouraging, has not yet established such treatment as being clinically significant.
- Meditation techniques of a wide variety all produce comparable degrees of relaxation, with associated physiological and metabolic changes. Currently, "non-cultist" adaptations of meditative procedures are being applied with some success in the treatment of anxiety, hypertension, and cardiac arrythmias. Again, findings must be viewed as tentative pending further research.
- The criteria of "growth," "self-actualization," and the attainment of transpersonal levels of consciousness remain ambiguous, and it is therefore difficult to measure them objectively.
- Apparent differences in the relative effectiveness of different psychotherapies gradually disappear with time.
- Although most studies report that similar proportions of patients benefit from all tested forms of therapy, the possibility remains open that different therapies may effect different kinds of change.

All forms of psychotherapy tend to be reasonably useful for patients who are highly motivated, experience acute discomfort, show a high degree of personality organization, are reasonably well educated, have had some history of social success and recognition, are reflective, and can experience and express emotion.

Jerome D. Frank has proposed that all therapies may incorporate the same common (non-specific) elements, although in differing degrees: an emotionally charged relationship with a helping person; a plausible explanation of the causes of distress; provision of some experiences of success; and use of the therapist's personal qualities to strengthen the patient's expectation of help.

This statement in no way endorses tactlessness, insensitivity, or psychological assault. The therapist has no license to humiliate—or to thrill. A large-scale, careful study of participants who suffered psychological injury during encounter groups (led by acknowledged experts) revealed that the incidence of such casualties was disproportionately high among clients of so-called charismatic therapists, with their often aggressive, impatient, and challenging confrontation techniques.

No matter how specific the theory, no matter how clearly prescribed the techniques for a given therapy, treatment is far from standardized. Psychotherapy is mediated by the individual therapist and further modified by the nature of the interaction with the particular patient.

When the patient is "therapist-shopping," it is wise for him to select carefully from among an array of qualified therapists the one whose style of relating is acceptable to him—and preferably from a school whose philosophy, values, and goals are most congenial to his own.

Bio-Feedback Training

Barnard Law Collier

Humans have always been fascinated by the body's ability to heal itself, and with some individuals' ability to control their bodily reaction to pain, stress, and other difficulties. Until recently, though, most of us in the Western world have considered such control to be the exclusive province of yogis, Indian fakirs, and other Eastern mystics, and perhaps a few of their followers in this part of the world. Now, through psychophysiological research in bio-feedback, individuals are learning to control their pulse rates, mental state, and other bodily functions in ways never thought possible here.

In this article, Barnard Collier summarizes some exciting recent research on bio-feedback, and speculates on the implications of that research—that someday all of us may be able to control our bodies' reactions to fear, disease, and other problems that today cause so much human misery.

Inside a darkened chamber in the laboratory of Dr. Lester Fehmi sits Ralph Press, a nineteen-year-old mathematics student at the State University of New York in Stony Brook, Long Island. Relaxed in an armchair with his eyes closed, Ralph is undergoing his eleventh session of bio-feedback training to help him learn to control his brain waves.

Four silver electrodes are pasted to Ralph's scalp, their orange lead wires plugged into an electroencephalograph that is tracing his brain-wave activity on thick ribbons of EEG paper in the next room. The silence in the soundproofed chamber is broken only by the long and short beepings of a rather high-pitched tone: the key to Ralph's bio-feedback training.

Dr. Fehmi, a professor of psychology at Stony Brook, has told Ralph that he can learn to increase his brain's output of an eight-to-fourteen-cycle-per-second brain sine wave called alpha. Alpha waves are one of four known brain waves. They are generated, billions of them, by the tiny electrical pulses that surge through the brain as it does its complex chores.

High production of alpha waves is often associated with the objective state of peak mental and physical performance, a relaxed yet extremely sensitive alertness.

Dr. Fehmi and George Sintchak, the Stony Brook psychology department's chief electronic engineer, have rigged the EEG machine and a computer so that each time Ralph's brain generates a burst of alpha activity the occurrence is recorded, timed, and almost instantly made known to Ralph by means of the beeping tone. The tone is Ralph's bio-feedback. It is an audible signal that lets Ralph be consciously aware of a visceral function, in this case the production of his alpha brain waves, which his mind ordinarily blocks out, ignores, or is unable to perceive without external assistance. When Ralph's brain generates only snippets of alpha radiation, the tone comes in staccato little blips. As he produces more and more alpha, the tone stays on longer and longer. Ralph, of course, wants to succeed by producing as much alpha as he can.

For nearly an hour, Ralph shows minute-by-minute improvement in his ability to keep the tone on. A computer read-out verifies that he is maintaining the tone for a cumulative average of twenty-eight seconds out of each minute. "He's one of our super-subjects," Dr. Fehmi remarks. "He's not the best, but he's getting pretty good."

Ralph's alpha waves are of high amplitude, very rhythmic and regular. This is what they look like as they are traced by the jiggling pens of the EEG machine:

"OK, Ralph," Dr. Fehmi says quietly over the intercom, "I want you to turn the tone off and keep it off."

The tone that Ralph has learned to sustain for upwards of three seconds now goes beep, beep, *blip;* within seconds, it has died away except for tiny random beeps. This is what it looks like on the EEG tracing as Ralph begins to stop his alpha waves:

"Now turn the tone back on," Dr. Fehmi says.

A pause of a second or so and the tone beeps back to life and stays on for seconds at a time. Then on, off, on, off. The tests continue until it is clear that Ralph is in personal command of his brain's alpha-wave activity as evidenced by the EEG machine's record.

A steady flow of new scientific findings indicates that, with the aid of the teaching technique called bio-feedback training, man can learn to control willfully his body and his state of consciousness to a degree that traditionally has been dismissed in Western cultures as mere trickery or condemned as somehow wicked or blasphemous.

Projects in hospitals and research laboratories around the world are convincingly demonstrating that it may be possible to learn personal mastery over the functions of our visceral organs—the heart, liver, kidneys, intestines, glands, and blood vessels—in the same specific way that we learn to manipulate our fingers to play Chopin or our legs to kick a field goal. There is also highly intriguing research going on in laboratories like Dr. Fehmi's to demonstrate that with bio-feedback training we can learn self-control over the electrical activity of our brain. These studies indicate that man may possess the ability to will himself into whatever state of consciousness seems most appropriate to his environment, to accomplishing a task at hand, or to some special pursuit.

The implications of bio-feedback training are proving terribly easy to overstate, given the limited amount of solid experimental evidence that presently exists. People seem peculiarly ready nowadays to lunge at the adventurous prospect of employing new methods and modern technology to explore and conquer one's own brain and body instead of, say, the moon or Southeast Asia. The propensity for exaggeration about progress in this area frightens prudent scientists. Already they are encountering the con artists, the charlatans, and the quacks who are taking people's money by glibly mouthing the jargon associated with bio-feedback research and similar studies of the mind's control over internal organs. This caveat is offered early because it is difficult to keep one's imagination reined in unless one is warned that much of the data accumulated so far are limited to experiments with rats, monkeys, rabbits, or other lab animals. And the remarkable results with animals may not travel well from the laboratory to humans. Nevertheless, research teams are reporting an ever increasing number of cases in which human subjects have unquestionably gained conscious control over visceral organs once thought beyond the mastery of the mind.

In Baltimore, for example, Dr. Bernard T. Engel, a psychologist, and Dr. Eugene Bleecker, a cardiovascular specialist, have conducted bio-feedback training sessions with eight patients suffering from premature ventricular contractions, a dangerous irregularity of the heartbeat involving the heart's main pumping chamber. With significant success, these patients have learned to speed, slow, and narrowly regulate their heart by force of mental discipline alone.

At the Gerontology Research Center of the National Institute of Child Health and Human Development, Dr. Engel and Dr. Bleecker use a visual form of bio-feedback training to help patients control their heart. In a typical experiment, the patient lies quietly on a hospital bed in a small, windowless laboratory near Dr. Engel's office. The electrodes of an electrocardiograph are attached to his chest and pulse points, and the EKG machine is hooked up with a specially programed computer. On the bed table in front of the patient sits a small metal box fitted with a red, a yellow, and a green light in the same pattern as a regular traffic signal. The display is hooked into the computer, which almost instantly analyzes the EKG readings and provides bio-feedback information to the patient by means of the flashing colored lights.

The first phase of the training is speeding the heart rate. The patient may be told that when the yellow light goes on he will know that his heart is beating faster; the green light flashing on means it is slowing down. A small meter next to the light box indicates to the patient what percentage of the time he is succeeding in keeping the yellow light lit. The goal for the heart patient, of course, is to gain control over the lights and his heartbeat in the same way Ralph Press controlled the beeping tone and his alpha-wave production: by sheer mental effort, and without any muscular exertion—which amounts to cheating.

After a patient learns to speed his heart, he is then taught to slow it down with the red light and later to keep it beating within narrow normal limits, with the three lights acting as too fast, too slow, and normal speeds. Some of Dr. Engel's patients have achieved a 20 percent speeding or slowing of their hearts—about sixteen beats a minute from an eighty-beat-per-minute base. This self-willed rate change in one direction or the other tends to even out the irregular beats. Why? Researchers are not quite sure, but it works.

But what happens when the patient goes home, away from Dr. Engel's bio-feedback light box? The final s of the five-phase training program is the stepped withdrawal of the bio-feedback light signals. The patient, after extensive training, finds he can deliberately alter his heartbeats in the desired direction without artificial feedback. One of Dr. Engel's patients could still remember how to control his rate after two years. That Dr. Engel's patients retain what they have learned without the aid of an electronic device to provide feedback is what excites many researchers who feel that we may be capable of discovering unknown mechanisms, or "feedback loops," within ourselves that will allow us, after some basic training, to monitor our viscera and their functions at will throughout life.

In Boston and New York City, scientists are trying to see how people with hypertension can effectively lower their abnormally high blood pressure by thinking it down. Under the direction of Dr. Neal E. Miller, a professor of physiological psychology at Rockefeller University in New York and a pioneer in the brain sciences, experiments are now proceeding to discover if human subjects can learn to control the contractions of their intestinal tract. Laboratory rats have learned to control these contractions with notable success. If humans can do as well, it could mean relief from much suffering for people with spastic colons and similar gastrointestinal ailments usually associated with stress and psychosomatic illness.

Dr. Miller was in the forefront of what seemed, just a decade or so ago, a vain and somewhat foolhardy challenge to the bedrock idea that the viscera and the autonomic nervous system that controls them operate entirely independently of an animal's deliberate control. Dr. Miller has traced back to Plato the dogma that the organs controlled by the autonomic nervous system function at a kind of cave-mannish level, learning only in classical Pavlovian fashion to react to such stimuli as sour lemons and growling bears. On the other hand, the somatic, or cerebrospinal, nervous system, which transmits nerve signals from the brain to the spinal cord and directly to the skeletal muscles, can learn by the sophisticated trial-and-error instrumental process. Perhaps the Greeks considered it an act of hubris to believe that they, not the gods, exercised command of their heart, brain, and guts. Dr. Engel, who also has studied the accumulated prejudices against the viscera, can recite a chain of erroneous proofs put forth until only a few years ago by scientists who, with a kind of religious fervor, had shunned anatomical facts and new information in order to steadfastly support Plato.

At the root of the research reports on bio-feedback training is what Dr. Miller describes as "an almost complete change in our way of thinking about our viscera and their ability to learn. We are now able to regard the activities of our internal organs as behavior in the same sense that the movements of our hands and fingers are behavior. This is the basic stem of it all, but just where this rather radical new orientation will lead, we can't be sure yet."

Some indications that we can possibly control our viscera have been around for centuries without anyone's grasping their import. Dr. Miller points out that actors and actresses can control their tear glands, which are visceral organs, to make themselves cry on cue. It is possible that some classical conditioning is involved: The actor recalls something sad and the sadness makes him cry. But many actors and actresses say they can cry without any recalling, that all they have to do is think "cry" and the tears flow.

Magicians and mystics and meditators have often gained mental control over visceral organs to a significant degree. Harry Houdini is said to have been able to swallow and regurgitate a key that would unlock him from some otherwise unopenable box. If he did this, it would mean he had gained mastery over the muscles of his esophagus and stomach, part of the viscera.

A few yogis, it would seem, can control their metabolism to some extent. But whether or not they "cheat" by using skeletal muscles instead of only their mind to perform their tricks is unknown. Scientists have found that some yogis who can "stop" their hearts so that no pulse or sound of beating can be detected are actually performing what is called the Valsalva maneuver. By taking a deep breath, closing their windpipe, and breathing hard to increase the pressure inside their chest and around their heart, they collapse the veins to the heart and clamp off the return of blood. This arrests heart sounds and the pulse, but an EKG shows that the heart is still beating and usually quite fast. "We must re-examine a lot of phenomena we may have dismissed as fakery before," Dr. Miller says.

The belief in a "superior" somatic nervous system and an "inferior" autonomic nervous system was so strong that, according to Dr. Miller, "for more than a dozen years I had extreme difficulty getting students or even paid assistants to conduct experiments on the control of internal organs." But Dr. Miller persisted, and his research has led many other scientists to abandon the old dogma. He has shown that the internal organs in animals and to a significant extent in man, as well, are capable of learning by trial and error—and with a startling degree of specificity and discrimination. In one experiment, which Dr. Miller particularly enjoys mentioning, he and his research colleague, Dr. Leo V. DiCara, tuned their instrumental conditioning process down so fine that a rat learned to blush one ear and blanch the other. In almost all of his animal experiments, Dr. Miller paralyzes the rats and other lab animals with curare, a powerful drug used by South American Indians to tip their poison darts. The curare interferes with all the nerve impulses that keep the skeletal muscles working—including respiration. The paralyzing of the skeletal muscles ensures that the animals do not "cheat" by somehow using their skeletal muscles to affect their visceral responses. (It is thus far a frustration for Dr. Miller and others that non-curarized animals are slower to learn viscerally than the curarized ones.)

The difference between the way the body learns by classical conditioning and by instrumental conditioning is crucial to understanding how bio-feedback training works. Classical conditioning, or learning, always demands a stimulus that elicits an innate response. For example, the first time you ever saw a lemon, nothing much happened with your saliva glands, which are visceral organs. But after you first tasted its sour juice, your saliva glands automatically secreted lots of saliva to dilute and wash away the puckering citric acid. You cannot control the response of your saliva glands to the lemon juice, and after you have tasted several lemons your mouth will start watering at the very sight of one. You have been classically conditioned to salivate at the sight of lemons. The same thing works for other such stimuli: a mad dog, for example. The sight of one will boost your heart rate, increase your adrenaline flow, and generally activate other innate fear responses.

The process of instrumental learning is much less limited since it requires no specific stimulus to provoke a response. If you want to sink a twelve-foot golf putt, for instance, there is nothing anyone can offer you, not a lemon or $5,000, that will get your body to hole the ball out with Pavlovian sureness. But by the process of trial and error, or instrumental conditioning, you can learn to coordinate your muscles and other responses. You stroke the ball toward the hole and it glides by. You try again and again. Each time you get closer. You are not aware of precisely what you are doing to improve; you cannot say which muscles are contracting or relaxing and in what order. But you get closer nonetheless, and each near success is a reward that is likely to keep you trying. At last you are in control of your muscles, your responses, and the golf ball. It plunks into the hole. This trial-and-error process is called instrumental learning.

Now imagine that you are trying to make the same putt blindfolded. Very difficult, if not impossible. Why? Because something essential is missing from the learning process: feedback. In this case, the feedback is the sight of the ball getting closer to the cup. Of course, you could learn to make the putt blindfolded if you substituted for the feedback of your visual perception the voice (feedback) of your caddy. He might, at the simplest level, say "yes" when your direction was right and say nothing or "no" when it wasn't. He might offer more guidance: "A little more to the right" or "A little to the left and harder." You would still be badly handicapped by the imprecision of your caddy's secondhand information, but eventually you would sink one and then perhaps quite a few.

Our mind is in some ways like the blindfolded golfer where the viscera are concerned. Scientists are trying to find new ways to remove the blindfold, which is enormously difficult indeed, or to substitute the guidance of the caddy-type feedback for sensory information about visceral organs that the mind for some reason dismisses or never perceives. Dr. Fehmi's beeping tone and the mini-volt currents of pleasurable brain stimulation that lab rats get are simple reward bio-feedback signals; Dr. Engel's colored lights represent more guidance. All are examples of bio-feedback used to instrumentally condition internal organs by letting the mind know, within predetermined limits, what those organs are up to.

One path of bio-feedback research has branched slightly away from the strictly therapeutic approach and is investigating the ability of human beings to exert purposeful control over their visceral functions, especially their brain functions, with the goal of making the essentially healthy person better able to cope with his world. At the United States Navy Medical Neuropsychiatric Research Unit in San Diego, California, Dr. Ardie Lubin and Dr. David Hord, both psychologists, are studying the relationship between the output of alpha waves and sleep. What they want to determine is whether or not a person deprived of sleep can be returned to a state of effectiveness and acceptable decision-making capacity by willing himself into an alpha state for a certain length of time. Some preliminary tests have shown that alpha states may be recuperative.

At the Langley Porter Neuropsychiatric Institute, part of the University of California Medical Center in San Francisco, a research group headed by Dr. Joe Kamiya is exploring the possibility that brain-wave control may have important effects on health, creativity, and such mental functions as perception and memory. Dr. Kamiya is regarded by most psychologists as the pioneer in the field of brain-wave control. Dr. Kamiya and his research team have found that subjects who do best at mastering their alpha-wave output are those who have had some training in meditation, as in Zen. At Stony Brook, Dr. Fehmi has noted that musicians, athletes, and artists are especially adept at control over their brain waves. Conversely, he has found that subjects who come into his chamber and slouch in their armchair in the spaced-out way associated with drug trips produce precious little alpha.

It is frustrating to researchers that the subjects who are most proficient in gaining brain-wave control are often strangely tongue-tied when it comes to telling just how they do it. Some say they relax and wipe everything from their mind. Others concentrate on some infinite point like a mystical third eye in the middle of their forehead. Some are unable to verbalize the experience at all.

"The best way I can describe the feeling of alpha," says Dr. Fehmi, "is a relaxed but alert and sensitive 'into-it-ness.'" Dr. Edgar E. Coons, a physiological psychologist at New York University and a musician, has been trained to produce alpha waves in Dr. Fehmi's lab; he says the alpha state "makes me feel as if I'm floating about half an inch above my seat." A talented young musician named David Rosenboom, who recently presented a bio-feedback brain-wave concert at Automation House in New York (brain-wave activity was fed into a computer and an ARP synthesizer;

the result was a weird but not unpleasing effect), is the reigning champion brain-wave producer for Dr. Fehmi. When his alpha is really going strong in all parts of his brain, Rosenboom says he is plugged in to a "great energy source." Another musician named LaMonte Young, who keeps a forty-cycle "home" tone going in his Manhattan studio at all times, explained that he had no trouble generating alpha the first time he ever tried it, because his mind "is tuned to frequencies and intervals."

At the University of Colorado Medical School, Dr. Hans Stoyva has had notable success in teaching his patients how to relax specific muscles that tense up and cause certain kinds of tension headaches. The easing of pain has been swift and dramatic.

Dr. Martin Orme, director of experimental psychiatry at the University of Pennsylvania Medical School in Philadelphia, is studying the alpha-wave phenomenon with an eye toward finding out what exactly an alpha state does to or for an individual and how it might be beneficial to him. "It's not enough to know you can contemplate your navel," Dr. Orme says. "You then have to ask, 'What happens?' " Experiments conducted with subjects who have been trained to produce a reliably high alpha-wave output show, according to Dr. Orme, that critical thinking tends to interfere with alpha waves, but that alpha-wave production does not mean blunted intellectual capacity. What alpha production seems to do best for the alpha producer is relax him, insulate him from stressful critical thought, and rehabilitate his autonomic nervous system to some degree.

"What this may mean," Dr. Orme says, "is that alpha might be used to bring down the level of a person's anxiety to a point where he can function at his best. We all need a certain amount of anxiety to function. It is well accepted that we function best as anxiety rises to a certain point on a bell-shaped curve, and past that point we do increasingly worse as anxiety increases. If alpha can be used to knock down anxiety to the point on the curve where we work most effectively, it can be a most important development." However, Dr. Orme is quick to point out that "this is three levels or more from where we are now, but it is something to consider."

Another prospect for visceral learning is its use as a possible alternative to drugs. If, for example, a high alpha output can cause deep relaxation, or a specific focusing of bio-feedback training can loosen up a taut muscle, this could well substitute for the billions of tranquilizers consumed to achieve essentially the same effect. The advantage over drugs might be considerable. For instance, while a tranquilizer acts in a general way on the whole body or an entire bodily system (perhaps with unwanted side effects), bio-feedback training might be specific enough to do the job required and let the rest of the body function undisturbed.

"There is also," says Dr. Orme, "the general question of personal control and how we might be able to bring our emotions under control. We want to know, of course, to what extent an individual can gain control with precision and reliability over the things he fears. A good part of fear is the fear of fear. If you know you are going to be hurt, you will hurt more with exactly the same degree of hurting stimulus. If we can break into some of the feedback loops that are part of the fear cycle, we may be able to control unpleasant and unproductive anxiety."

To Dr. Orme, the goal is clear. "We may be able to become actual masters of our destiny. As a psychiatrist, my purpose is to enable man to decide his own fate instead of his juices deciding for him."

At Rockefeller University, Dr. DiCara, a burly ex-football player, is attempting to unravel some of the whys and hows of visceral learning. In one recent experiment, he and Dr. Eric Stone found that rats trained to increase their heart rate had significantly more of a powerful group of chemicals called catecholamines in their brains and hearts than rats who learned to lower their heart rates. In humans, catecholamines are associated with hypertension and coronary artery disease. The possibility of learning to slow the heart rate to achieve beneficial effects on hypertension and heart ailments is intriguing; however, a major obstacle still to be overcome is the inability at present to measure catecholamines in the human brain.

An equally intriguing possibility has been raised by an experiment conducted by Dr. DiCara and Dr. Jay M. Weiss. Rats that had learned to slow their heart rates subsequently showed excellent ability to learn to move back and forth in a shuttle box to avoid an electric shock. Rats trained to speed their hearts learned very poorly and exhibited signs of extreme fearfulness by leaping into the air, squealing, and turning toward their tails with each pulse of shock instead of getting away from it. In contrast, the slow heart rate rats took each shock in stride, with only "mild jerks," and slowly walked out of the electrified side of the box.

"It is crystal-clear," says Dr. Miller, with whom Dr. DiCara has worked as co-experimenter on many projects, "that heart rate training affects rats' learning. What is further indicated is that the training also affects their emotionality. We cannot jump from the laboratory to the clinic, but we may indeed find that in human subjects trained to lower their heart rates there could be an increased capacity to adapt to stressful situations and a corresponding decrease in emotionality."

The field of bio-feedback training and visceral learning is still only crudely charted. New research teams are forming to explore further; the mechanical and electronic spin-offs of the space age are providing the new tools and infinitely more sensitive measuring devices that are required for progress. But most of all there seems to be a new attitude.

"We have brought four to five thousand years of cultural myths into the laboratory to be investigated," says Dr. Miller, who, in just a few years, has seen the pendulum of interest swing from "great resistance to great readiness." Although he is understandably reluctant to speculate on what the future holds, he is nonetheless confident that the new knowledge about our internal organs will stimulate much more research into the astonishing ability of human beings to learn.

The Appeal of the Theory

Anthony Barton

Are there any similarities in different approaches to psychotherapy? If so, what are they, and what, if anything, unites all or most of the major approaches?

In this excerpt from his book The Three Worlds of Therapy, *Anthony Barton compares and contrasts the theories of Sigmund Freud, Carl Jung, and Carl Rogers.*

Coherence, Clarity, Control, Objectivity

In all of the therapies a patient-client who is more or less lost, confused, and unable to live as he wishes turns hopefully to a skilled, professional, knowing other. The patient's expectation, hope, and urgent need for expert principled treatment is already given culturally in the situation. That is, the fact that he seeks a professional therapist already points to his felt need for objective help. He does not need merely friendship or a shoulder to cry on, though these may be part of what is called for therapeutically. He wants his therapist to be genuinely knowledgeable about what is helpful and unhelpful in life. Hence, for the therapist to respond with a specific, coherent, consistent orientation and style of treatment already accords with his needs.

For his part, the therapist also needs a guide for dealing with the complex problematics of people who are difficult to help. He cannot proceed on the basis of whim, guess, or hunch, and he does not wish simply to repeat cultural clichés to his patients. In order to help as many patients as he possibly can, with their varieties of difficulties, modes of expression,

Reprinted from *The Three Worlds of Therapy*, by Anthony Barton, by permission of National Press Books.

and cultural backgrounds, he needs some mode of simplifying, ordering, and managing the complex field of interaction. All therapeutic orientations are responses to this need.

Both therapist and patient, then, need a mutually guiding frame of reference, and this knowledgeable guiding is rationally grounded in the therapist's theory, which he lives in his every response—in his questions and silences, in his mode of empathy, in his way of noticing or not noticing, in the index of meanings that the patient's utterances have for him. This is not to suggest that the therapist lives in a world of pure clarity but only to suggest that he is oriented and knows his way. Further, it is precisely this way of the therapist that the patient hopes will become a useful way for himself. To the patient's "How shall I get better, learn to live more amply, become less inhibited?" the therapist answers with his oriented, expert, more or less consistent ordering of the world that is constituted between them.

In Jungian therapy, for example, the constant turning of the therapist to the patient's inward sense of the symbolic—to his dreams and fantasies and their symbolic meanings—provides a coherent emphasis, language, and way of approach for therapist and patient alike. The way in which the therapist constantly looks for the "other side" encourages and helps to articulate a consistently expanding world of symbolic meanings. By means of this emphasis and style of interaction fundamentally given within Jungian thought, both the therapist and patient find a coherent, clear, controlled, and objective way of proceeding. They are thus engaged in a clearly structured process of interaction which has rules for uncovering truth about the patient.

Transcendent Truth

All three theorists [followers of Freud, Jung, and Carl Rogers] describe the patient as a split, nonintegrated being. Different aspects of his life are at war with, in some way isolated from, one another, which makes his commerce with the world tenuous and difficult. In the Freudian view, he is seen as living his particular idiosyncratic past history. In the Jungian view, he is seen as living his onesided face and striving desperately to keep the other sides at bay.[1] In the Rogerian view, he is seen as trying to maintain the self

1. A person's particular idiosyncratic past history would be the unconscious conflicts he experienced, brought about by his relationship with his parents and the unresolved conflicts he experienced through the oral, anal, phallic, and genital stages of development. Jung viewed man's developing one side of his personality as the experience of keeping the other side underdeveloped. A man would develop his logical, independent, unsympathetic side, and his ability to be intuitive, dependent, and empathetic would be underdeveloped.

he ought to be according to false values he has adopted from others, instead of finding his true feeling-self and authentic inner values. Thus, the patient lives a double life. "Being-more-than-he-lets-himself-be" means that he strives "to-be-what-he-cannot-be," disowning what he could be and most fundamentally is. This disordered, false, neurotic mode of being has its counterpart in a too narrow, incoherent vision of the world and of truth.

The three theorists also agree, though in very different ways, that the patient must come to know, and to feel a wider, truer, fuller, more ample world. This coming to the truth is not only ideational [a matter of ideas], but must involve lived-conviction, affective [emotional] substantiality, and thereby a transformed life. . . .

When the Rogerian therapist refuses simply to answer his client's question but resolutely attends and responds to the client's feeling-life, he is expressing more than just his client and himself in an individual way. They stand together in a tradition of truth and value, a way of living, a language, a culture with its own standards. The therapist, especially, stands for a truth that transcends his whim, impulse, momentary thought, or feeling, and his personal appeal as a likable, admirable human being. This stand in something beyond and greater than himself is absolutely necessary for the therapeutic process because it is just this vision of the world within which the client's disorder can find principled integration and order. It is the therapist's world as opening on the truth and as able to comprehend the client's disunity in a living way that is necessary to the help of therapy.

The patient must be more than casually influenced; he must be introduced into a world of truth that is not subject to whim, not evanescent, and not caught in the grip of his own split self. For an effective therapy, this lived-vision of the world must be able to unite and integrate the "self-in-the-world" into a vision of truth and reality. Each theory provides a more or less adequate vision within which the patient can find a greater unity or harmony, a greater openness and receptivity, a greater amplitude of life and of truth than he has been able to live before, because each theory is more unified and principled than the world view the usual patient brings into therapy.

The patient, having lost himself in disunity and the conflict of his split life, turns to the therapist, after all, for a principled, unified, expert pathway of help. It is already presupposed by the patient and the therapist that this will not be arbitrary help but will be grounded in the search for the true and the good. Further, it is expected that the therapist will be somewhat a specialist in getting people better in touch with what is really real and really important.

Special Paths of Life

For the student of psychotherapy, it is obvious that each orientation and approach has a grip on *some* reality and that persons in each orientation can and do shape helpful relationships, even though each therapy is unique, special, and strange. In the pursuit of their special visions and special experience, each engages the patient in out-of-the-ordinary pursuits, leads him to experience the world at peculiar angles, and brings him to twists and turns of consciousness which take him out of the everyday world.

The Jungian will typically get the nonartist patient to paint, to make up imaginative stories, to daydream and talk about his daydreams as they are occurring, to pay close attention to his dreams and write them out, to develop an interest in the symbolic-imaginative collective realism of human existence, and so on. While this can be, and often is, helpful to individuals, it is also a highly specialized group of activities aimed at a highly specialized style of consciousness. In some way, each therapy orientation tends to introduce the patient to a specialized view of reality by employing a special, unusual mode of "living-in-relation" to the patient.

It is not immediately obvious, however, why each orientation sustains itself as separate from the other orientations to psychotherapy. As each plausibly expresses some truth about man, it would seem that they could be fruitfully combined in some way. To this end, many therapists and therapeutic thinkers have sought increasingly more comprehensive and adequate ways of dealing with patients and comprehending their varieties. Jung, especially, understands that each school of therapy constitutes a certain way of being a person. Within Jung's thought, this means that Freudian theory is appropriate to certain persons at certain stages of their development, whereas Adlerian theory is more appropriate to others.

There is certainly some truth in this idea; the reader may have noticed that he himself found one or another of the different theories in this text most convincing. Careful examination reveals, however, that logical coherence or objective evidence are not the only grounds for this preference. These special views are not just abstractive or purely scientific theories. They are ways of experiencing and living in the world; styles of interacting with people; modes of understanding, comprehending, and making sense of the world; they are even effectively toned colorations of certain modes of life. As such, they attract or repel.

The world that we bring to these specialized worlds is already a special world shaped by our own particular histories, specific sensitivities, cultural backgrounds, habits of thought, and social ways. Before we ever read

Freud, Jung, or Rogers, our way of life is already in hidden harmony or disharmony with the ways of living which they open up. Thus, our ease of understanding or not understanding the theories, our liking or disliking of them, our response to the specialized worlds they open up, is not based on a neutral objectivity or logic. As specialized worlds with special emphases and specific values, they appeal to us as ways to life, and we respond intuitively, and quite properly, in terms of our sense of whether they would be helpful in describing, unifying, or making sense of our own lives.

Some of the divergencies in therapeutic orientation can be understood in this way. Each offers not only a scientific theory, an expert approach to working helpfully with people, but also a whole world view of goals, values, and meanings. Each offers a specification of thought within a specific style or group of styles of life. Hence, the Freudian theory offers more than certain ideas about the inner psychic life, a certain view of development from infancy to adulthood, and a certain empiric-scientific idea about the distribution of energy in the body-mind of persons. The Freudian way of thinking offers itself as a mode of seeking to be reasonable and rational in a world that can be chaotic and irrational as a skepticism about values, traditional truths, and religious views; as a mode of suspicion, doubtfulness, and an attempt to penetrate the deceptive surfaces of things. Hence, liking or not liking the Freudian approach, finding it inwardly and importantly convincing to one's life, is primarily a question of the consonance of that life with these value-laden attitudes. In this sense, a person is predisposed toward or away from Freudian, Jungian, or Rogerian thought and practice before his formal exposure to them as theorists, therapists, or thinkers.

Little Brother Is Changing You

Farnum Gray with Paul S. Graubard and Harry Rosenberg

One criticism of behavior modification is that its practitioners can sometimes exercise too much control over other people's lives. Ordinarily, the accounts of how "behavior mod" is used deal with parents' and teachers' shaping children's or young people's behavior, prison guards' or psychologists' modifying inmate behavior, and so on. In other words, the technique is usually used to maintain and promote the existing power structure.

This article tells about a new and exciting use of the technique: to help students change their own environments and the behavior of the people (including parents and teachers) around them, to make life more rewarding and change others' perceptions of them. In the end, both the students and their "environments" benefited.

Jess's eighth-grade teachers at Visalia, California, found him frightening. Only 14 years old, he already weighed a powerful 185 pounds. He was easily the school's best athlete, but he loved fighting even more than he loved sports. His viciousness equaled his strength: he had knocked other students cold with beer bottles and chairs. Jess's catalog of infamy also included a 40-day suspension for hitting a principal with a stick, and an arrest and a two-and-a-half-year probation for assault.

Inevitably, Jess's teachers agreed that he was an incorrigible, and placed him in a class for those with behavioral problems. Had they known that he had begun secret preparations to change *their* behavior, they would have been shocked.

The New Jess

His math teacher was one of the first to encounter his new technique. Jess asked for help with a problem, and when she had finished her explanation, he looked her in the eye and said, "You really help me learn when you're nice to me." The startled teacher groped for words, and then said, "You caught on quickly." Jess smiled, "It makes me feel good when you praise me." Suddenly Jess was consistently making such statements to all of his teachers. And he would come to class early or stay late to chat with them.

Some teachers gave credit for Jess's dramatic turnaround to a special teacher and his rather mysterious class. They naturally assumed that he had done something to change Jess and his "incorrigible" classmates.

Rather than change them, the teacher had trained the students to become behavior engineers. Their parents, teachers and peers in the farm country of Visalia, California, had become their clients.

A Reward System

Behavior engineering involves the systematic use of consequences to strengthen some behaviors and to weaken others. Jess, for example, rewarded teachers with smiles and comments when they behaved as he wanted; when they were harsh, he turned away.

People often call reward systems immoral because they impose the engineer's values upon those conditions. But the Visalia Project turns things around, according to Harry Rosenberg, head of the project and Director of Special Education for the school district. "The revolutionary thing here is that we are putting behavior-modification techniques in the hands of the learner. In the past, behavior modification has been controlled more or less by the Establishment. It has been demanded that the children must change to meet the goodness-of-fit of the dominant culture. We almost reverse this, putting the kid in control of those around him. It's kind of a Rogerian [after Carl Rogers] use of behavior modification."

Rosenberg was born and reared in Visalia and has been teacher and principal in a number of schools in that area. He began using behavior modification nine years ago, and he has kept experimentation going in the district with modest grants, mostly Federal. His proposals have emphasized that Visalia is an isolated district that, to avoid provincialism, needs contact with innovative educators from around the country. The grants have paid a variety of consultants to work with Visalia schools over the years.

Reinforcing Opponents

The idea of training kids as behavior engineers arose from a single incident with a junior high school student. He was in a behavior-modification program for the emotionally disturbed. His teacher told Rosenberg that although the boy was responding fairly well to the class, he was getting into fights on the playground every day. As they discussed ways of helping the boy, the teacher suggested that they identify the kids with whom he was fighting and teach him to reinforce those kids for the behaviors that he wanted. The process worked.

Rosenberg mentioned the incident to Paul Graubard of Yeshiva University, who was a consultant to the district. The incident intrigued him and he thought that training students as behavior engineers could have widespread implications in education, answering some philosophical objections to the use of behavior modification in schools.

Rosenberg had long believed that many students who were segregated in special education classes should be reintegrated into regular classes. Graubard agreed. He designed an experiment to help children diagnosed as retardates, or as having learning or behavior problems, change their teachers' perceptions of them. This, predicted Graubard, would enable the child to be reintegrated into regular classes.

Special Classes: Incorrigibles and Deviants

For the pilot project, Rosenberg selected a local junior high school with an unfortunate but accurate reputation. It was the most resistant in the district to the integration of special education students; it had a higher percentage of students assigned to special classes than any other in the district. Classes for those labeled incorrigible held 10 percent of the school's 450 students; Rosenberg saw this as a disturbing tendency to give up on pupils too easily. He also found that minority children were more likely to be labeled incorrigible or tagged with some other form of deviancy. Directives from the principal and supervisors to treat all children alike regardless of race or ability had failed. To make matters worse, the school also had the highest suspension and expulsion rates in the district.

Graubard and Rosenberg selected seven children, ages 12 to 15, from a class for children considered incorrigible, to be the first behavior engineers. Jess and one other child were black, two were white, and three were Chicanos. A special education teacher gave the seven students instruction and practice in behavior modification for one 43-minute class period a day. He then moved them into regular classes for two periods each day. The teachers of these classes became their clients. The teachers ranged in age from 26 to 63, and had from two to 27 years of teaching experience.

Shaping Teachers' Behavior

Stressing the idea that the program was a scientific experiment, the special teacher required each student to keep accurate records. During the experiment, they were to record daily the number of both positive and negative contacts with their clients. The students would not try to change the teachers' behavior during the first period; instead, they would keep records only to determine the norm. For the next phase, the students were to work at shaping the teachers' behaviors and to continue to keep records. For the last phase the students were not to use any of the shaping techniques.

Rosenberg had estimated that record-keeping could begin after two weeks of training students to recognize and to record teachers' positive and negative behavior. But this preliminary training took twice as long as he expected. While the students quickly learned to score negative behavior, they were seldom able to recognize positive behavior in their teacher-clients. Without the knowledge of the teachers or of the student-engineers, trained adult aides also kept records of teacher behavior in classes. Rosenberg compared their records to those of the students to determine accuracy;

he found that the aides recorded substantially more instances of positive teacher behavior than did the students. For example, an aide reported that a teacher had praised a child, but the child reported that the teacher had chewed him out. Rosenberg determined through closer monitoring that the aides were more accurate. He speculated that students were unable to recognize positive teacher behavior because they were accustomed to failure and negative treatment.

The students learned to identify positive teacher behavior accurately by role playing and by studying videotapes. This eventually brought about a high correlation between their records and those kept by adult teacher aides.

Building a New Smile

Rosenberg and Graubard taught the students various reinforcements to use in shaping their teachers' behavior. Rewards included smiling, making eye contact, and sitting up straight. They also practiced ways of praising a teacher, for example, saying, "I like to work in a room where the teacher is nice to the kids." And they learned to discourage negative teacher behavior with statements like, "It's hard for me to do good work when you're cross with me."

Each student studied techniques for making himself personally more attractive. One of the hardest tasks for Jess, for example, was learning to smile. Through use of a videotape, he learned that instead of smiling at people, he leered at them menacingly. Although he thought the process was hilarious, he practiced before the camera, and eventually developed a charming smile.

Learning to praise teachers with sincerity was difficult for the children. They were awkward and embarrassed at first, but they soon became skillful. Rosenberg said that the teachers' responses were amazing, and added that "the nonverbal cues make the difference between being a wise guy and being believable. They had to *sincerely* mean it so it would be accepted by the teacher as an honest statement of a kid's feelings, not as smarting off." Besides learning to praise and to discourage teachers, they also learned to make small talk with them. This was a new skill for these students and, after considerable training, they excelled at it.

Ah Hah!

The students enjoyed using a device that Fritz Redl, a child psychologist, has called "the Ah-Hah reaction." When a pupil was sure that he already understood a teacher's explanation, he would say that he did not

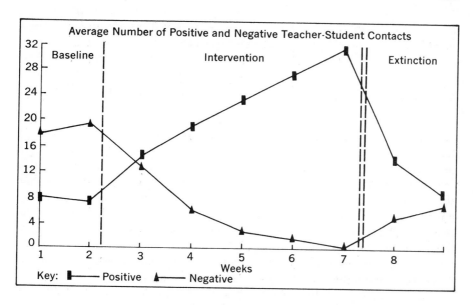

understand. When the teacher was halfway through a second explanation, the pupil would exclaim, "Ah hah! Now I understand! I could never get that before." Unlike some of the other reinforcements used, this one does not directly help the teacher improve his teaching, and it is less than honest. But it does encourage the teacher to like the student who gave him a feeling of accomplishment, and it is hoped, will lead to a better relationship between them.

Rosenberg recorded the results of the project on a graph. It showed that during each of the five weeks of shaping, the number of positive comments from teachers increased while the number of negative comments decreased. The seven students in Jess's group felt that they had succeeded in engineering their teachers' behavior more to their liking. The "extinction" period proved to be a good indicator of the effects of this engineering. During those two weeks, there was a sharp drop in positive comments, but a marked rise in negative comments. The engineering had indeed caused the changes in teacher behavior. As the extinction period showed, the teachers were like other people. Most were backsliders and they needed persistent reinforcement to maintain their new behavior.

When the project was over, the students resumed conditioning of the teachers, but they no longer kept formal records. Positive behavior increased once again, they reported; and in many cases, the negative comments ceased entirely. Rosenberg stressed the importance of requiring the children to keep data while teaching them reinforcement techniques. Projects that do not require data have failed. A student's success with a full, formal project, on the other hand, increases his ability to continue informal use of the behavior-engineering techniques that he has learned.

Who Really Changed?

The teacher-clients were enthusiastic about the project, and Rosenberg reported that so far, none had expressed hostility or displeasure. Some teachers did question the right of aides to observe and to record their teaching methods. But Rosenberg pointed out that it was "justified by the necessity for scientific validation of the procedure." He assured them that the district did not use data from the project for evaluation of their abilities, and so it would not affect their careers. When he explained the project to teachers afterwards, two or three said that it did change them. They admitted that they had become more positive toward their engineers. It is interesting to note, however, that most teachers tended to think of the projects as having changed the *children* rather than themselves.

Children, especially those in special education classes, often suffer feelings of impotence when they encounter the school environment. The crucial goal of the project was to instill within the student a feeling of power, the ability to control the controllers, i.e., his teachers and the school. As a result of their training in behavior engineering, the students reported feeling more power in their relationships with their teachers and the school than ever before. And with that feeling of power came a new feeling of self-confidence.

Parents as Clients

When children shape the behaviors of their parents, procedures are much the same as they are in the teacher-training projects. One difference, however, is that Rosenberg first asks the parents to let him work with the child. He does not tell them, though, that their children will be shaping them.

After the parents grant permission, the student decides what he wants to change in their behavior. Then, Rosenberg, or a special teacher will help him to design a project to bring about that change. After the child completes his project, Rosenberg talks with the parents in their home, and tells them what the child has been trying to accomplish. For example, one girl's mother seldom had meals on time, nor did she wash or iron the girl's clothes. Through systematic use of praise and other conditioning techniques, the girl made her mother into a much better homemaker. After more than a year, the mother had maintained her improvement and gained new self-respect.

Rosenberg cited other examples of adolescents who have shaped their parents to be less restrictive. But the critical result of each of these parent-shaping projects was the parents' increased awareness of their child's needs as a person. One father said that the project had really helped them with their child; for the first time the child talked to them about the different ways that they could help him.

Switch, Don't Fight

Since children have problems with each other as well as with adults, the students at Visalia have used the same conditioning techniques on their classmates.

"We can teach kids systematically how to make friends, how to get along with other students," Rosenberg said. "If they're being teased, we can teach them how to extinguish that permanently. If they're getting in fights, we can teach them to use basic learning principles to get the same thing they were trying to get by fighting."

He cited the example of Peggy, an attractive, intelligent girl who nevertheless encountered extreme problems in school. Her sixth-grade teachers sent her to the office frequently, and she was unable to make friends with the other students, whose hostility towards her made her miserable. She was gifted academically, but apparently because of her unhappiness in school, she had never ahieved even an average report card.

The special teacher helped her to design and to carry out a project to change her classmates' attitudes towards her. She was spectacularly successful. She spoke of the experience later: "They told me it was a scientific experiment, but I really didn't know what that meant. At first I was confused, and I really didn't think it would help me. But then I thought I might as well try it. At least I would get out of the classroom for part of the time."

The teacher asked Peggy to name three people whom she would like to have as friends. She named Arthur, Elwyn and Doris, all of whom frequently insulted her. For two weeks, she and her teacher recorded both positive and negative contacts with them. Then they discussed how they could increase the number of nice things that those students said to her. She began to apply the behavior-modification theory and techniques that her teacher had taught her. "I ignored Doris if she said anything bad to me. But when she said anything nice to me, I'd help her with her work, or compliment her, or sit down and ask her to do something with me. She's been increasing saying the nice things about me and now we can ride on the bus together, and she'll sit by me in the class. I'll tell you that really helps me a lot."

She engineered Elwyn's behavior in much the same manner; she would turn her back on him whenever he said something bad to her. But the first time he walked past her without saying something bad, she gave him a big smile and said, "Hi, Elwyn, how are you today?" After he recovered from his initial shock at Peggy's overtures, he eventually became her friend.

Arthur proved to be a much tougher subject than the other two. As Peggy stated, "He calls *everybody* names. I don't think anybody likes Arthur." She attempted to ignore him whenever he called her names, but with Arthur, this tactic was unsuccessful. If the other children laughed, it just gave Arthur more encouragement. As she discussed her shaping of Arthur, Peggy showed her grasp of behavioral learning theory. She realized that the reward of the other children's laughter far outweighed her attempts to extinguish Arthur's teasing by ignoring it. They, not she, were reinforcing Arthur. She came up with a clever solution. "If Arthur was standing around with some kids, I tried to stay away from him. I'd wait until Arthur was by himself, and then I'd walk up to him, say "Hi" and smile. He just didn't know what to do! The first time, though, he still called me a name, because he thought I was being mean to him . . . I'd never said anything nice to Arthur . . . hardly anybody ever does. I guess the only way [he] ever gets anybody's attention is by calling people names . . . being mean, and fighting."

Arthur was a small sixth-grader and apparently his stature caused him a great deal of self-consciousness. Peggy continued her positive reinforcement of Arthur, who is now friendly and no longer calls her names.

Peggy's social difficulties disappeared with dramatic speed as she made use of behavior-modification techniques. The teachers who once reported her attitude as disagreeable now found her charming and delightful. Her grade average rose to B, and the following year, she was elected president of the seventh grade.

Gifted Students

Rosenberg also instructed a class of gifted children in the use of behavior engineering; each child chose as a client a classmate, an adult, or a sibling. The children met frequently to discuss ways of handling problems and to report on the progress of their projects.

One student related how he had modified the disruptive behavior of a fellow math student. "I compliment him when he's not disruptive, and when he is, I say things to him like, 'You know, you could be a real bright student, and I like you a lot more when you don't disrupt the class.' He doesn't do it so much now, and he makes good grades."

One student was near despair over her efforts to change a teacher who, the other students agreed, was a difficult person. This teacher seemed impervious to any type of conditioning technique. "His latest thing is to send everybody out to sit under a table," she reported. "The first minute you open your mouth, he sends you out, and he doesn't really give you a chance." She had tried unsuccessfully to tell him that she was not learning math while sitting under the table, or she would apologize for saying something she should not have. But his response was usually, "You're not sorry, you're *ignorant!*" or "You're a knothead!"

The special education teacher asked the girl to name the behavior she most wanted to change. "Sending me out without a chance," the girl replied. "That's what bothers me most. I'm out in the *first 10 minutes* of the class!"

The special teacher then suggested that she say to the problem teacher, "I'd really appreciate it if you'd give me a warning before sending me out of the room, because I have trouble about talking anyway." It was necessary for her to repeat this several times, but it wasn't long before the teacher stopped sending kids out of the room.

Dignity and Worth

In *Beyond Freedom and Dignity,* B.F. Skinner points out that "Any evidence that a person's behavior may be attributed to external circumstances seems to threaten his dignity or worth. We are not inclined to give a person credit for achievements over which he has no control."

The people at Visalia are very concerned with maintaining the dignity of their clients. They believe that dignity is lost if the reinforcements given in behavior engineering are insincere. The individual must feel that he has earned rewards by his own actions, not because the engineer is using a technique. Otherwise the gesture lacks dignity and worth.

A junior high school boy drew agreement from his fellow students when he said, "If the person knows you're doing it, it won't work. At least not very well. He'll figure, 'Oh, he's trying to do it on me. He's not going to change the way I am!' " The boy cited his little brother as an example. He was trying to condition him not to curse, but the child found out about the conditioning techniques, and said, "Oh, you dumb little psychologist!"

Sincerity is also an integral part of instruction in behavior engineering. Rosenberg recalled with amusement that the teachers working with him on the experiment have at times doubted each other's sincerity. "One person compliments another, who says, 'You're just reinforcing me!' And the response is, 'Oh, the hell if I am! I really mean it.' With the kids, and with our own staff," Rosenberg said, "we've had to continually stress being sincere. You should really want the other person to change."

Many of the teachers felt that the engineering by the students created a more positive working environment; it eliminated the ever-present cutting and sarcasm. It also eliminated the meanness that is so often characteristic of junior high school students, according to a humanities teacher. He found that children of that age often conform by being meaner than they would really like to be. "I feel these projects are very effective in giving kids an excuse to be positive. At this age, that seems very helpful to them."

The Visalia project revived the issue of whether it is *moral* for people to condition each other. Certainly, behavior engineering could appear to be a harbinger of *A Clockwork Orange*, or *Brave New World*. But Rosenberg, Graubard, and other behaviorists believe that people are always conditioning each other, and that often, in their ignorance, they strengthen behaviors that no one wants. Proponents believe that to make really *constructive* changes in behavior, people should be conscious of what they are doing.

Future Projects

Rosenberg envisions another three or four years of research on this project before its techniques are disseminated in the school district. The current research is to provide information for the effective matching of the student with the technique for behavioral conditioning. In the future, this "prescription" will aid the counselor in helping the student.

Additional experiments planned will compare the teacher-training effectiveness of a single child to that of two or three children working as a team. And in some projects, teachers will know that the students are trying to change them. In this instance, Rosenberg wants to find out if that will make a difference in the effectiveness of the conditioning.

Having students train teachers is inexpensive and effective. Since the students spend more time with their teachers than does any professional supervisor, they have more opportunity to change them. Students also have the most to gain or to lose from the quality of teaching. Rosenberg estimates that the students are doing about as well in exercising control over human behavior as professionals who charge fifty dollars an hour.

11 The Loving Self

Love is the final word. Having said it, you've said it all. Health is what emerges as people know and love themselves. They experience and express themselves most fully in the love relationship.

To the billions of words that have been written about love, what can we hope to add? We have attempted, in this section, only to portray what we feel are some of the deepest meanings of love.

The late Marshall Hodge, a psychologist in private practice in Claremont, California, wrote our first selection, an excerpt from Your Fear of Love, *a sensitive and lucid discussion of what intimacy is all about, and why we seem to shy away from it even though we desire it.*

The second reading is an essay written by one of the editors of this volume, John Brennecke, who is also a psychologist. In his teaching and clinical work, he has experienced some of the satisfactions of seeing "love in action," especially in the learning of the fuller meanings of love.

A short poem by David Throckmorton gives us a view of the contrast between love and duty, roles, and form.

The next piece is an excerpt from Sylvia Plath's The Bell Jar, *a young woman's view of the relationship between sexual and emotional love, and her expectations as to how a sexual relationship may change her.*

Rollo May heightens our awareness of the beauty and rewards of a fulfilling sexual experience in the last reading in this chapter, an excerpt from his book Love and Will.

Loving and Trembling

Marshall B. Hodge

Why do we avoid each other? Why do people shy away from closeness and intimacy? Are there secret fears that keep us from loving? How do we recognize love, and how do we root out the obstacles that interfere with our fullest appreciation of each other?

Marshall B. Hodge offers us some of his deeper insights, gleaned from his practice of psychotherapy and marriage counseling. We must love in order to be full and free persons. Yet many of us don't love, either because we don't know how or are afraid to try.

Ted, a man in his middle twenties, sought the help of a psychotherapist because he was having difficulty in his marriage. One week, after he had had several sessions with the therapist, sudden and dramatic changes occurred in his relationship with his wife, Patti.

Both of them began to talk to each other about events and feelings that they had never discussed before. In some ways it was an agonizing week for them. Anger that had been pent up for months, and even years, poured forth. In the course of their self-disclosures each of them revealed that they had had brief sexual "flings" with another since their marriage. More expressions of anger and hurt burst forth, reaching an intensity they had never experienced before. But when the anger and hurt had been expressed other feelings began to manifest themselves. They became aware that they felt closer and more sexually alive to each other than they ever had before. As they moved toward each other they found themselves exquisitely sensitive to each other's touches and caresses.

Sexual intercourse had always been marred for the couple by the fact that Ted invariably had his orgasm almost immediately after entering the vagina, leaving both Patti and himself feeling frustrated and cheated. Now, suddenly, this, too, was changed. To his amazement he found that during intercourse he now remained for many minutes at the peak of the most delicious sexual enjoyment he had ever experienced, yet he was not aware of making any effort to control the timing of his sexual climax, but was caught up completely in the enjoyment of his own sensations and Patti's obvious enjoyment.

All of this occurred in one week between Ted's sessions with the therapist. When he appeared for his next hour it was natural that he describe what had happened. He did so with great enthusiasm, but then he said, "It was such a great week that I just can't understand what happened to me today. I discovered that my hands were literally shaking, and I just felt scared to death."

Ted's bewilderment was understandable. He assumed that he would feel more confident because of his new-found ability to be more completely himself and more expressive of his love and his sexual desire. The last thing he expected of himself was that he would become very frightened. He did not reckon with his fear of love, which he has in common with the rest of us.

Time and again experiences such as this confirm that we are most frightened by that for which we most long—the experience of intimacy. What can we do about this fear of love, which so often confronts us in ourselves and in those we love?

Perhaps one of the most helpful things we can do about it is to become clearly aware of it. Our relationships would often be more understandable if we could see these fears clearly in ourselves and others. For example, couples frequently report sequences of events in which they first felt very close and then shortly thereafter began arguing or nagging one another about some seemingly insignificant thing. These experiences mystify them and often lead to doubts about their love for each other. It would be helpful if we could recognize that for most of us the exquisite experience of intimacy is a razor's edge, which we cannot allow to exist for more than a few moments. When intimacy does occur, then we frequently trump up some "reason" for moving away from it.

In other instances we prevent ourselves from even momentary experiences of intimacy by finding something (almost anything!) to be angry, hurt, irritated, nervous, or busy about any time love comes threateningly close.

Anna, a woman in her early forties who was seeing a psychotherapist, followed a constant pattern for many weeks in her sessions. It would often be obvious during her weekly hour that she had some inclination to respond to the feelings of warmth and acceptance that he felt for her. Invariably, however, toward the end of the session she would find some reason to become violently angry with him. She would read some manipulative or rejecting meaning into some innocuous statement or glance of his. She would then explode at him, accuse him of being a phony and a charlatan, and stomp out of the room after hurling all manner of invectives at him. On one occasion when she was angry she refused to leave; and it was necessary for him to call the police to force her to do so.

But some dogged persistence in Anna kept her coming back week after week. And despite the anger that her behavior aroused in the therapist, which frequently led him to shout back and threaten never to see her again, he allowed the appointments to continue. Finally, after the pattern of her behavior had been pointed out many times, Anna gradually became aware of the fact that she was desperately frightened of caring. She began to recognize that she had to reject and hurt anyone who gave evidence of caring for her lest she be caught in the trap of the vulnerability of caring and be hurt again as she had been hurt many times before. Once this awareness began to dawn on her, Anna's moments of anger toward the therapist became less frequent, less violent, and more quickly over and done with when they did occur.

Gaining awareness of our fear of love is often a difficult task, for we tend to disguise it from ourselves and others by employing many defenses against intimacy.

One man, Bill, invariably sounded angry in any discussion with his wife. The two of them had been seeing a marriage counselor together for a number of sessions. During these sessions the two of them often clashed, and the arguments frequently seemed to start because Bill sounded so angry. Finally the therapist became suspicious of this, and when the husband spoke out loudly and with apparent anger toward his wife, the therapist interrupted to ask, "Bill, are you really angry right now?" Bill replied that he was not. "You sound as though you are." To this remark Bill replied, "I'm just speaking positively and with conviction, I'm not mad."

It appeared on further exploration that Bill was often not angry when he sounded as though he were. Perhaps he did have a reservoir of hostility built up over the years that had something to do with this behavior, but the function that it appeared to serve in relation to his wife and other people he cared for was one of keeping it virtually impossible to experience intimacy.

There are many similar defenses against intimacy. We may keep people at a distance by seeming indifferent to them, by being rigid or legalistic, or by playing the role of martyr. As long as we are successful at employing these ways of keeping others away, it is hard for us to become aware of our fear of love, for we make the possibility of intimacy so remote that there is little "danger" of our experiencing it. With the lion so successfully caged, we do not become aware of our fear of it!

Recognizing Our Fear of Love

If we can begin to see what we are doing and begin to give up some of our defenses, then we will be more likely to experience our fear of love directly. Once this occurs we are in a much better position to do something about it. It will also be helpful if we can not only be aware of our fear of love, but also accept it both in ourselves and in others. Here, as elsewhere, caring for ourselves seems to be the starting point for personality growth.

If we can experience and accept our fear of love, we will have less need of indirect ways of expressing it, which are almost invariably harmful to relationships. Instead of finding some pretext for withdrawing when we experience more intimacy than our fear will permit, we can admit our fear to ourselves and often to the other person as well. This direct way of responding to our fear will be far less destructive to the relationship. A natural ebb and flow of the experience and expression of love will then be possible, as we experience such intimacy as we are ready for and then withdraw for a time as our fear asserts itself too strongly. As we see this pattern clearly we will be far more able to take in stride apparent setbacks in our associations with others.

It also makes a big difference when we can recognize that when someone we love acts destructively or hurtfully toward us it is almost certainly an indication that he, too, is afraid rather than that he does not care for us. We may be just as hurt or express as much anger as we would if we did not have this insight. The chances of resolving the situation are much better, however, because we ourselves will not be likely to react as though we have been completely rejected and unloved. This is when we often play that "he loves me, he loves me not" game in which we tally up what we consider to be indications of how the other person feels about us. Often our feelings of worth become involved, as we say to ourselves, "There must be something the matter with me or he wouldn't treat me this way."

This game is pointless, for the problem does not usually lie in the absence of caring but rather in the fear of love, which leads the person to act as though he does not care. Of course, recognizing the existence of the fear of love does not always lead to a resolution of interpersonal difficulties. A woman, for example, might see that her husband belittles her constantly as a means of avoiding intimacy and as a way of coping with his own self-hate. Yet if she saw no crack in the wall of this defense, she might ultimately come to the conclusion that it would be self-destructive for her to continue the marriage. And a child might still have to be taken from a cruel father even though it might be recognized that his brutality is rooted in a terrible fear of love.

It will also be helpful if we can discover that the potential hurt of not experiencing and expressing love ultimately far outweighs the risks that accompany intimacy. We can never eliminate the possibility that we will be hurt when we dare to love. The emotional involvement of caring always includes vulnerability; in fact we can be certain that we will sometimes be hurt if we allow ourselves to love. Someone we love will die; someone we love will be injured; someone we love will be incurably and painfully ill; someone we love will be so frightened and mistrustful of our caring that they will react in ways that are hurtful or even destructive to us.

These are painful experiences, and we cannot avoid them if we choose to love. It is part of the human dilemma that love always includes the element of hurt. We are invariably hurt by those we love, and, as the song has it, "You always hurt the one you love, the one you shouldn't hurt at all." So it is not surprising that we are frightened of love and tend to shy away from it. The self-disclosure and involvement of love is a sometimes painful joy.

What are the alternatives to a life in which hope is experienced and expressed? Does such a life hold out the hope of any less hurt? Only two other alternatives appear to be available. One would be, if it is possible, to cut one's self off completely from the experience of love. Such persons would say in effect to themselves, "I won't allow anyone to mean anything to me. I may have business relationships of one kind or another, but no one will be important to me beyond the immediate dealings in which we find each other useful, and no one will learn anything of a personal nature about how I feel or who I really am. I'll never allow myself to experience the desire or need for love." Perhaps this kind of life could be achieved, but it sounds like a desperately lonely existence. Perhaps a person could keep so busy or be so controlled that he could even block the loneliness out of awareness, but what kind of life is that? The viewpoint suggested here does, of course, involve a value judgment that meaningfulness is found above all else in human relationships, although it does appear that few of us would *choose* to live so isolated an existence.

The other alternative is more often practiced, but it seems almost equally unsatisfying. This way of life would be to love guardedly and almost secretly. Although he may not be aware of it, such a person says to himself, "All right, so I admit *to myself* that I care for my children and my wife. And maybe there are a few other people in the world who mean something to me. But I'm going to play it cool. I'll never reveal too much of myself or let them know how much I care. No sense getting too far out on a limb or being too enthusiastic about our relationship. No use letting them see how much they mean to me. They'd be likely to find some way of using it to push me around or hurt me." A lot of us settle for this approach to love. But this, too, makes for a kind of loneliness and cheats us out of the deepest and most satisfying experiences of love. And since it involves a guardedness and calculated dullness in our relationships, it cheats us of the free, unburdened feeling that spontaneity in our actions and words could give us. All of life becomes toned down and the exhilarating excitement is taken away.

The risks of love are ever-present, but the alternatives are not inviting. So from the standpoint of satisfying living it *is* better even "to have loved and lost than never to have loved at all."

Taking a Chance on Love

If we postponed the experience and expression of love until we no longer feared it, we would postpone it forever. Some people do appear to use their fear of love as a perpetual excuse for stalemated living—loving and trembling seem to go together. If we desire love we must learn to love in spite of our fears.

This process of "taking a chance on love" might be compared to the experience of a person who wants to make parachute jumps. If he is not a fool, he is frightened. And no amount of prejump training will eradicate that fear. When the time comes to make the leap he will be trembling internally and, quite possibly, externally. No amount of reassurance by experienced jumpers will make it otherwise. Making the leap of love is not too unlike this. No amount of advance preparation or reassurance from others will keep us from experiencing fear. It is different, however, in that we can make some tentative leaps in the direction of self-disclosure and the involvement of love and withdraw back into the security of emotional distance if the experience is too frightening. The parachutist, once committed, doesn't have that option!

When we make our first moves toward deeper experiences and more open expressions of love, it may seem at first that our fear is greatly intensified. This is a very critical time, for we may become so frightened that we choose to withdraw permanently and not allow ourselves another chance to feel so deeply.

This sometimes happens in psychotherapy. After a few sessions a person may begin to respond to the therapist's warmth with feelings of caring. Perhaps the individual does not even allow himself to verbalize these feelings but suddenly "discovers" he cannot afford the sessions or does not have sufficient time to work them into a busy schedule.

It is understandable that the experience of fear is intensified at first when we allow ourselves to love more deeply. In the past our defenses—the devices we used to keep ourselves emotionally distant from others—protected us not only from the experience of love but also from the full awareness of our fear. As we allow the defenses to crumble we stand naked and vulnerable before our fear.

One thing that will help as we begin to allow ourselves the experience of love will be the awareness that we are no longer in the same circumstances as we were when the fear developed within us. When we were first exposed to the risks of love, we were children. And when we experienced the hurts of feeling rejected, we were relatively helpless to do anything about the situation. No wonder we were frightened and built whatever defenses against hurt we could by walling ourselves off emotionally.

We Aren't Helpless

Often as adults we still feel helpless, as though we were still children. But we are not helpless. If we express love and are rejected, we can do something about it—we can express our anger and frustration. If our loving proves unsatisfying we can withdraw from that person if we choose to and express our love to others more able to respond. We can also discover that another person's inability to express love to us when we love them has nothing to do with our value as a person. Perhaps most important of all we can learn that we can survive hurt and that, while it is never pleasant, it need not be catastrophic.

Our fear of love will never completely disappear any more than would the fear of the parachutist. In both instances there is always a realistic fear of hurt, but as we are able to enter into more and more emotionally intimate relationships, the fear will gradually lessen. We will learn from experience that the satisfactions far exceed the occasional hurts we experience, and we will have so much fun enjoying the intimacy and the freedom of spontaneous living, we will give decreasing attention to the hurts or our fear of them.

We will find it increasingly easy to be ourselves and to express all our feelings, for we will have increasing confidence that people will generally like us as we are. And when we are frightened, we will likely find it comfortable to express that feeling, too—and expressing it will help to dissipate it.

A sentence in the New Testament reads, "There is no fear in love, but perfect love casts out fear." (I John 4:18) It is true. There is no fear *in* love—only fear *of* love and the vulnerability it involves. And the repeated experience of love reduces fear.

Whether the central message of the New Testament, which revolves around the crucifixion of Jesus, is regarded as the literal truth or as a myth growing out of man's yearning for meaning in life, the theme is a deeply moving one. It is often garbled by theological lingo, but it finally comes down to relationships and appears to be essentially this: God risked creating persons so independent that they could love him or thumb their noses at him. He went even further and chose to love them. As it always does, the decision to love necessarily included suffering. But it must have been worth the risk, for perhaps the alternative even for God was the ultimate loneliness of having no one to love.

We can discover for ourselves that it is worth the risk to love, even though we tremble and even though we know we will sometimes experience the hurt we fear.

The Mysteries of Love

John H. Brennecke

*Love's ecstasies, agonies, highs, lows, ins and outs, all are
extolled by writers of every kind, in every language, from every land.
The most used (and abused) word is still the least understood
concept.*

*Love is a mystery and contains many other mysteries. The
following article, written especially for this book, attempts to describe
some of these mysterious properties of love. The author, a
psychologist and college teacher, has been engaged in marriage and
family counseling and psychotherapy for the past eleven years.
Throughout his work, Mr. Brennecke has attempted to show people
that love is still one of the most important and productive things
people have going for them. When everything else has failed, we still
have love to try. Most of us don't really try it.*

Most of us don't love. This isn't a statement designed to stir up con-
troversy or stimulate debate: it's a statement of information. I don't pretend
to be wise; I claim a certain intelligence, a bit of practical knowledge, a
smattering of common sense. But I have not yet lived fully enough to claim
wisdom. What I am claiming in my opening sentence is a beginning of
wisdom.

Many of us lust. We can, most of us, stir up enough animal drive and
physical power to seek, find, and consummate a physical erotic experience.

Many of us feel desire. Almost any healthy person can know what it
feels like to want to be with someone, to touch and hold and experience him
fully. We also can know what it's like to be desired. That feels nice. You can
go all day on that feeling.

Many of us know affection. We can pat and touch, hug and kiss, nuzzle
and snuggle, grip and grapple: it's fun, and nearly everyone enjoys it. It
feels good to get it and it also feels very nice to give it.

Many of us enjoy the company of another person, or many others. This
involves shared interests, shared symbols (like words and ideas), and some
emotions that we can have in common.

Many of us feel good about another person. We appreciate him, value

Written especially for this anthology by John H. Brennecke.

him, like him, enjoy him (possibly, though who's to say this is a necessity?),
or want to express some kind of good feeling about him.

Many people feel respect for others, too. They stand in some kind of
awe or reverence, possibly, or maybe just a simple feeling of deference.

But, these things, whatever else they are, don't really qualify as love.
Why not?

The reasons are complex, but they *can* be described. Most of us don't
really know what love is. Many people claim to love, to be in love, to write
on, preach about, teach about, or counsel in, love. But if my own life and
loving tells me anything, it's that love is a "sweet, elusive butterfly," as the
song says.

Love is a fragile and intangible "something." Like Zen, "that which can
be expressed in words *isn't*" love. This smacks of mysticism and fantasy.
Possibly there is a lot of both involved in love. Certainly what Dr. Harlow
calls "love" when he writes about the need for contact comfort in his
monkeys isn't all there is to it. Certainly, the moods and emotions sung
about, poetized about, and dreamed about aren't all there is to it.

Erich Fromm tells us that to really experience love you must *trust* the
loved one. Trust, or the willingness to put yourself into the keeping of
someone else, is a fairly rare commodity today. We are into a mood of
distrust and skepticism. We are caught up in a form of suspiciousness and
social distance that really makes trust seem like a naïve and, therefore,
impractical behavior. Trusting people, we're told, get caught, used, taken
advantage of, and they certainly stand a damned good chance of getting
hurt. Moreover, they lose. We live in a society that worships winning,
achieving. Losers are scorned, pitied, spit on, and relegated to the cellar,
whether in baseball ("Nice guys finish last!") or business ("Dog eats dog in
this game, Charlie!") or politics.

Nonetheless, trust we must, or love just doesn't happen. If we're going
to take this matter of loving seriously, then we may just have to take the
risky course of trusting. You must be willing to "put yourself into the hands
of" somebody else. You must be ready, willing, and able to open yourself up
to that person, to expose yourself, to set yourself up, to drop whatever
protective defenses you may have acquired to enter into an authentic
relationship, naked and unarmed. To trust, of course, means to become
vulnerable. Vulnerable means open to being hurt or used. Most of us can't
let this happen. Most of us are "controllers" or manipulators. We aren't used
to, nor willing to try, being under someone else's control or at another's
disposal. Yet this is partly what love is all about.

Fromm says we have to accept four traits if the love thing is going to be
real and give us pleasure. We have to know the other, respect the other, care
for the other, and be responsible for the other. Knowing means more than
intellectual knowledge; it means deep, intimate, personal knowing, and it

often takes time. Take heed, you impetuous and impatient young lovers! Love at first sight is more a fantasy, a screenplay, than a reality. It rarely happens.

Respect means appreciation for the unique individuality and character of another person. It means you want him to become everything he can be. It means setting him up for fulfillment, and being willing to be an active partner in that process. It's plain hard work, and it calls for a degree of unselfishness.

Caring means concern-in-action. You can't just wish a person well. That's important, but you've got to be willing to *do* something in his best interests, in his behalf. You've got to show concern and act on it. It may mean protecting him, it may mean defending or helping or interceding for him. Whatever form it takes, it means *doing* something, actively and personally, to enhance the well-being of the one you love. As Eliza Doolittle says in *My Fair Lady*, "Show me!"

Responsibility is better spelled response-ability. It means you are able and willing to respond to the emotional needs of your loved one. It means seeing or sensing his needs and following through in trying to meet them. This is where most of us fall down on the job. We like the hugging or kissing, the sexual and sensual pleasures, but we don't all like to follow through with the difficult part of it.

Fromm also cautions us against one-sided "love affairs." They don't exist. Love is a relationship, and as such, it involves two people at least. Each person in the relationship must give and get as much as the other. The words for this are mutuality and reciprocity, but they are rather cold and intellectual. Most simply, I must get as much out of this relationship as you do, and you also must get as much pleasure and satisfaction and comfort and joy as I do.

All of the above is probably right, maybe even true, but there is something about love that just can't be defined or even explained.

Abraham Maslow, a very loving and wise man, tells us that young people today have extracted a lot of the "juices" out of love. By claiming to know it, easily and cheaply, they claim to have had it all. Yet what many of them (and us) have done is to "desacralize" love, especially the sexual expression of it:

> These youngsters mistrust the possibility of values and virtues. They feel themselves swindled or thwarted in their lives. Most of them have, in fact, dopey parents whom they don't respect very much, parents who are quite confused themselves about values and who, frequently, are simply terrified of their children and never punish them or stop them from doing things that are wrong. So you have a situation where the youngsters simply despise their

elders—often for good and sufficient reason. Such youngsters have learned to make a big generalization: They won't listen to anybody who is grown up, especially if the grown-up uses the same words which they've heard from the hypocritical mouth. . . .

The youngsters have learned to reduce the person to the concrete object and to refuse to see what he might be or to refuse to see him in his symbolic values or to refuse to see him or her eternally. Our kids have desacralized sex, for example. Sex is nothing; it is a natural thing, and they have made it so natural that it has lost its poetic qualities in many instances, which means that it has lost practically everything.[1]

We don't mean anything religious or spiritual here, and neither does Maslow, at least not in the conventional sense of those terms. What has to be involved in love is some mystery, some feeling that even though we can't understand everything going on, it still feels good. There should be something about the person, about the relationship, that can't quite be identified, that we just can't put our finger on, that goes beyond words. True lovers know this and tend to enjoy the experience. Most of us would sit around and brood about the mystery: we've just got to make sense—mathematical and logical sense—out of everything we do. Pity, that!

To get a glimpse of why this is so, we have to dig into mythology. Rollo May helps us here. He reminds us that Eros, whom we call the god of love, was a puzzling creature. He wasn't human, but he wasn't quite divine. He was what the ancient Greeks called a *daimon*. Plato says it: "Eros is a daimon. He is neither mortal nor immortal, but a mean between the two. . . . He is the mediator between men and gods, and therefore in him all is bound together."

Rollo May defines the *daemonic* (or *daimonic*) as any natural function in the individual

which has the power of taking over the whole person. . . . Eros is the daemon which constitutes man's creative spirit, the drive that not only impels him to sexual union and to other forms of love, but also incites in him the yearning for knowledge and drives him to seek union with the truth, to become poet, or artist, or scientist. Sex and Eros, anger and rage, and the craving for power are daemonic and thus *either* creative or destructive.[2]

All this means that love and sex are extremely powerful forces in our

1. Abraham Maslow, "Self-Actualization and Beyond," in James F.T. Bugental, *The Challenges of Humanistic Psychology.* (New York: McGraw-Hill, 1967), p. 284.

2. Quoted in Erich Fromm, "The Daemonic: Love & Death," in *Psychology Today*, February 1968, pp. 16 – 17.

lives. They are sources of sublime satisfaction and hellish frustrations—often at the same time. Most people who love know that they experience the fullest frustration and anger, even hatred, with the ones they love.

The opposite of love isn't hate; they go together and are complementary parts of the whole. The opposite of love is *indifference* or apathy. If love is deep feeling ("pathos") then its opposite is no feeling ("apathy"). Hate and love are parts of the same kind of involvement. This means that there's a tremendous amount of tension and conflict in a love relationship. It isn't all peace and calm and nice, gooey feelings; it may mean hurt and bother and upset and anxiety and even fear. But since it also means joy and fondness and pleasure and peace and Candyland, it's certainly well worth all the "bad" parts.

Love is often wild and unexplainable. It should be! Nothing is so unsatisfying as a placid, taken-for-granted relationship. I would join Maslow and May and Fromm and many, many real lovers in saying that to love is to know (and yet not know) a lot of wild and unpredictable, sensual and cognitive, joyous and unrehearsed, spontaneous and free kinds of feelings and experiences.

As a teacher and certainly as a therapist, there is nothing more important I can give my students and clients than this insight: Love, and love well. It can mean all the difference between a full or an empty life. Since "what the world needs now is love, sweet love," I wish you real love, wild and full and free and *warm! Take love;* take life!

Gee, You Didn't Have to Get Nasty About It

David B. Throckmorton

This is a poem by a young man whose marriage did not work out, expressing where he feels it went wrong.

> I gave you love,
>   you gave me responsibility,
>   role expectations,
>   obligations,
>   commitments,
>   codes of conduct,
>   duty,
>   and other vulgarities
>   too horrible to mention.

Printed by permission of the author.

from *The Bell Jar*

Sylvia Plath

Many of us have strange and wonderful expectations as to what effect falling in love, being married, or even having sex with someone may have on us. None of these experiences is likely to turn anyone into an angel or devil, despite the individual's expectations. In this brief, humorous excerpt from her book, The Bell Jar, *Sylvia Plath describes one young girl's feelings about how different she might be if she were seduced by an attractive man.*

The more I thought about it the better I liked the idea of being seduced by a simultaneous interpreter in New York City. Constantin seemed mature and considerate in every way. There were no people I knew he would want to brag to about it, the way college boys bragged about sleeping with girls in the backs of cars to their roommates or their friends on the basketball team. And there would be a pleasant irony in sleeping with a man Mrs. Willard had introduced me to, as if she were, in a roundabout way, to blame for it.

When Constantin asked if I would like to come up to his apartment to hear some balalaika records I smiled to myself. My mother had always told me never under any circumstances to go with a man to a man's rooms after an evening out, it could mean only one thing.

"I am very fond of balalaika music," I said.

Constantin's room had a balcony, and the balcony overlooked the river, and we could hear the hooing of the tugs down in the darkness. I felt moved and tender and perfectly certain about what I was going to do.

I knew I might have a baby, but that thought hung far and dim in the distance and didn't trouble me at all. There was no one hundred percent sure way not to have a baby, it said in an article my mother cut out of the *Reader's Digest* and mailed to me at college. This article was written by a married woman lawyer with children and called "In Defense of Chastity."

It gave all the reasons a girl shouldn't sleep with anybody but her husband and then only after they were married.

The main point of the article was that a man's world is different from a woman's world and a man's emotions are different from a woman's emotions and only marriage can bring the two worlds and the two different sets of emotions together properly. My mother said this was something a girl didn't know about till it was too late, so she had to take the advice of people who were already experts, like a married woman.

This woman lawyer said the best men wanted to be pure for their wives, and even if they weren't pure, they wanted to be the ones to teach their wives about sex. Of course they would try to persuade a girl to have sex and say they would marry her later, but as soon as she gave in, they would lose all respect for her and start saying that if she did that with them she would do that with other men and they would end up by making her life miserable.

The woman finished her article by saying better be safe than sorry and besides, there was no sure way of not getting stuck with a baby and then you'd really be in a pickle.

Now the one thing this article didn't seem to me to consider was how a girl felt.

It might be nice to be pure and then to marry a pure man, but what if he suddenly confessed he wasn't pure after we were married, the way Buddy Willard had? I couldn't stand the idea of a woman having to have a single pure life and a man being able to have a double life, one pure and one not.

Finally I decided that if it was so difficult to find a red-blooded intelligent man who was still pure by the time he was twenty-one I might as well forget about staying pure myself and marry somebody who wasn't pure either. Then when he started to make my life miserable I could make his miserable as well.

When I was nineteen, pureness was the great issue.

Instead of the world being divided up into Catholics and Protestants or Republicans and Democrats or white men and black men or even men and women, I saw the world divided into people who had slept with somebody and people who hadn't, and this seemed the only really significant difference between one person and another.

I thought a spectacular change would come over me the day I crossed the boundary line.

I thought it would be the way I'd feel if I ever visited Europe. I'd come home, and if I looked closely into the mirror I'd be able to make out a little white Alp at the back of my eye. Now I thought that if I looked into the mirror tomorrow I'd see a doll-size Constantin sitting in my eye and smiling out at me.

Well, for about an hour we lounged on Constantin's balcony in two separate slingback chairs with the victrola playing and the balalaika records stacked between us. A faint milky light diffused from the street lights or the half moon or the cars or the stars, I couldn't tell what, but apart from holding my hand Constantin showed no desire to seduce me whatsoever.

I asked if he was engaged or had any special girlfriend, thinking maybe that's what was the matter, but he said no, he made a point of keeping clear of such attachments.

At last I felt a powerful drowsiness drifting through my veins from all the pine-bark wine I had drunk.

"I think I'll go in and lie down," I said.

I strolled casually into the bedroom and stooped over to nudge off my shoes. The clean bed bobbed before me like a safe boat. I stretched full length and shut my eyes. Then I heard Constantin sigh and come in from the balcony. One by one his shoes clonked on to the floor, and he lay down by my side.

I looked at him secretly from under a fall of hair.

He was lying on his back, his hands under his head, staring at the ceiling. The starched white sleeves of his shirt, rolled up to the elbows, glimmered eerily in the half dark and his tan skin seemed almost black. I thought he must be the most beautiful man I'd ever seen.

I thought if only I had a keen, shapely bone structure to my face or could discuss politics shrewdly or was a famous writer Constantin might find me interesting enough to sleep with.

And then I wondered if as soon as he came to like me he would sink into ordinariness, and if as soon as he came to love me I would find fault after fault, the way I did with Buddy Willard and the boys before him.

The same thing happened over and over:

I would catch sight of some flawless man off in the distance, but as soon as he moved closer I immediately saw he wouldn't do at all.

That's one of the reasons I never wanted to get married. The last thing I wanted was infinite security and to be the place an arrow shoots off from. I wanted change and excitement and to shoot off in all directions myself, like the colored arrows from a Fourth of July rocket.

I woke to the sound of rain.

It was pitch dark. After a while I deciphered the faint outlines of an unfamiliar window. Every so often a beam of light appeared out of thin air, traversed the wall like a ghostly, exploratory finger, and slid off into nothing again.

Then I heard the sound of somebody breathing.

At first I thought it was only myself, and that I was lying in the dark in my hotel room after being poisoned. I held my breath, but the breathing kept on.

A green eye glowed on the bed beside me. It was divided into quarters like a compass. I reached out slowly and closed my hand on it. I lifted it up. With it came an arm, heavy as a dead man's, but warm with sleep.

Constantin's watch said three o'clock.

He was lying in his shirt and trousers and stocking feet just as I had left him when I dropped asleep, and as my eyes grew used to the darkness I made out his pale eyelids and his straight nose and his tolerant, shapely mouth, but they seemed insubstantial, as if drawn on fog. For a few minutes I leaned over, studying him. I had never fallen asleep beside a man before.

I tried to imagine what it would be like if Constantin were my husband.

It would mean getting up at seven and cooking him eggs and bacon and toast and coffee and dawdling about in my nightgown and curlers after he'd left for work to wash up the dirty plates and make the bed, and then when he came home after a lively, fascinating day he'd expect a big dinner, and I'd spend the evening washing up even more dirty plates till I fell into bed, utterly exhausted.

This seemed a dreary and wasted life for a girl with fifteen years of straight A's, but I knew that's what marriage was like, because cook and clean and wash was just what Buddy Willard's mother did from morning till night, and she was the wife of a university professor and had been a private school teacher herself.

Once when I visited Buddy I found Mrs. Willard braiding a rug out of strips of wool from Mr. Willard's old suits. She'd spent weeks on that rug, and I had admired the tweedy browns and greens and blues patterning the braid, but after Mrs. Willard was through, instead of hanging the rug on the wall the way I would have done, she put it down in place of her kitchen mat, and in a few days it was soiled and dull and indistinguishable from any mat you could buy for under a dollar in the five and ten.

And I knew that in spite of all the roses and kisses and restaurant dinners a man showered on a woman before he married her, what he secretly wanted when the wedding service ended was for her to flatten out underneath his feet like Mrs. Willard's kitchen mat.

Hadn't my own mother told me that as soon as she and my father left Reno on their honeymoon—my father had been married before, so he needed a divorce—my father said to her, "Whew, that's a relief, now we can stop pretending and be ourselves"?—and from that day on my mother never had a minute's peace.

I also remembered Buddy Willard saying in a sinister, knowing way that after I had children I would feel differently, I wouldn't want to write poems any more. So I began to think maybe it was true that when you were married and had children it was like being brainwashed, and afterward you went numb as a slave in some private, totalitarian state.

As I stared down at Constantin the way you stare down at a bright, unattainable pebble at the bottom of a deep well, his eyelids lifted and he looked through me, and his eyes were full of love. I watched dumbly as a shutter of recognition clicked across the blur of tenderness and the wide pupils went glossy and depthless as patent leather.

Aspects of the Love Act

Rollo May

One of the closest experiences one can share with another human being—as well as one of the most potentially alienating—is the sexual act. In this moving excerpt from his book Love and Will, *Rollo May talks of some of the best things that can emerge out of a satisfying sexual experience—an expanded sense of identity, a new enrichment of self, the pleasure of being able to give to another person.*

Let us summarize how the love act contributes to the deepening of consciousness. First, there is the tenderness which comes out of an awareness of the other's needs and desires and the nuances of his feelings. The experience of tenderness emerges from the fact that the two persons, longing, as all individuals do, to overcome the separateness and isolation to which we are all heir because we are individuals, can participate in a relationship that, for the moment, is not of two isolated selves but a union. In this love act, the lover often cannot tell whether a particular sensation of delight is felt by him or his loved one—and it doesn't make any difference. A sharing takes place which is a new *Gestalt*, a new field of magnetic force, a new being.

The second aspect of the deepened consciousness comes from the affirmation of the self in the love act. Despite the fact that many people in our culture use sex to get a short-circuited, ersatz identity, the love act can and ought to provide a sound and meaningful avenue to the sense of personal identity. We normally emerge from love-making with renewed vigor, a vitality which comes not from triumph or proof of one's strength but from the expansion of awareness. Probably in lovemaking there is always some element of sadness—to continue an analogy suggested in an earlier chapter—as there is in practically all music no matter how joyful (precisely because it does not last; one hears it at that moment or it is lost forever). This sadness comes from the reminder that we have not succeeded absolutely in losing our separateness; and the infantile hope that we can recover the womb never becomes a reality. Even our increased self-awareness can also be a poignant reminder that none of us ever overcomes his loneliness completely. But by the replenished sense of our own personal significance in the love act itself, we can accept these limitations laid upon us by our human finiteness.

This leads immediately to the third aspect, the enrichment and fulfillment—so far as this is possible—of personality. Beginning with the expansion of awareness of our own selves and our feelings, this consists of experiencing our capacity to give pleasure to the other person, and thereby achieving an expansion of meaning in the relationship. We are carried beyond what we were at any given moment; I become literally more than I was. The most powerful symbol imaginable for this is *procreation*—the fact that a new being may be conceived and born. By new being I mean not simply a literal "birth," but the birth of some new aspect of one's self. Whether literal or partially metaphorical, the fact remains that the love act is distinguished by being procreative, and whether casual and ephemeral or faithful and lasting, this is the basic symbol of love's creativity.

A fourth aspect of new consciousness lies in the curious phenomenon that being able to give to the other person in lovemaking is essential to one's own full pleasure in the act. This sounds like a banal moralism on our age of mechanization of sex and emphasis on "release of tension" in sexual objects. But it is not sentimentality; it is rather a point which anyone can confirm in his own experience in the love act—that to give is essential to one's own pleasure. Many patients in psychotherapy find themselves discovering, generally with some surprise, that something is missing if they cannot "do something for," give something to, the partner—the normal expression of which is the giving in the act of intercourse itself. Just as giving is essential to one's own full pleasure, the ability to receive is necessary in the love relationship also. If you cannot receive, your giving will be a domination of the partner. Conversely, if you cannot give, your receiving will leave you empty. The paradox is demonstrably true that the person who can only receive becomes empty, for he is unable actively to appropriate and make his own what he receives. We speak, thus, not of receiving as a passive phenomenon, but of active receiving; one knows he is receiving, feels it, absorbs it into his own experience whether he verbally acknowledges it or not, and is grateful for it.

A corollary of this is the strange phenomenon in psychotherapy that when the patient feels some emotion—eroticism, anger, alienation, or hostility—the therapist normally finds himself feeling that same emotion. This inheres in the fact that when a relationship is genuine, they empathetically share a common field of emotion. This leads to the fact that, in everyday life, we normally tend to fall in love with those who love us. The meaning of "wooing" and "winning" a person is to be found here. The great "pull" to love someone comes precisely from his or her loving you. Passion arouses an answering passion.

Now I am aware of all the objections which will immediately be raised to this statement. One is that people are often repulsed by someone's loving them. Another is that my statement does not take into account all the added things one is motivated to *do* for the beloved and that it places too great an emphasis on passivity. The first objection, I answer, is the reverse proof of my point; we inhabit a *Gestalt* with the one who loves us, and to protect ourselves against his emotion, possibly with good reason, we react with revulsion. The second objection is merely a footnote to what I am already saying—that if someone loves us, he *will* do the many things necessary to show us that this is so; the actions are not the cause, however, but part of the total field. And the third objection will be made only by people who still separate passive and active and who have not accepted or understood active receiving. As we all know, the love experience is filled with pitfalls and disappointments and traumatic events for most of us. But all the pitfalls in the world do not gainsay the point that the given effect going out to the other does incite a response, positive or negative, in him. To quote Baldwin again, we are "like lovers [who] insist on, or create, the consciousness of the others." Hence, making *love* (with the verb being neither a manipulative nor accidental one) is the most powerful incentive for an answering emotion.

There is, finally, the form of consciousness which occurs ideally at the moment of climax in sexual intercourse. This is the point when the lovers are carried beyond their personal isolation, and when a shift in consciousness occurs which they experience as uniting them with nature itself. There is an accelerating experience of touch, contact, union to the point where, for a moment, the awareness of separateness is lost, blotted out in a cosmic feeling of oneness with nature. In Hemingway's novel, *For Whom the Bell Tolls*, the older woman, Pilar, waits for the hero and the girl he loves when they have gone ahead into the mountain to make love; and when they return, she asks, "Did the earth shake?" This seems to be a normal part of the momentary loss of awareness of the self and the surging up of a sudden consciousness that includes the earth as well. I do not wish my account to sound too "ideal," for I think it is a quality, however subtle, in all lovemaking except the most depersonalized sort. Nor do I wish it to sound simply "mystic," for despite limitations in our awareness, I think it is an inseparable part of actual experience in the love act.

12 The Transcending Self

Humans are one in their nature, but often experience themselves in other ways. All people everywhere have found it necessary to relate themselves to something outside or other than themselves. People do many things in their attempt to "get outside" their ordinary flesh-locked existence. They utilize religion and a variety of "cultic" behaviors to experience something more.

People have always been interested in the mystical, the odd, the exotic, the other-worldly. In their interest, partly from curiosity and partly because they hoped to relate themselves to something Other, they have done many interesting and also desperate things.

Psychiatrist Ronald Laing discusses the transcendent experience in an excerpt from his book, The Politics of Experience. He makes a strong case for the necessity of getting out of one's self and relating to a larger reality.

Alan Watts is a many-faceted man: Zen devotee, Taoist, Anglican priest, lay psychologist, and writer. He is an advocate of the larger reality, feeling that humans have a "metaphysical instinct."

The last article summarizes some research that may revolutionize our thinking about personality as it is affected by the brain. It is quite possible that each individual has two separate interpreters of the environment, built into the two sides of the brain. One side tends to be intuitive and creative, the other logical and rational—and they do not always function as a unified and coordinated whole.

Transcendental Experience

Ronald Laing

*People are insecure because they are limited in their knowledge
of many things; about none of these things are they as ignorant as they
are about themselves.*

*How do we find ourselves? We do it in the way advocated by
mystics of old, by "losing ourselves." Laing believes that the
experience of psychosis may be a necessary one for some people.
Others may have to experiment with transcending behavior, which
includes drugs, alcohol, music, and other types of "skinless"
behavior. We present his views for their value in provoking your
thinking, not as final answers to this enormous problem.*

We are living in an age in which the ground is shifting and the
foundations are shaking. I cannot answer for other times and places.
Perhaps it has always been so. We know it is true today.

In these circumstances, we have every reason to be insecure. When
the ultimate basis of our world is in question, we run to different holes
in the ground, we scurry into roles, statuses, identities, interpersonal relations. We attempt to live in castles that can only be in the air because
there is no firm ground in the social cosmos on which to build. We are
all witnesses to this state of affairs. Each sometimes sees the same fragment of the whole situation differently; often our concern is with different presentations of the original catastrophe.

In this chapter I wish to relate the transcendental experiences that
sometimes break through in psychosis, to those experiences of the divine
that are the living fount of all religion. . . .

Experience may be judged as invalidly mad or as validly mystical.
The distinction is not easy. In either case, from a social point of view,
such judgments characterize different forms of behavior, regarded in our
society as deviant. People behave in such ways because their experience
of themselves is different. It is on the existential meaning of such unusual experience that I wish to focus.

Psychotic experience goes beyond the horizons of our common, that
is, our communal, sense.

What regions of experience does this lead to? It entails a loss of the
usual foundations of the "sense" of the world that we share with one an-

From *The Politics of Experience* by Ronald D. Laing, pp. 131–145. Reprinted by permission
of Penguin Books Ltd.

other. Old purposes no longer seem viable; old meanings are senseless; the distinctions between imagination, dream, external perceptions often seem no longer to apply in the old way. External events may seem magically conjured up. Dreams may seem to be direct communications from others; imagination may seem to be objective reality.

But most radical of all, the very ontological foundations are shaken. The being of phenomena shifts and the phenomenon of being may no longer present itself to us as before. There are no supports, nothing to cling to, except perhaps some fragments from the wreck, a few memories, names, sounds, one or two objects, that retain a link with a world long lost. This void may not be empty. It may be peopled by visions and voices, ghosts, strange shapes and apparitions. No one who has not experienced how insubstantial the pageant of external reality can be, how it may fade, can fully realize the sublime and grotesque presences that can replace it, or that can exist alongside it.

When a person goes mad, a profound transposition of his place in relation to all domains of being occurs. His center of experience moves from ego to self. Mundane time becomes merely anecdotal, only the eternal matters. The madman is, however, confused. He muddles ego with self, inner with outer, natural and supernatural. Nevertheless, he can often be to us, even through his profound wretchedness and disintegration, the hierophant of the sacred. An exile from the scene of being as we know it, he is an alien, a stranger signaling to us from the void in which he is foundering, a void which may be peopled by presences that we do not even dream of. They used to be called demons and spirits, and they used to be known and named. He has lost his sense of self, his feelings, his place in the world as we know it. He tells us he is dead. But we are distracted from our cozy security by this mad ghost who haunts us with his visions and voices which seem so senseless and of which we feel impelled to rid him, cleanse him, cure him.

Madness need not be all breakdown. It may also be breakthrough. It is potentially liberation and renewal as well as enslavement and existential death.

There are now a growing number of accounts by people who have been through the experience of madness.[1]

The following is part of one of the earlier contemporary accounts, as recorded by Karl Jaspers in his *General Psychopathology*.

---

1. See, for example, the anthology *The Inner World of Mental Illness*, edited by Bert Kaplan (New York and London: Harper & Row, 1964), and *Beyond All Reason*, by Morag Coate (London: Constable, 1964; Philadelphia: Lippincott, 1965).

I believe I caused the illness myself. In my attempt to penetrate the other world I met its natural guardians, the embodiment of my own weaknesses and faults. I first thought these demons were lowly inhabitants of the other world who could play me like a ball because I went into these regions unprepared and lost my way. Later I thought they were split-off parts of my own mind (passions) which existed near me in free space and thrived on my feelings. I believed everyone else had these too but did not perceive them, thanks to the protective successful deceit of the feeling of personal existence. I thought the latter was an artifact of memory, thought-complexes, etc., a doll that was nice enough to look at from outside but nothing real inside it.

In my case the personal self had grown porous because of my dimmed consciousness. Through it I wanted to bring myself closer to the higher sources of life. I should have prepared myself for this over a long period by invoking in me a higher, impersonal self, since "nectar" is not for mortal lips. It acted destructively on the animal-human self, split it up into its parts. These gradually disintegrated, the doll was really broken and the body damaged. I had forced untimely access to the "source of life," the curse of the "gods" descended on me. I recognized too late that murky elements had taken a hand. I got to know them after they had already too much power. There was no way back. I now had the world of spirits I had wanted to see. The demons came up from the abyss, as guardian Cerberi, denying admission to the unauthorized. I decided to take up the life-and-death struggle. This meant for me in the end a decision to die, since I had to put aside everything that maintained the enemy, but this was also everything that maintained life. I wanted to enter death without going mad and stood before the Sphinx: either thou into the abyss or I!

Then came illumination. I fasted and so penetrated into the true nature of my seducers. They were pimps and deceivers of my dear personal self which seemed as much a thing of naught as they. A larger and more comprehensive self emerged and I could abandon the previous personality with its entire entourage. I saw this earlier personality could never enter transcendental realms. I felt as a result a terrible pain, like an annihilating blow, but I was rescued, the demons shriveled, vanished and perished. A new life began for me and from now on I felt different from other people. A self that consisted of conventional lies, shams, self-deceptions, memory images, a self just like that of other people, grew in me again but behind and above it stood a greater and more comprehensive self which impressed me with something of what is eternal, unchanging, immortal and inviolate and which ever since that time has been my protector and refuge. I believe it would be good for many if they were acquainted with such a higher self and that there are people who have attained this goal in fact by kinder means.[2]

Jaspers comments:

Such self-interpretations are obviously made under the influence of delusion-like tendencies and deep psychic forces. They originate from profound experiences and the wealth of such schizophrenic experience calls on the observer as well as on the reflective patient not to take all this merely as a chaotic jumble of contents. Mind and spirit are present in the morbid psychic life as well as in the healthy. But interpretations of this sort must be divested of any casual importance. All they can do is throw light on content and bring it into some sort of context.

This patient has described, with a lucidity I could not improve upon, a very ancient quest, with its pitfalls and dangers. Jaspers still speaks of this experience as morbid and tends to discount the patient's own construction. Yet both the experience and the construction may be valid in their own terms.

Certain *transcendental experiences* seem to me to be the original wellspring of all religions. Some psychotic people have transcendental experiences. Often (to the best of their recollection), they have never had such experiences before, and frequently they will never have them again. I am not saying, however, that psychotic experience necessarily contains this element more manifestly than sane experience.

We experience in different modes. We perceive external realities, we dream, imagine, have semiconscious reveries. Some people have visions, hallucinations, experience faces transfigured, see auras and so on. Most people most of the time experience themselves and others in one or another way that I shall call *egoic*. That is, centrally or peripherally, they experience the world and themselves in terms of a consistent identity, a me-here over against a you-there, within a framework of certain ground structures of space and time shared with other members of their society.

This identity-anchored, space-and-time-bound experience has been studied philosophically by Kant, and later by the phenomenologists, e.g.

2. Manchester: Manchester University Press, 1962, pages 417–18.

Husserl, Merleau-Ponty. Its historical and ontological relativity should be fully realized by any contemporary student of the human scene. Its cultural, socioeconomic relativity has become a commonplace among anthropologists and a platitude to the Marxists and neo-Marxists. And yet, with the consensual and interpersonal confirmation it offers, it gives us a sense of ontological security, whose validity we experience as self-validating, although metaphysically-historically-ontologically-socio-economically-culturally we know its apparent absolute validity as an illusion.

In fact all religious and all existential philosophies have agreed that such egoic experience is a preliminary illusion, a veil, a film of maya—a dream to Heraclitus, and to Lao Tzu, the fundamental illusion of all Buddhism, a state of sleep, of death, of socially accepted madness, a womb state to which one has to die, from which one has to be born.

The person going through ego-loss or transcendental experiences may or may not become in different ways confused. Then he might legitimately be regarded as mad. But to be mad is not necessarily to be ill, notwithstanding that in our culture the two categories have become confused. It is assumed that if a person is mad (whatever that means) then ipso facto he is ill (whatever that means). The experience that a person may be absorbed in, while to others he appears simply ill-mad, may be for him veritable manna from heaven. The person's whole life may be changed, but it is difficult not to doubt the validity of such vision. Also, not everyone comes back to us again.

Are these experiences simply the effulgence of a pathological process or of a particular alienation? I do not think they are.

In certain cases, a man blind from birth may have an operation performed which gives him his sight. The result—frequently misery, confusion, disorientation. The light that illumines the madman is an unearthly light. It is not always a distorted refraction of his mundane life situation. He may be irradiated by light from other worlds. It may burn him out.

This "other" world is not essentially a battlefield wherein psychological forces, derived or diverted, displaced or sublimated from their original object-cathexes, are engaged in an illusionary fight—although such forces may obscure these realities, just as they may obscure so-called external realities. When Ivan in The Brothers Karamazov says, "If God does not exist, everything is permissible," he is not saying, "If my superego, in projected form, can be abolished, I can do anything with a good conscience." He is saying, "If there is only my conscience, then there is no ultimate validity for my will."

Among physicians and priests there should be some who are guides, who can educt the person from this world and induct him to the other. To guide him in it and to lead him back again.

One enters the other world by breaking a shell: or through a door: through a partition: the curtains part or rise: a veil is lifted. Seven veils: seven seals, seven heavens.

The "ego" is the instrument for living in *this* world. If the "ego" is broken up or destroyed (by the insurmountable contradictions of certain life situations, by toxins, chemical changes, etc.), then the person may be exposed to other worlds, "real" in different ways from the more familiar territory of dreams, imagination, perception or fantasy.

The world that one enters, one's capacity to experience it, seem to be partly conditional on the state of one's "ego."

Our time has been distinguished, more than by anything else, by a drive to control the external world, and by an almost total forgetfulness of the internal world. If one estimates human evolution from the point of view of knowledge of the external world, then we are in many respects progressing.

If our estimate is from the point of view of the internal world and of oneness of internal and external, then the judgment must be very different.

Phenomenologically the terms "internal" and "external" have little validity. But in this whole realm one is reduced to mere verbal expedients—words are simply the finger pointing at the moon. One of the difficulties of talking in the present day of these matters is that the very existence of inner realities is now called in question.

By "inner" I mean our way of seeing the external world and all those realities that have no "external," "objective" presence—imagination, dreams, fantasies, trances, the realities of contemplative and meditative states, realities of which modern man, for the most part, has not the slightest direct awareness.

For example, nowhere in the Bible is there any argument about the *existence* of gods, demons, angels. People did not first "believe in" God: they experienced His presence, as was true of other spiritual agencies. The question was not whether God existed, but whether this particular God was the greatest god of all, or the only God; and what was the relation of the various spiritual agencies to each other. Today, there is a public debate, not as to the trustworthiness of God, the particular place in the spiritual hierarchy of different spirits, etc., but whether God or such spirits *even exist* or ever have existed.

Sanity today appears to rest very largely on a capacity to adapt to the external world—the interpersonal world, and the realm of human collectivities.

As this external human world is almost completely and totally estranged from the inner, any personal direct awareness of the inner world already has grave risks.

But since society, without knowing it, is *starving* for the inner, the demands on people to evoke its presence in a "safe" way, in a way that need not be taken seriously, etc., is tremendous—while the ambivalence is equally intense. Small wonder that the list of artists, in say the last 150 years, who have become shipwrecked on these reefs is so long— Hölderlin, John Clare, Rimbaud, Van Gogh, Nietzsche, Antonin Artaud. . . .

Those who survived have had exceptional qualities—a capacity for secrecy, slyness, cunning—a thoroughly realistic appraisal of the risks they run, not only from the spiritual realms they frequent, but from the hatred of their fellows for anyone engaged in this pursuit.

Let us *cure* them. The poet who mistakes a real woman for his Muse and acts accordingly. . . . The young man who set off in a yacht in search of God. . . .

The outer divorced from any illumination from the inner is in a state of darkness. We are in an age of darkness. The state of outer darkness is a state of sin—i.e., alienation or estrangement from the *inner light*.[3] Certain actions lead to greater estrangement; certain others help one not to be so far removed. The former used to be called sinful.

The ways of losing one's way are legion. Madness is certainly not the least unambiguous. The countermadness of Kraepelinian psychiatry is the exact counterpart of "official" psychosis. Literally, and absolutely seriously, it is as *mad*, if by madness we mean any radical estrangement from the totality of what is the case. Remember Kierkegaard's objective madness.

As we experience the world, so we act. We conduct ourselves in the light of our view of what is the case and what is not the case. That is, each person is a more or less naive ontologist. Each person has views of what is and what is not.

There is no doubt, it seems to me, that there have been profound changes in the experience of man in the last thousand years. In some ways this is more evident than changes in the patterns of his behavior. There is everything to suggest that man experienced God. Faith was never a matter of believing He existed, but of trusting, in the presence that was experienced and known to exist as a self-validating datum. It

---

3. M. Eliade, *The Two and the One* (London: Harvill Press, 1965), especially Chapter 1.

seems likely that far more people in our time experience neither the presence of God, nor the presence of his absence, but the absence of his presence.

We require a history of phenomena, not simply more phenomena of history.

As it is, the secular psychotherapist is often in the role of the blind leading the half-blind.

The fountain has not played itself out, the frame still shines, the river still flows, the spring still bubbles forth, the light has not faded. But between us and It, there is a veil which is more like fifty feet of solid concrete. *Deus absconditus.* Or we have absconded.

Already everything in our time is directed to categorizing and segregating this reality from objective facts. This is precisely the concrete wall. Intellectually, emotionally, interpersonally, organizationally, intuitively, theoretically, we have to blast our way through the solid wall, even if at the risk of chaos, madness and death. For from *this* side of the wall, this is the risk. There are no assurances, no guarantees.

Many people are prepared to have faith in the sense of scientifically indefensible belief in an untested hypothesis. Few have trust enough to test it. Many people make-believe what they experience. Few are made to believe by their experience. Paul of Tarsus was picked up by the scruff of the neck, thrown to the ground and blinded for three days. This direct experience was self-validating.

We live in a secular world. To adapt to this world the child abdicates its ecstasy. *("L'enfant abdique son extase":* Mallarmé.) Having lost our experience of the spirit, we are expected to have faith. But this faith comes to be a belief in a reality which is not evident. There is a prophecy in Amos that a time will come when there will be famine in the land, "not a famine for bread, nor a thirst for water, but of *hearing* the words of the Lord." That time has now come to pass. It is the present age.

From the alienated starting point of our pseudo-sanity, everything is equivocal. Our sanity is not "true" sanity. Their madness is not "true" madness. The madness of our patients is an artifact of the destruction wreaked on them by us and by them on themselves. Let no one suppose that we meet "true" madness any more than that we are truly sane. The madness that we encounter in "patients" is a gross travesty, a mockery, a grotesque caricature of what the natural healing of that estranged integration we call sanity might be. True sanity entails in one way or another the dissolution of the normal ego, that false self competently adjusted to our alienated social reality; the emergence of the "inner" archetypal mediators of divine power, and through this death a rebirth, and the eventual re-establishment of a new kind of ego-functioning, the ego now being the servant of the divine, no longer its betrayer.

It

Alan W. Watts

Is there in any of us an instinct to get "outside" of our own physical being? Is there a justification for escape, for getting away from it all? Alan W. Watts thinks so. We have a need to relate ourselves to something outside, something other, something Watts calls "It."

Human history includes far too many references to mysticism and transcendent experiences for today's behavioral scientist to ignore this area, troublesome and unempirical as it may seem.

The Book: On the Taboo Against Knowing Who You Are is one of Watts' varied attempts to help Westerners to know the larger Self. Again, you are invited to explore this area and make up your own mind.

Just as true humor is laughter at oneself, true humanity is knowledge of oneself. Other creatures may love and laugh, talk and think, but it seems to be the special peculiarity of human beings that they reflect: they think about thinking and know that they know. This, like other feedback systems, may lead to vicious circles and confusions if improperly managed, but self-awareness makes human experience resonant. It imparts that simultaneous "echo" to all that we think and feel as the box of a violin reverberates with the sound of the strings. It gives depth and volume to what would otherwise be shallow and flat.

Self-knowledge leads to wonder, and wonder to curiosity and investigation, so that nothing interests people more than people, even if only one's own person. Every intelligent individual wants to know what makes him tick, and yet is at once fascinated and frustrated by the fact that oneself is the most difficult of all things to know. For the human organism is, apparently, the most complex of all organisms, and while one has the advantage of knowing one's own organism so intimately—from the inside—there is also the disadvantage of being so close to it that one can never quite get at it. Nothing so eludes conscious inspection as consciousness itself. This is why the root of consciousness has been called, paradoxically, the unconscious.

The people we are tempted to call clods and boors are just those who seem to find nothing fascinating in being human; their humanity is incomplete, for it has never astonished them. There is also something incomplete about those who find nothing fascinating in *being*. You may say that this is a philosopher's professional prejudice—that people are defective who lack a sense of the metaphysical. But anyone who thinks at all must be a philosopher—a good one or a bad one—because it is impossible to think without premises, without basic (and in this sense, metaphysical) assumptions about what is sensible, what is the good life, what is beauty, and what is pleasure. To hold such assumptions, consciously or unconsciously, is to philosophize. The self-styled practical man of affairs who pooh-poohs philosophy as a lot of windy notions is himself a pragmatist or a positivist, and a bad one at that, since he has given no thought to his position.

If the human organism is fascinating, the environment which accompanies it is equally so—and not merely as a collection of particular things and events. Chemistry, biology, geology, and astronomy are special fascinations with the details of our environment, but metaphysics is fascination with the whole thing. I find it almost impossible to imagine a sensitive human being bereft of metaphysical wonder, a person who does not have that marvelous urge to ask a question that cannot quite be formulated. If, as we have been arguing, the only real atom—as de Chardin put it—is the universe, and the only real thing is everything, then what is it?

Yet the moment I have asked this question, I must question the question. What sort of answer could such a question have? Ordinarily, one answers the question "What is it?" by putting the designated thing or event into a class—animal, vegetable, or mineral, solid, liquid, or gas, running, jumping, or walking. But what class will fit *every*thing? What can possibly be said about everything? To define is to limit, to set boundaries, to compare and to contrast, and for this reason the universe, the all, seems to defy definition. At this point, the mind runs into an apparently absolute limitation, and one may well argue that it is therefore a misuse of the mind to ask such a question. Just as no one in his senses would look for the morning news in a dictionary, no one should use speaking and thinking to find out what cannot be spoken or thought. Logically, then, the question "What is everything?" has no meaning, even though it seems to be profound. As Wittgenstein suggested, people who ask such questions may have a disorder of the intellect which can be cured by philosophical therapy. To "do philosophy," as he put it, is to think about thinking in such a way that we can distinguish real thinking from nonsense.

But this neat logic does not get rid of the urge to know which expresses itself—however ineptly—in the question. As I said at the beginning, it is just unbelievably odd that anything is happening at all. Yet how am I to express this feeling in the form of a sensible question which could have a satisfactory answer? The point is, perhaps, that I am not looking for a *verbal* answer, just as when I ask for a kiss, I do not want a piece of paper with "A kiss" written on it. It is rather that metaphysical wonder looks for an experience, a vision, a revelation which will explain, without words, why there is the universe, and what it is—much as the act of loving explains why we are male and female.

It could be said, then, that the best answer to "What is everything?" is "Look and see!" But the question almost always implies a search for something *basic* to everything, for an underlying unity which our ordinary thinking and feeling do not grasp. Thought and sensation are analytical and selective, and thus present the world as no more than a multiplicity of things and events. Man has, however, a "metaphysical instinct" which apparent multiplicity does not satisfy.

> What guarantee is there that the five senses, taken together, do cover the whole of possible experience? They cover simply our actual experience, our human knowledge of facts or events. There are gaps between the fingers; there are gaps between the senses. In these gaps is the darkness which hides the connection between things. . . . This darkness is the source of our vague fears and anxieties, but also the home of the gods. They alone see the connections, the total relevance of everything that happens; that which now comes to us in bits and pieces, the "accidents" which exist only in our heads, in our limited perceptions.[1]

Man is therefore intuitively certain that the entire multitude of things and events is "on" or "in" something as reflections are on a mirror, sounds on a diaphragm, lights and colors in a diamond, or the words and music of a song in the singer. This is perhaps because man is himself a unified organism, and that if things and events are "on" anything at all, they are on his nervous system. Yet there is obviously more than one nervous system, and what are all nervous systems on? Each other?

This mysterious something has been called God, the Absolute, Nature, Substance, Energy, Space, Ether, Mind, Being, the Void, the Infinite— names and ideas which shift in popularity and respectability with the winds of intellectual fashion, of considering the universe intelligent or stupid, superhuman or subhuman, specific or vague. All of them might be dismissed as nonsense-noises if the notion of an underlying Ground of Being were no more than a product of intellectual speculation. But these names are often used to designate the content of a vivid and almost sensorily concrete experience—the "unitive" experience of the mystic, which,

---

1. Idris Parry, "Kafka, Rilke, and Rumpelstiltskin." *The Listener*. British Broadcasting Corporation, London, December 2, 1965, p. 895.

with secondary variations, is found in almost all cultures at all times. This experience is the transformed sense of self which I was discussing in the previous chapter [of the original work], though in "naturalistic" terms, purified of all hocus-pocus about mind, soul, spirit, and other intellectually gaseous words.

Despite the universality of this experience and the impressive regularity with which it is described in the same general way,[2] tough-minded types regard it as a commonly recurring hallucination with characteristic symptoms, like paranoia, which adds nothing to our information about the physical universe. Just as we cannot say anything about everything, so, they argue, one cannot feel or experience anything about everything. For all our senses are selective. We experience by contrast just as we think by contrast. To experience something underlying *all* experiences would thus be like seeing sight itself, as something common to everything seen. In terms of what color, what shape—other than all mutually contrasting colors and shapes—could we see sight itself? . . .

But the underlying assumption, that all knowledge is in terms of contrasts, is as metaphysical as an assumption can be. Put it in another way: "All knowledge is a recognition of the mutual relations between sense-experiences and/or things and events." This comes perilously close to being a meaningful statement about everything. "All things are known by their differences from the likenesses to each other." Backed up into this position, the antimetaphysician can be carried, albeit with screams of protest, to an even deeper metaphysical level. . . .

I have sometimes thought that all philosophical disputes could be reduced to an argument between the partisans of "prickles" and the partisans of "goo." The prickly people are tough-minded, rigorous, and precise, and like to stress differences and divisions between things. They prefer particles to waves, and discontinuity to continuity. The gooey people are tender-minded romanticists who love wide generalizations and grand syntheses. They stress the underlying unities, and are inclined to pantheism and mysticism. Waves suit them much better than particles as the ultimate constituents of matter, and discontinuities jar their teeth like a compressed-air drill. Prickly philosophers consider the gooey ones rather disgusting—undisciplined, vague dreamers who slide over hard facts like an intellectual slime which threatens to engulf the whole universe in an "undifferentiated aesthetic continuum" (courtesy of Professor F.S.C. Northrop). But gooey philosophers think of their prickly colleagues as animated skeletons that rattle and click without any flesh or vital juices, as dry and desiccated mechanisms bereft of all finer feelings.

2. For which the reader is directed to such works as Bucke's *Cosmic Consciousness*, James' *Varieties of Religious Experience*, and Johnson's *Watcher on the Hills*.

Either party would be helplessly lost without the other, because there would be nothing to argue about, no one would know what his position was, the whole course of philosophy would come to an end.

As things now stand in the world of academic philosophy, the prickly people have had the upper hand in both England and the United States for some years. With their penchant for linguistic analysis, mathematical logic, and scientific empiricism, they have aligned philosophy with the mystique of science, have begun to transform the philosopher's library or mountain retreat into something nearer to a laboratory, and, as William Earle said, would come to work in white coats if they thought they could get away with it. The professional journals are now as satisfactorily unreadable as treatises on mathematical physics, and the points at issue as minute as any animalcule in the biologist's microscope. But their sweeping victory over the gooey people has almost abolished philosophy as a discipline, for we are close to the point where departments of philosophy will close their offices and shift the remaining members of their faculties to the departments of mathematics and linguistics. . . .

To go anywhere in philosophy, other than back and forth, round and round, one must have a keen sense of *correlative vision*. This is a technical term for a thorough understanding of the Game of Black-and-White, whereby one sees that all explicit opposites are implicit allies—correlative in the sense that they "go with" each other and cannot exist apart. This, rather than any miasmic absorption of differences into a continuum of ultimate goo, is the metaphysical unity underlying the world. For this unity is not mere one-ness as opposed to multiplicity, since these two terms are themselves polar. The unity, or inseparability, of one and many is therefore referred to in Vedanta philosophy as "non-duality" (*advaita*) to distinguish it from simple uniformity. True, the term has its own opposite, "duality," for insofar as every term designates a class, an intellectual pigeonhole, every class has an outside polarizing its inside. For this reason, language can no more transcend duality than painting or photographs upon a flat surface can go beyond two dimensions. Yet by the convention of perspective, certain two-dimensional lines that slant towards a "vanishing-point" are taken to represent the third dimension of depth. In a similar way, the dualistic term "non-duality" is taken to represent the "dimension" in which explicit differences have implicit unity. . . .

Is it possible that myself, my existence, so *contains* being and nothing that death is merely the "off" interval in an on/off pulsation which must be eternal—because every alternative to this pulsation (e.g., its absence) would in due course imply its presence? Is it conceivable, then, that I am basically an eternal existence momentarily and perhaps needlessly terrified by one half of itself because it has identified all of itself with the other half? If the choice must be either white or black, must I so commit myself to the white side that I cannot be a good sport and actually play the Game of Black-and-White, with the implicit knowledge that neither can win? Or is all this so much bandying with the formal relations between words and terms without any relation to my physical situation?

To answer the last question affirmatively, I should have to believe that the logic of thought is quite arbitrary—that it is a purely and strictly human invention without any basis in the physical universe. While it is true, as I have already shown, that we do project logical patterns (nets, grids, and other types of calculus) upon the wiggly physical world—which can be confusing if we do not realize what we are doing—nevertheless, these patterns do not come from *outside* the world. They have something to do with the design of the human nervous system which is definitely in and of the world. Furthermore, I have shown that correlative thinking about the relation of organism to environment is far more compatible with the physical sciences than our archaic and prevalent notions of the self as something confronting an alien and separate world. To sever the connections between human logic and the physical universe, I would have to revert to the myth of the ego as an isolated, independent observer from whom the rest of the world is absolutely external and "other." Neither neurology nor biology nor sociology can subscribe to this.

If, on the other hand, self and other, subject and object, organism and environment are the poles of a single process, THAT is my true existence. As the *Upanishads* say, "That is the Self. That is the real. That art thou!" But I cannot think or say anything about THAT, or, as I shall now call it, IT, unless I resort to the convention of using dualistic language as the lines of perspective are used to show depth on a flat surface. What lies beyond opposites must be discussed, if at all, in terms of opposites, and this means using the language of analogy, metaphor, and myth.

The difficulty is not only that language is dualistic, insofar as words are labels for mutually exclusive classes. The problem is that IT is so much more myself than I thought I was, so central and so basic to my existence, that I cannot make it an object. There is no way to stand outside IT, and, in fact, no need to do so. For so long as I am trying to grasp IT, I am implying that IT is not really myself. If it were possible, I am losing the sense of it by attempting to find it. This is why those who really know that they are IT invariably say they do not understand it, for IT understands understanding—not the other way about. One cannot, and need not, go deeper than deep!

But the fact that IT eludes every description must not, as happens so often, be mistaken for the description of IT as the airiest of abstractions, as a literal transparent continuum or undifferentiated cosmic jello. The most concrete image of God the Father, with his white beard and golden robe, is better than that. Yet Western students of Eastern philosophies and religions persistently accuse Hindus and Buddhists of believing in a featureless and gelatinous God, just because the latter insist that every conception or objective image of IT is void. But the term "void" applies to all such conceptions, not to IT. . . .

You were probably brought up in a culture where the presiding image of IT has for centuries been God the Father, whose pronoun is HE, because IT seems too impersonal and She would, of course, be inferior. Is this image still workable, as a functional myth to provide some consensus about life and its meaning for all the diverse people and cultures of this planet?

Frankly, the image of God the Father has become ridiculous—that is, unless you read Saint Thomas Aquinas or Martin Buber or Paul Tillich, and realize that you can be a devout Jew or Christian without having to believe, literally, in the Cosmic Male Parent. Even then, it is difficult not to feel the force of the image, because images sway our emotions more deeply than conceptions. As a devout Christian you would be saying day after day the prayer, "Our Father who art in heaven," and eventually it gets you: you are relating emotionally to IT as to an idealized father—male, loving but stern, and a personal being quite other than yourself. Obviously, you must be other than God so long as you conceive yourself as the separate ego, but when we realize that this form of identity is no more than a social institution, and one which has ceased to be a workable life-game, the sharp division between oneself and the ultimate reality is no longer relevant.

Furthermore, the younger members of our society have for some time been in growing rebellion against paternal authority and the paternal state. For one reason, the home in an industrial society is chiefly a dormitory, and the father does not work there, with the result that wife and children have no part in his vocation. He is just a character who brings in money, and after working hours he is supposed to forget about his job and have fun. Novels, magazines, television, and popular cartoons therefore portray "Dad" as an incompetent clown. And the image has some truth in it because Dad has fallen for the hoax that work is simply something you do to make money, and with money you can get anything you want.

It is no wonder that an increasing proportion of college students want no part in Dad's world, and will do anything to avoid the rat-race of the salesman, commuter, clerk, and corporate executive. Professional men, too—architects, doctors, lawyers, ministers, and professors—have offices away from home, and thus, because the demands of their families boil down more and more to money, are ever more tempted to regard even professional vocations as ways of making money. All this is further aggravated by the fact that parents no longer educate their own children. Thus the child does not grow up with understanding of or enthusiasm for his father's work. Instead, he is sent to an understaffed school run mostly by women which, under the circumstances, can do no more than hand out mass-produced education which prepares the child for everything and nothing. It has no relation whatever to his father's vocation....

Hitherto the poets and philosophers of science have used the vast expanse and duration of the universe as a pretext for reflections on the unimportance of man, forgetting that man with "that enchanted loom, the brain" is precisely what transforms this immense electrical pulsation into light and color, shape and sound, large and small, hard and heavy, long and short. In knowing the world we humanize it, and if, as we discover it, we are astonished at its dimensions and its complexity, we should be just as astonished that we have the brains to perceive it.

Hitherto we have been taught, however, that we are not really responsible for our brains. We do not know (in terms of words or figures) how they are constructed, and thus it seems that the brain and the organism as a whole are an ingenious vehicle which has been "given" to us, or an uncanny maze in which we are temporarily trapped. In other words, we accepted a definition of ourselves which confined the self to the source and to the limitations of conscious attention. This definition is miserably insufficient, for in fact we know how to grow brains and eyes, ears and fingers, hearts and bones, in just the same way that we know how to walk and breathe, talk and think—only we can't put it into words. Words are too slow and too clumsy for describing such things, and conscious attention is too narrow for keeping track of all their details.

Thus it will often happen that when you tell a girl how beautiful she is, she will say, "Now isn't that just like a man! All you men think about is bodies. OK, so I'm beautiful, but I got my body from my parents and it was just luck. I prefer to be admired for myself, not my chassis." Poor little chauffeur! All she is saying is that she has lost touch with her own astonishing wisdom and ingenuity, and wants to be admired for some trivial tricks that she can perform with her conscious attention. And we are all in the same situation, having dissociated ourselves from our bodies and from the whole network of forces in which bodies can come to birth and live.

Yet we can still awaken the sense that all this, too, is the self—a self, however, which is far beyond the image of the ego, or of the human body as limited by the skin. We then behold the Self wherever we look, and its image is the universe in its light and in its darkness, in its bodies and in its spaces. This is the new image of man, but it is still an image. For there remains—to use dualistic words—"behind," "under," "encompassing," and "central" to it all the unthinkable IT, polarizing itself in the visible contrasts of waves and troughs, solids and spaces. But the odd thing is that this IT, however inconceivable, is no vapid abstraction: it is very simply and truly yourself.

In the words of a Chinese Zen master, "Nothing is left to you at this moment but to have a good laugh!" As James Broughton put it:

> This is It
> and I am It
> and You are It
> and so is That
> and He is It
> and She is It
> and It is It
> and That is That.[3]

True humor is, indeed, laughter at one's Self—at the Divine Comedy, the fabulous deception, whereby one comes to imagine that a creature *in* existence is not also *of* existence, that what man is is not also what everything is. All the time we "know it in our bones" but conscious attention, distracted by details and differences, cannot see the whole for the parts.

The major trick in this deception is, of course, death. Consider death as the permanent end of consciousness, the point at which you and your knowledge of the universe simply cease, and where you become as if you had never existed at all. Consider it also on a much vaster scale—the death of the universe at the time when all energy runs out, when, according to some cosmologists, the explosion which flung the galaxies into space fades out like a skyrocket. It will be as if it had never happened, which is, of course, the way things were before it *did* happen. Likewise, when you are dead, you will be as you were before you were conceived. So—there has been a flash, a flash of consciousness or a flash of galaxies. It happened. Even if there is no one left to remember. . . .

I presume, then, that with my own death I shall forget who I was, just as my conscious attention is unable to recall, if it ever knew, how to form the cells of the brain and the pattern of the veins. Conscious memory plays little part in our biological existence. Thus as my sensation of "I-ness," of being alive, once came into being without conscious memory or intent, so it will arise again and again, as the "central" Self—the IT—appears as the self/other situation in its myriads of pulsating forms—always the same and always new, a here in the midst of a there, a now in the midst of then, and one in the midst of many. And if I forget how many times I have been here, and in how many shapes, this forgetting is the necessary interval of darkness between every pulsation of light. I return in every baby born.

Actually, we know this already. After people die, babies are born—and, unless they are automata, every one of them is, just as we ourselves were,

---

3. From *The Bard and the Harper*, recorded by James Broughton and Joel Andrews. LP–1013, produced by Musical Engineering Associates, Sausalito, California, 1965.

the "I" experience coming again into being. The conditions of heredity and environment change, but each of those babies incarnates the same experience of being central to a world that is "other." Each infant dawns into life as I did, without any memory of a past. Thus when I am gone there can be no experience, no living through, of the state of being a perpetual "has-been." Nature "abhors the vacuum" and the I-feeling appears again as it did before, and it matters not whether the interval be ten seconds or billions of years. In unconsciousness all times are the same brief instant.

This is so obvious, but our block against seeing it is the ingrained and compelling myth that the "I" comes into this world, or is thrown out from it, in such a way as to have no essential connection with it. Thus we do not trust the universe to repeat what it has already done—to "I" itself again and again. We see it as an eternal arena in which the individual is no more than a temporary stranger—a visitor who hardly belongs—for the thin ray of consciousness does not shine upon its own source. In looking out upon the world, we forget that the world is looking at itself—through our eyes and ITs.

Now you know—even if it takes you some time to do a double-take and get the full impact. It may not be easy to recover from the many generations through which the fathers have knocked down the children, like dominoes, saying, "Don't you dare think that thought! You're just a little upstart, just a creature, and you had better learn your place." On the contrary, you're IT. But perhaps the fathers were unwittingly trying to tell the children that IT plays IT cool. You don't come on (that is, on stage) like IT because you really are IT, and the point of the stage is to show on, not to show off. To come on like IT—to play at being God—is to play the Self as a role, which is just what it isn't. When IT plays, it plays at being everything else.

Two Brain Studies Hint We're Two Personalities

Newsday

When we speak of "transcendence," we may assume that there is a single, more or less unified "self"–controlled by a single brain–to transcend. This last reading has been included as a reminder that scientists are finding out more every day about how diverse and multifaceted each of us is–even in our brains–and how strongly affected our personalities and emotions may be by physical factors about which, as yet, we know very little.

According to the research summarized in this article, your brain is actually two distinct halves connected by nerve fibers. Until recently, it was assumed that the two halves worked as one "mind." However, split-brain operations performed to arrest epileptic seizures have changed this thinking. It now seems probable that each side works independently, and each of us may have two "minds."

This is the story of two quite different persons who inhabit each of our heads. One is found in the left side of the branin, the other in the right. Each has its own peculiar talents, but normally the two work together like a smoothly polished vaudeville team.

About a decade ago, researchers began to explore what happens when the communications line between those two halves of the brain is cut. For example, one California housewife afflicted with severe epilepsy underwent an operation in 1961 in which the nerve fibers connecting the two sides of the roof of her brain were cut. The woman's seizures subsided. There were virtually no lasting side effects to the operation. The woman is able to do housework, swim, ride a bicycle, cook—all with no apparent difficulties.

Such split-brain operations had been performed as early as the 1930s and apparently had been effective in stopping the spread of epileptic seizures from one side of the brain to another. For many years, however, the implications of "splitting" the brain remained unknown.

Using some intriguing tests, researchers at the California Institute of Technology in Pasadena began to draw out the character of the two half-brains of the California woman, and a handful of others like her. In some situations, the left side of the woman's brain literally did not know what the right side was doing. Yet both sides of her brain seemed capable of independent action, as though she had two minds instead of one.

The left side of the brain's team has long been considered the star, the dominant force in directing human action. It is the side that controls speech. It also controls movement of the body's right side. Fully 90% of the population is right-handed, which means their handwriting and other skilled tasks are controlled by the left side of the brain. The right side controls movements of the left hand and the left side of the body, but its other functions were unclear. The right side of the brain remained mysterious and mute.

But as tests on the California housewife and others continued, researchers, led by psychologist Roger Sperry, found that the right side of the brain may play a more important role in the way we cope with the world than previous suspected. It began to take on a character of its own. In one test, the California housewife was asked to identify objects by using her left hand to feel the items hidden behind a screen. She was unable to do so. Her right brain, which controls the left hand, has no apparent capacity to transfer its findings into verbal thoughts.

But that does not mean that the right brain is dumb. If the woman is allowed to identify the hidden objects in a manner other than using words (by pointing at pictures, for example), it turns out that the left hand-right brain combination is very effective. She consistently indicates the correct object she is touching. In fact, she is more often able to recognize the objects using the mute right brain-left hand combination than if she is allowed to use her right hand and talk about what she is touching (since that hand is controlled by the verbal left side of her brain).

In other tests, Michael Gazzaniga, then a young postdoctoral student at Cal Tech, began to work in 1961 with a man identified only as W.J. He was a World War II veteran whose brain had been damaged by bullet fragments during combat. He had been subject to violent epileptic seizures, which subsided after he underwent a split-brain operation.

Gazzaniga, who recently joined the psychology faculty at the State University at Stony Brook, New York, found that W.J., like the California housewife, demonstrated some unusual traits. When asked to read a page of printed matter, W.J. could read only those words that were in his right visual field. Those words were transmitted to the left half of his brain, where the ability to organize and interpret them apparently lies. W.J. was unable to read words in his left visual field, those words which are transmitted to the right half.

W.J. also was unable to write any words with his left hand, not even those in the halting manner of most persons who are, as he is, right-handed. So again the temptation is to consider the right brain as not only silent but also illiterate. But when Gazzaniga asked W.J. to draw geometrical figures with his left hand, he was able to do so swiftly and correctly. His nondominant right-brain, in control of his left hand, proved to be more clever than first suspected.

From such tests researchers are starting to find that the right brain may be skilled in such nonverbal areas as spatial perception—the ability to recognize faces, shapes and textures. The housewife's ability to recognize objects by touch and W.J.'s ability to draw intricate geometric patterns are just two examples of right-side brain abilities.

At the same time, Gazzaniga and others have found that there are some language abilities hibernating in the right brain as well. They worked with patients who had lost their ability to speak because of damage to the speech center in their left brain. By painstaking work, they have been training these patients to recognize various geometric shapes and to associate them with certain words. Although still speechless, the patients have been learning a crude language by using such symbols. And that language is being directed by their right brains.

Since the two brains of the split-brain patients appear to be quite different in character—the one talkative and analytical, the other nonverbal and mysterious—it is likely that each of us also has similarly contrasting halves of the brains in our heads.

The work of Sperry, Gazzaniga and others is starting to show that the right brain is more versatile than had been thought. The more enthusiastic adherents of split-brain work even talk of trying to draw out this ability of the nonverbal right half of the brain in normal persons as well.

They talk of trying to reverse the dominance of the left half of the brain in normal persons, of trying to find ways to train persons to become less analytical and more creative by using their right halves. By monitoring the minute electrical impulses in each half of the brain, some researchers hope to give persons ways to determine when their right halves are active. It is unclear whether such work, called biofeedback training, will prove successful.

Gazzaniga is more cautious about the implications of the split-brain work. "The split-brain is a powerful research tool," he said. "It encourages you to think of different modes of consciousness and breaks up the idea of unity in the brain."

By studying the unique abilities of the split-brain patients, researchers are able to localize some of the processes of the brain they hope to learn more about. At one time, brain research concentrated on trying to pin down the precise location in the brain of various thought processes and emotions. By destroying small sections of brain cells in animals, researchers sought to trace the location of such processes as memory and learning. This research was carried to almost absurd extremes and there was a backlash, starting in the early 1950s, against such techniques.

Researchers came to view the brain as an integrated, complex system in which many subtle processes could not be traced to a particular region. Now, the split-brain seems to offer researchers a way in which local areas of the brain can be studied without the controversial destruction of cells. Even with this unique research (Gazzaniga estimates that there are only about 25 split-brains in the United States), scientists find the brain remains marvelously unpredictable. With the split-brain patients, for example, there appears to be a transfer of subtle emotional information between the two halves of the brain, even though researchers contrive ways to prevent it.

This transfer may occur via the brain stem, a remaining link between the two halves.

One woman with a split brain was asked to look at a point on a movie screen. In her right visual field, nothing was shown, but in her left visual field, a picture of a nude woman was projected. When the researchers asked the woman what she had seen, she replied, as expected, that she had seen nothing. The image of the nude woman had gone to her mute right brain.

But the woman began to laugh. Her talkative left brain apparently was reacting to something. When she was asked what, she replied, "I don't know. . . . Oh, that funny machine." Her left brain had not "seen" the nude, but it did react to it. The silent right brain had somehow let its talkative partner in on the joke.